Spurs to Glory

A Florida Scout. 1836.

Spurs to Glory

THE STORY OF
THE UNITED STATES CAVALRY

By James M. Merrill

RAND McNALLY & COMPANY

CHICAGO · NEW YORK · SAN FRANCISCO

The following sources have given permission for use of the photographs appearing in this book, on the pages listed: Henry E. Huntington Library and Art Gallery, 25 (top), 63, 73 (bottom), 129, 245; Library of Congress, 25 (bottom), 125, 171, 249 (bottom); West Point Museum, 53, 231, 255 (top), 263 (top); National Archives, 73 (top), 79, 101 (top, left), 239, 263 (bottom); Utah State Historical Society, 83; Frank Fiske Collection, Courtesy Mrs. Frank Fiske, 101 (top right and bottom); Collection of Edgar William & Bernice Chrysler Garbisch, National Gallery of Art, 151; Western Reserve Historical Society, 175; Custer Battlefield National Monument, 189; State Historical Society of North Dakota, 193 (top); The Kansas State Historical Society, Topeka, 193 (bottom), 205; Pennell Collection, University of Kansas, 249 (top); Bancroft Library, University of California, 255 (bottom).

Dedicated with
affectionate thanks to
Harry Hayes Hillman

Lancer Fort Jesup. 1843.

"Prepare to Mount."

U
NTIL THE YEAR 1833 THE UNITED STATES CAVALRY HAD AN uncertain existence. Horse units were recruited for emergencies and hastily disbanded when their services were no longer required. The fledgling nation with meager financial resources felt the maintenance of even one mounted regiment was too expensive. Thrifty-minded congressmen, wanting the most protection for the least money, depended primarily upon the foot soldier in times of national crisis. The heavily forested eastern half of the United States was another obstacle to the successful employment of heavily equipped horse soldiers operating in the orthodox European tradition.

The story of the United States Cavalry prior to 1833 is one of feeble beginnings and sudden retrenchments. In combat during the American Revolution, the cavalry was too weak numerically to play a significant part.

When peace came with Great Britain, the government in Washington reduced the military establishment and, after 1789, there was no cavalry at all. Several years later the United States Army, faced with Indian uprisings in the Northwest Territory, organized detachments of dragoons which fought with General Anthony Wayne at the Battle of Fallen Timbers in 1794. The number of horse outfits was expanded, but as a result of Jeffersonian economy in the 1800's, the cavalry again disappeared from the scene.

In 1808 the United States reactivated one regiment of light dragoons and, in January, 1812, on the eve of the war with Great Britain, added another. But the cavalry forces employed during the conflict were so few that their accomplishments, however bold, left little impression upon official military thinking.

On the banks of the Thames River, Canada, in 1814, Colonel Richard M. Johnson's volunteer Kentuckians demonstrated the type of mounted troops best suited for the North American terrain. Johnson's men, a band of skilled sharpshooters, were lightly equipped, well-drilled in hit-and-run tactics and, more importantly, were so armed and organized that they were capable of fighting dismounted. For fifty years their tactics, which were to become fixed principles in United States Cavalry doctrine, were forgotten and had to be relearned.

In 1815 the cavalry was disbanded. It was not until Andrew Jackson's administration that the government, pressured by Indian troubles in the West, revived the mounted arm of the service. From 1833 onward the cavalry held a permanent place in the United States Army and expanded steadily throughout the nineteenth century.

This book is a popular history of the horse cavalry from its beginnings in 1833. To write an exhaustive chronicle of the cavalry would require volumes. Redefining the problem, I have selected episodes which, in my judgment, best describe the many facets of the horse regiments and which underscore the cavalry's contribution to American history.

My hearty thanks for their efforts go to Dr. Benjamin Whitten and his associates at the Bonnie Bell Wardman Library, Whittier College, for supplying me with hard-to-find books, and to Mrs. Ann Dahlstrom Farmer of Whittier College, who spent precious time correcting my misspelled words and helped type the final manuscript. My gratitude, too, goes to Professor Brainerd Dyer for his counsel and suggestions, to Professor Max Hyman for his technical advice, and to Ann, my wife, who listened patiently to endless readings of the various drafts and whose suggestions, despite frequent heated arguments, remain in the text.

JAMES M. MERRILL
Whittier, California

December 2, 1965

Table of Contents

List of Illustrations

Spurs to Glory

One of the "Forty 1841.

chapter 1

"We meet you as friends, not as enemies."

🐴 🐴 🐴

IT WAS A DAY OF STILL HEAT AND WHITE SKY, JUNE 15, 1834. Colonel Henry Dodge, eyeing his waiting command, crossed the parade of Fort Gibson. Dragoons stood silently beside their horses, reins in hand. Henry Dodge, a thickset, graying veteran of many campaigns who commanded the First Dragoon Regiment, kept walking until he came to the columns, where his orderly saluted and handed over the reins.

Saluting again, the orderly stepped away. Dodge was silent while he looked the troopers over. They were a sensation to behold, dressed in double-breasted dark-blue coats with rows of shiny buttons and blue-gray trousers trimmed with stripes of yellow in each outside seam. Their caps were ornamented with silver eagles, gold cords, and stars worn in front with drooping pompons. Each dragoon wore ankle boots, spurs, and a saber sheathed in its scabbard. Yellow silk sashes, black patent-leather belts, black silk socks, and white gloves completed their outfits.

The troopers watched the colonel. Stepping into his saddle, Dodge glanced across the parade through the gates, off into the distance where lay the prairies. Two hundred and fifty miles to the west of Fort Gibson, Arkansas Territory, were the Pawnee Pict and Comanche villages.

Between the Missouri and Arkansas frontiers and the Rocky Mountains, beyond the reach of infantrymen, roamed these restless tribes, who had never recognized the authority of the United States government. In the same region Osage warred with Kiowa. The War Department in Washington had decided to impress the redman with a majestic show of might. A secondary objective was the recovery of Matthew Martin, a lad of nine years, whose father,

Judge Martin, had been brutally murdered by savages during the summer of 1833.

Dodge sat on his roan at the head of 500 dragoons, tenderfeet fresh from the city streets of the East, poorly trained and ill-equipped for a rough western campaign. The mounts stirred a bit. Onlookers heard the jingle of bit chains and the clatter of equipment. Raising his hand, the colonel looked at the trumpeter, who rode into position immediately behind. Dodge's hand dropped and at the same instant the trumpet gave forth a muted *Forward* and the expedition, the first in dragoon history, began to canter across the parade. Outside the gates it picked up additional companies.

It was an imposing cavalcade. Bugles carried a blinding polish. The quickened *clop-clop* of the horses mingled with the commands of the officers.

Dodge sat stiffly. Behind him a company of white horses contrasted sharply with another of blacks; while sorrels, bays, grays, and creams splashed the expedition with color. Fanning out north and south, four bands of Indians—Seneca, Osage, Cherokee, Delaware—galloped ahead to serve as guides and hunters. To the rear of the columns rode two young Indian girls, a Kiowa aged 15, and a Pawnee, 18, who were to be restored to their families.

Covered baggage wagons groaned forward. The loads were much of a pattern—tents, officers' personal effects and bedrolls, ration cases, and ammunition boxes. Ambulances carried hospital and medical supplies. Trailing the wagons were seventy head of beeves.

In that prancing procession was George Catlin, the famous painter of Indians, who had gained the Secretary of War's permission to ride with the command. Exuberant, Catlin rode off with friends to the top of a hill to observe the troopers as they started:

> Beneath us, and winding through the waving landscape was seen with peculiar effect, the 'bold dragoons,' marching in beautiful order, forming a train of a mile in length. Baggage waggons and Indians helped to lengthen the procession. From the point where we stood, the line was seen in miniature; and the undulating hills over which it was bending its way, gave the appearance of a huge black snake, gracefully gliding over a rich carpet of green.

These columns symbolized safety and civilization on the frontier.

The recently formed dragoons, weaving their way westward, were the forerunners of the United States Cavalry. Usually garrisoned on the extreme frontier, the blue-clad troopers opened the highways and byways of America, carved new roads, searched the recesses of the darkest canyons, marched across immense tracts of wasteland. Pressed by the encroaching flood of immigrants, the cavalry penetrated farther and farther into Indian country, defending settlers in their perpetual war with the redmen, campaigning in fearful blizzards and under relentless summer suns. Without the skilled and disciplined trooper, the progress of the unending line of wagon trains rolling toward the Pacific would have been grievously impeded and the West could scarcely have been won.

The United States Congress in 1832 had authorized the organization of a battalion of Mounted Rangers to guard the western frontier and put an end to the Black Hawk War then in progress. The battalion, six companies strong, trotted off for Wisconsin under the command of Major Henry Dodge.

Prior to the formation of these rangers the Army lacked a regular mounted arm. This negative policy was forced upon the military by congressional economy and by civilian fears that a cavalry, the most aristocratic segment of European armies, would menace the very core of democracy. But the victory of Colonel Richard Johnson at the Thames River, Canada, during the War of 1812 showed clearly that mounted troops were essential to the rapid settlement of the West.

The hazards faced by infantry-escorted wagon trains along the Santa Fe trail in the late 1820's led Congress to establish a battalion of Mounted Rangers. This outfit, in its brief career, demonstrated that horsemen, even untrained horsemen, were more effective on the frontier than the best-drilled infantry or artillery.

Secretary of War Lewis Cass, however, in his report of 1832, seriously questioned the financing of the rangers. He pointed to the one-year enlistment and argued that the cost of the rangers was $150,000 greater annually than a regular dragoon regiment. Interested in economy, Congress merged the rangers with the First Regiment of Dragoons and on that day, March 2, 1833, the United States Cavalry was born.

Dragoon officers rode across every state of the Union beating recruiting drums. Hundreds of youngsters and a few old-timers, thirsting for adventure, signed enlistment papers. At Jefferson Barracks in St. Louis, Missouri, they drilled with firearms long condemned, and in off hours went to work with saws, hammers, and shovels constructing stables and corrals.

At headquarters Colonel Henry Dodge of the First Dragoons and Stephen Watts Kearny, the regiment's lieutenant colonel, mapped the campaign which lay ahead. They realized that it would be especially rough and hazardous with their outfit of greenhorns.

The Western Department of the United States Army was composed of 3,000 men, including infantry, artillery, and dragoons on duty at sixteen posts. Seven of these establishments formed the defense line of the western perimeter, a line stretching from Fort Snelling, Minnesota Territory, in the north to Fort Gibson, Arkansas Territory, in the south. The duty of the First Dragoons was to keep the peace with the Indian tribes and to protect over 1,000 miles of frontier. On their first expedition in the summer of 1834, Dodge and his troopers were charged with the responsibility of impressing the restless Pawnee, Kiowa, and Comanche.

Two days out from Fort Gibson the command was delighted with the sight of June wild flowers growing in the lush green countryside. At the Canadian River on June 25, the force overtook General Leavenworth who commanded the Army's Western Department. Leaving behind twenty-seven sick men, the dragoons forded the river and continued westward, marching daily at eight and breaking off and encamping at four.

It was past midafternoon on June 27, when General Leavenworth was stirred by the sight of a buffalo herd grazing just over a hill ahead. Shouting orders, the general spurred his horse and galloped off with Dodge in hot pursuit. They shot and killed a fat cow.

George Catlin, the artist, was charged by a buffalo. He aimed his rifle, fired, missed. The muzzle then became entangled in his mount's mane and broke in two. He whipped out his pistol and fired, severely wounding the beast, which bounded off into the safety of a thicket, leaving Catlin empty-handed and thankful to have escaped injury.

At midmorning the following day, Leavenworth, Dodge, and Catlin, complaining about their sore bones, were jogging along with the command. "Well, Colonel," said the general casually, "this running for buffaloes is bad business for us—we are getting too old, and should leave such amusements to the young men; I have had enough of this fun in my life, and I am determined not to hazard my limbs or weary my horse any more with it."

The dragoons marched to the top of a hill. Leavenworth turned sharply, trotted back to Dodge, and whispered that a band of buffalo were grazing on the other side.

Dodge and Catlin, along with the general, who disregarded his own advice, dug in their spurs and charged across the plain. Guns barked. Swooping in beneath a tree limb, Catlin was unceremoniously brushed off his mount. Dodge returned without success.

"I'll have that calf before I quit!" roared Leavenworth as he galloped off. The calf dodged and veered. The general's horse crashed into a hole. Catlin, seeing the accident, raced to the spot and saw Leavenworth struggling on his hands and knees, gasping, breathing irregularly. The general's hands shook as though his entire body was in the grip of a frenzied excitement.

Catlin dismounted and helped him to his feet. Asked if he were hurt, Leavenworth replied, "no, but I might have been," before his knees buckled and he passed out. Catlin revived the old soldier and helped him back to the regiment.

Westward across prairies, through broken plains the command marched. The sun glared. Temperatures soared to 105 degrees in the shade. The humidity seemed unbearable. The heat began to sear through their blue blouses, causing the men to crouch forward in their saddles and often to shrug their shoulders, loosening their sticky, sweat-blotched shirts.

On they went day after day in the implacable sun and heat. Mirages emerged and shrank from sight. The splendor and pomp of the dress parade vanished on the parched, trackless plains. Each time the expedition halted during the day, Dodge heard the dry, leathery blowing of the horses as they lowered their heads. Then came silence, a silence broken only by the buzz of insects and the switching of tails. Suddenly, officers' voices would tear through the regiment. A bugle would blare in the noonday heat, individual buglers taking up the call one by one. The expedition would be in motion again.

Disease and death pursued them. The sick, halt, and unfit

were sent back to Fort Gibson. Sergeant Hugh Evans grumbled:

> *We would travel whole days at a time without coming to any water at all, what we came to occationally was the worst kind of top covered over with green slime—when sturd up [it] was perfectly muddy and unfit for the use of man or horse— These days were incesently warm . . . when the sun was pouring down with all his scourching rays upon us.*

Sundown, June 29. A brilliant sunset, a fantastic spray of color running from the brightest reds to delicate pastels crowned the whole western sky. The expedition limped sore-footed into Captain Dean's camp, 200 miles from Fort Gibson, where two companies of infantry were garrisoned. Dodge was grim-faced at the medical reports. His men died daily. Failure was stalking the campaign.

Leavenworth, unwell since his fall, was unable to continue the march. George Catlin watched him as he lay pallid and emaciated, writhing with fever, his orderly fanning him. Three other officers and forty-five men were ill. Seventy-five horses and mules were too disabled to move on.

The regiment rested at this site, renamed Camp Leavenworth, to nurse the invalids and to reorganize and reform the command. The sick were to remain here near the Washita River, 180 miles from Fort Gibson, while six companies of forty-two men each were to march forward with Colonel Dodge. The roughest stage of the campaign lay ahead.

On Independence Day, 1834, the contingent plunged into the Washita River, a deep stream with muddy shores and steep banks. Dodge lost a whole day in crossing the left wing of his command; another, for the right wing, and it was well past midnight before the weary men floated the last white-topped wagon to the far side.

Equipped with ten days rations, jotted Sergeant Evans in his journal, "we mounted our horses [and] commenced the line of march filled up with anthusiasm and a apperent prospect of acquiring fame."

Throughout the month of July, Dodge's columns slowly but doggedly moved across the plains. The blazing heat never diminished. Water was rationed. It was rough and exhausting, yet no one complained. Few of the troopers had ever ridden so far at a stretch. Many developed sores and chapped thighs. During the hourly halts, horses and mules responded to the pressures of bladder and bowel as casually as ever, and the granddaddy of all stinks was produced in the blistering sun.

Each day was practically the exact duplicate of the last. Frequently, in the distance, scouts saw stray bands of Indians or herds of wild horses and buffalo. One lieutenant stumbled upon pieces of a saddlebag, grisly evidence of a Pawnee scalping.

Gray with dust and fatigue, Colonel Dodge worried. The expedition was now venturing into the hunting grounds of the western tribes. "No man . . ." wrote Sergeant Evans, "[knew] where or what was to be his future destination—whether he was to leave his dead body a prey to the foracious wild animals . . . . Whether utter starvation was to be his lot or to perish at the hands of the merciless savages."

Night brought relief from the sun's glare, but not from the heat. Each evening the dragoons bivouacked uniformly in four lines forming a square. Troopers laid out saddles and packs and after grazing their horses, fastened them with ropes to stakes.

Once as the horsemen slept soundly on a warm evening, they heard the report of a gun and a horrid yell. "Indians! Indians! Pawnees!" Snorting and bellowing, the horses snapped their ropes and stampeded through and around the confused soldiers. Gradually the excitement subsided and silence was restored.

Officers checked the sentries' stories and reconstructed the incident. A private standing watch saw what he supposed to be an Indian crawl out from the underbrush. The shadowy figure failed to advance to give the countersign. The sentry aimed and fired a bullet into a dragoon horse which had strayed away the night before. The rifle blast and the terrifying screech of the dying animal had panicked the camp. It was not until noon that the scattered horses were again rounded up.

On July 14, the dragoons, having ridden hard most of the morning, halted on a hill. Colonel Dodge took his spyglass. Far to the left, he made out a group of mounted Indians, forty in number. He gave the hand signal and the column moved forward cautiously. A mile from the red men, the troopers reined in their horses and a guard trotted toward an escort of Indians who, becoming suspicious, veered off and retreated. Dodge then sent forward a single man, a lieutenant, who was met by the head man of the warriors. It was a moment of anxiety. Out in front of the waiting command the lieutenant halted, face to face with the chief. He offered his hand in friendship. It was accepted.

With shrill yelps the savages galloped toward the Americans, swirling about them, gesturing, panhandling tobacco and trinkets. They were Comanche. After these preliminaries, the copper-colored, powerfully built Indians fell silent to listen to the colonel through an interpreter. The President of the United States, the great American captain, Dodge reiterated, had dispatched him to shake hands with the Indians and to establish peace between Americans and their red brothers.

After the colonel's oratory, bugles sounded and the dragoons and their Indian friends marched toward the Comanche village. The column was dwarfed by the bold, rugged landscape. To the right and rear stretched a prairie of tall grass, swaying gently in the breeze to the very end of the horizon. To the left in the distance through the haze of clouds, they saw the Rockies, magnificent and awe inspiring. Directly in front stood two hundred wigwams of poles covered with tanned buffalo hides. Few Americans had ever seen a genuine Comanche village. Actually, few other white men had had a chance to see one as large as this. But traders had been there before the dragoons, for through the morning fog the troopers saw the Stars and Stripes floating over an Indian lodge.

As the horse soldiers dismounted and strolled about the wigwams, Comanche crowded up with as much curiosity, remarked George Catlin, as if the Americans "had come from the moon." Most of the redmen were stocky and bandy-legged so that they waddled when they walked. To the dragoons the Comanche appeared clumsy until they jumped on their horses.

The Americans gaped as the Indians, galloping full speed, dropped their bodies to the sides of their mounts, lying horizontally with their heels over the horses' backs, screening themselves from make-believe enemies. Abruptly they flung themselves up, slid down the other side, and shot arrows from beneath their horses' necks. This war strategem, remarked Catlin in astonishment, "completely puzzled the whole of us; and appeared to be the result of magic, rather than of skill acquired by practice."

Resting here at the Indian village, Dodge surveyed his men and counted thirty-nine of them sick, including George Catlin. The dragoons could not afford to jeopardize the success of their mission by delaying and nursing them to health so the colonel ordered Lieutenant James Izard and twenty-six volunteers to remain and protect the fever-stricken. With 183 troopers, Dodge rode out for the Pawnee Pict village.

Across the granite hills, through ravines and difficult passes, the columns dug their way. The sun was as harsh as ever, the temperature a little lower than it had been the week before. Others fell sick. Horses went lame and sore as they picked their way over the granite rocks. The country was destitute of game. "Our situation," commented Lieutenant James Hildreth, "was now extremely precarious; starvation seemed to stare us in the face on the one hand, and should the Indians prove unfriendly, we had little chance of escape on the other."

The terrain was not genuinely flat, yet neither was it really hilly or even rolling. To the slow, shuffling columns, it seemed never to deviate but actually it did change, although differences were not immediately discernible. The long, undulating rises did grow gradually steeper. Standing alone on an elevation, Dodge adjusted his spyglass and took a long survey to the west. There before him stood the mountains, stretching jagged and impressive from right to left, as far as the eye could reach.

"We were obliged," recalled a trooper, "to force our way through the narrow defiles, natural arches, and almost subterraneous passages sometimes almost shut out from the light. . . ."

"From the loftiest of these peaks," he continued, "I took occasion to look back upon our small force who now extended themselves in all directions, with little regard to order, some worn with fatigue had halted to rest themselves & horses—Others wandered from the main column to seek some passage of easier access."

Tediously the command worked up through the crags and rocks and suddenly they entered a level prairie, almost as high as the surrounding mountains. Dodge estimated that they had climbed to within five miles of the Pawnee village.

The colonel sat stolid in his saddle, arms akimbo. The scouts reported nothing. No one had seen any vestige of the Pawnee, and Dodge was worried that they had either fled or were preparing to strike. That afternoon the dragoons were ordered to check their guns and sabers.

The sun dropped over the horizon and the swift mountain night cloaked everything. Campfires flickered in the darkness as Dodge, after doubling the sentries, made an informal inspection of the bivouac. By midnight the camp was as quiet as it ever became.

Bugles echoed in the stillness, arbitrarily ending the short night. There was a streak of pale light along the eastern horizon, not daylight but its beginning. The command, its men prepared for instant action, began moving again. Scouts maintained a screen to the front and on either flank.

The columns had not gone far when Dodge observed his scouts coming back at a dead run. Behind them pounded sixty Pawnee. Straight and fast they cut across the prairie. Waving their hands frantically, the scouts charged up yelling "Hold fire!" and reined in their mounts. The Pawnee were friendly.

Dodge and the detachment, guided by the Pawnee, spurred lightly and let the horses lope the rest of the way. Five miles farther on they approached vast cultivated fields. Hopefully they urged their weary mounts forward and entered the Pawnee Pict village, their final objective.

The savages were dazzled by the Americans' display of trinkets, clothes, and tobacco and gladly traded corn and horsemeat for these luxuries. Quickly the hungry and thirsty soldiers gulped down Indian dishes of corn and beans and buffalo meat and savored liberal portions of watermelon and wild plums.

As they passed through the center of the village, between rows of wigwams, women turned from their labors to stare silently and then bent again to their work. A band of children rushed out to meet the Americans, capering and yelling, their faces daubed with streaks of soot as they played at being warriors. Older boys and men jumped from the lodges, and fell into stride, whispering, pointing, edging forward to see the dragoons. The tribe was clean, well-clothed, and well-fed.

Gaudily dressed in full ceremonials, Indian chiefs from the Pawnee and the neighboring Kiowa and Comanche tribes met in council with the dragoon officers. "We are the first American officers who have ever come to see the Pawnees," said the colonel solemnly. "We meet you as friends, not as enemies, to make peace with you, to shake hands with you. The great American Captain is at peace with all the white men in the world."

ABOVE: *Colonel Dodge's expedition approaching the Comanche village, 1834. Painting by George Catlin.* BELOW: *Troops fording Lake Ocklawaha, in the Seminole War.*

"We have come to your town . . ." the veteran campaigner continued, "[to acquire] the boy at your hands, for we are told he is in your town. Give us the white boy and we will give you the Pawnee girl that we have brought with us; we wish all that has passed to be put behind us—to be forgotten; we wish to shake hands with you and be friends; you must now give me a positive and direct answer in regard to . . . the white boy who was taken last spring."

Chief We-ter-ra-shah-ro grinned and replied, "The white boy is here."

"I wish the boy brought to me; I will then give to you the Pawnee girl; this act . . . will be the best proof that you can give of the sincerity of your disposition to shake hands and be at peace with us. I cannot leave the country until we obtain possession of the boy. . . ."

Pushing through the crowd of savages and troopers, a chief led out a naked white boy who, looking around, exclaimed with surprise, "What! Are there white men here?"

Dodge smiled and asked his name. The lad answered, "My name is Matthew Wright Martin."

Once the question of the boy was settled, Dodge pursued the problem of selecting members of the tribes to accompany him back to Fort Gibson. If they sent delegates to sign peace treaties, the colonel assured the Indians, the American captain would establish trading posts among them. No longer would they be dependent upon Mexican commerce from Santa Fe.

In midafternoon, a Comanche chief visited Dodge in his tent, wishing to exchange a Spanish girl for the young Kiowa beauty whom the troopers had brought along. The colonel jerked his head in dissent. The girl was Kiowa. "I mean to give her to her relations and friends without price," he said abruptly. "I will give the girl to her tribe; they shall see how much their friends we are."

Sitting cross-legged in the tent, Dodge and the Comanche turned to other matters. Suddenly thirty whooping Kiowa thundered past Dodge's quarters, encircled the camp, and halted. The fierce-looking creatures, believing the Americans in league with the hated Osage and holding the Kiowa girl prisoner, had their bows strung and their quivers filled with arrows. The dragoons eased toward their weapons. Dodge calmly stepped forward to assure them that the Kiowa girl would be restored to her father. Leaping from their saddles, the red men embraced the colonel warmly.

Much later in the afternoon the Indians passed the peace pipe. American officers looked strange in their hastily brushed blue uniforms, sitting among their almost-naked, copper-skinned hosts. Indian and American pledged everlasting friendship.

The dragoons, refreshed and eager for the return march, clattered eastward on July 25 accompanied by fifteen Kiowa, one Comanche, and three Pawnee chiefs, who had consented to return with the expedition. They journeyed over 100 miles the first week, arriving at their sick camp near the Comanche village. Lieutenant Izard, commanding the detachment left behind, was himself bedded down with the fever. George Catlin's condition had deteriorated and he was reported critically ill. Quickly, Dodge broke camp and with the invalids started out for Fort Gibson. Before night fell on the first day out, the sick list had doubled. Forty-two men, debilitated by fever, sat hunched in their saddles. Seven were past riding and had to be carted on litters suspended between mules.

The days dragged. The land was depressingly bare. The columns stumbled across the buffalo range where guides picked off two deer, a buffalo, and a panther. The "cry of buffalo was heard," recalled Lieutenant T. B. Wheelock, "and never was the cheering sound of 'land' better welcomed by wearied mariners, than this by our hungry columns." As the cooks carved the appetizing meat, the command's morale soared.

The dragoons waded and swam across the Canadian River on the first day of August and, after waiting there three days, struck out south down the river, killing buffalo, curing meat, plagued by quick-burning prairie fires. They were intercepted by a hard-charging courier. He brought the news of the tragic death of General Leavenworth from bilious fever. Dodge dispatched an express to Camp Leavenworth on the Washita River and ordered the sick there to start at once for Fort Gibson.

The expedition veered from the Canadian River after resting five days and set a course for home. They struggled over the Cross Timbers, slashing their way with axes through thickets of blackjack saplings. Eastward the grass was scorched, dried up, affording no forage for the animals. The only water was stagnant pools, where buffalo had lain and wallowed, like hogs in a mud puddle. Thirsty horses dashed toward these holes, plunged their noses into the stinking water, and sucked up the poisonous draft until some fell dead in their tracks. The men, parched-lipped and sun burnt, sprang from their mounts, scooping up the tepid water, drinking to almost fatal excess.

The columns straggled into Camp Holmes on the Little River where, to their relief, they discovered fresh water, pork, and flour. Without tarrying, the command moved out into a hot wind, alternately walking, leading, and riding the exhausted horses.

On August 15, a thin, high cloud filtered the sun's light as the staggering ranks, shaggy and emaciated, shorn of the pomp and circumstance which had marked their exit two months before, gradually recognized the familiar line of a roof, the posts of the corral, the blocks of buildings, the rod of the flagpole.

Everyone at Fort Gibson had turned out. The troopers were solemn lumps in their saddles as they rode through the lane of onlookers. Cheers broke from well-wishers—hearty, thankful, sincere cheers. The Dodge expedition had returned.

chapter 2.

"The Dragoon Bold"

♞ ♞ ♞

T WO YEARS LATER WAR ERUPTED IN THE STINKING HELL OF the Florida swamps. Seminole Indians pillaged and burned, fighting when they pleased, where they pleased. The American military was unable to anticipate their movements. Detachments of infantry and artillery were impotent against an enemy that would not stand and permit himself to be engaged.

The Second Regiment of Dragoons, organized in 1836 to subdue the Seminole, received its baptism of fire at Micanopy when Company D assisted in the defeat of 200 hatchet-swinging savages who struck at dawn on June 10. Mounting horses, the troopers rushed out from the stockade and enveloped the hostiles' right as an artillery company encircled the left. The dragoons, slashing through the forest, firing rapidly, repulsed the attacking warriors.

Again in July, Company D fought the Seminole at Welika Pond near Fort Defiance. Twenty-six horsemen and a detachment of artillery, escorting a train from Fort Drane, were bushwhacked. Retreating, refusing to surrender, the Americans beat off the redskins until reinforcements arrived.

The war against the Seminole dragged on, a war of countless skirmishes, of wading through morasses, of fighting the deadly mosquito as well as the treacherous Indian. Detachments of dragoons, artillery, and infantry marched and countermarched, battled fatigue, exposure, and privation.

On December 19, 1837, the entire regiment of Second Dragoons, part of a force under General Thomas S. Jesup, commanding the Army in Florida, moved out from Fort Mellon. Two companies of troopers and a battalion of Fourth Artillery, sent ahead of the main columns, constructed bridges and hacked out corridors through the untamed forest. Their course paralleled the St. John's River.

The woods grew thickly to the river's edge. The command had to dismount, lead the horses yard by yard through natural avenues under a canopy of branches interlaced with creeper vines. The woods broke away at intervals, leaving cleared patches in which grass rose waist high.

The force skirted Lake Harney, picking up an old trail, which straggled off in a southwesterly direction. Each morning as they looked about them, the landscape presented the same familiar picture, and they felt as if they had not moved from the campsite one day back. Maps were useless. They had no way of knowing the distance marched each day. Now and then they could make a rough guess through information gleaned from settlers and friendly Indians, but for the most part they had to make inaccurate calculations.

Splashing along the banks of the Locha Hatchee River, much of the time wading in the water, the infantry and dragoons surprised the redmen at Jupiter Inlet. The troops charged through the stream until they suddenly blundered into deep water. Through the confusion rang the curses of the noncoms who tried futilely to rally their sinking men. The Seminole fired from the banks. Frantically the Americans swam for the shore where a group of dragoons crawled from the water to charge the enemy's left and rear. But the wily Indians had merged with the forest and vanished.

General Jesup was relieved by General Zachary Taylor, "Old Zeke," in May, 1838. On the shores of Lake Okeechobee, Taylor and his army tracked down and defeated the Seminole. But fast-striking bands of savages continued to terrorize. Plantations went up in flames. White settlers were slaughtered without mercy, their homes reduced to blackened heaps, their crops devastated, their cattle destroyed.

At Charlotte Harbor on the banks of the Caloosahatchee River a detail of Second Dragoons had the tedious task of guarding a prosperous trading post. Here friendly Indians drifted in from the woods and bartered for American goods. In July, 1839, Lieutenant Colonel William S. Harney, second in command of the dragoon regiment, stopped to inspect the garrison on the way to his post at Cape Florida.

On the evening of July 22, after the stew pots were scoured, the troopers rolled up in their blankets and went to sleep. Colonel Harney stayed awake watching the stars wheel through the sky and listening to the night. The wilderness behind was alive with muffled cries and the horses grunted nervously at the forest sounds. Harney stirred the fire before returning to his tent. Tossing his blankets together for a bed of sorts, he fell asleep.

He awoke abruptly. The cry began on a short raucous note and rose to pierce his ears. Whooping Seminole came in firing guns, arrows singing. The lead man raced into camp, his painted face twisted in an inhuman grin which disappeared under the impact of Sergeant Bigelow's rifle butt. A crescendo swelled from the other side of the camp. Above it Harney heard the maddened cries of the frightened horses.

A white trader ran from the post, stumbling, mumbling to himself. A savage fired at him. The trader kept on moving his lips until the warrior broke the rifle butt on his head.

Harney heard someone calling, "Run to the water! Run to the water!" He started for his boots and coat, but thought better of it. Charging from the tent he dodged for the river. In a split second he glimpsed the chalk-white, crimson-splashed face of a trooper. He saw past the burning tents to the walls of the trading post. Flames shot from the structure, lapping at the veins of pitch, and running along the wood. Tents collapsed into heaps of flames. Fire spread, feeding on the grass and pine needles. The grotesque figures of Indians spun and twirled and charged.

Horror-struck and unarmed, the dragoons tried vainly to protect themselves in the river. Warriors on the banks emptied their guns and shot their arrows at them. Dropping down in the water, paddling for the opposite shore, the Americans swam out of rifle range. Hideous-looking Indians lined the other bank, screeching and waving their guns. A warrior who spoke English bellowed to Sergeant Bigelow, "Sergeant come ashore and bring you the men; we are friends, and will not hurt you." Corporal Haywood feared treachery, but Bigelow and eight others struggled ashore. Fleetingly Haywood saw a savage strolling arm in arm with Sergeant Simmons before Haywood and the others in the river slipped downstream, rounded a point, and clambered to safety on board an American sloop, which had dropped down when the attack commenced.

From the underbrush Harney had watched the drama. Certain he couldn't help his men, he ran down the bank a quarter of a mile where he walked into the water and down a few paces, then stepped out, backward, and up the bank to deceive the Indians into believing by the tracks that two men had gone into the river and drowned. As he raced through the trees, he could hear the triumphant cries of the Seminole. He ran, dodging between trunks until he had cleared the grove and was in the open scrub. All that mattered was to escape, to lose himself in the heavy brush.

Frequently he turned as he ran and looked back. Harney sensed someone was following. By midday there was no longer any doubt. He dropped flat on the ground, drew his pocket knife, and waited. To his relief, his tracker turned out to be Corporal Al Britton. Camouflaging themselves by blacking their faces with charred wood left by Indian fires, they snaked back along the river bank, stumbling over roots and grass, lacerating their bare feet.

Britton suddenly signaled for silence and stopped short. Crawling down to the river, Britton peered from beneath the undergrowth, then slithered back to the colonel and reported. A canoe was approaching.

"Britton, can you fight?" whispered Harney.

"I will die with you, colonel," he replied.

Harney asked where it was.

"Under the wild fig tree," Britton said, pointing.

Harney stole to the tree, knife in hand, and looked toward the water. He spotted the canoe. It was his own dugout, abandoned, drifting downstream. Splashing out and manhandling it to shore, he found his harpoon and rations undisturbed.

He and Britton scrambled in and paddled between a tangle of forest festooned with Spanish moss that all but shut out the sun. The gnarled trunks and twisting branches of trees shot upward, enveloped in clinging shrouds. Such light as penetrated through from above was without warmth. The river flowed swiftly without sound, a dark stream running through the misty grotto.

Harney and Britton overtook the same sloop boarded by Haywood and the escaped dragoons. The colonel arranged a sneak visit to the trading post that night to discover what had become of the rest of his force. A handful of men, badly shaken, yet determined, volunteered to accompany him.

The colonel and the troopers started out armed only with knives and, silently approaching, crept into camp and looked about. Where the tents had stood only mounds of ash remained. The trading post was a charred ruin. The men, working their way toward the outer rim of the camp, found the bodies of their comrades sprawled face down, arms outstretched. The Seminole had killed Sergeant Simmons by ripping out his bowels. Other had been tied to pine trees. After torturing them by igniting slivers thrust into their bodies, the savages had set them ablaze by tossing torches at their feet. A grim-faced detachment buried them at dawn and started back.

Depredation followed depredation. On a bright April day in 1840, a well-mounted Uchee Indian crossed the Hillsboro River at Tampa Bay, trotted to the commanding general's quarters, and halted. He dismounted, entered, and reported that he had passed the dead and mutilated body of an express rider, forty miles north on the Fort Clinch road.

Ordered to investigate, Captain Benjamin Beall and Company I, Second Dragoons, swung into their saddles. The road they followed was little more than a single set of deeply rutted tracks gouged into the earth. It wandered and curled, taking advantage of every small clearing with little regard for distance or direction.

They rode throughout the night and, just as the first streaks of light colored the eastern sky, their guides gestured ahead. After a short gallop, the company reined in to stare at a grisly sight— the head of the express rider stuck atop a pyre, blackened and charred, surrounded by fragments of his body, apparently first hacked to pieces by hostiles, then torn and devoured by wolves. The spectacle so infuriated Captain Beall that he vowed if he caught the rascals, he would skin them alive, literally.

A burial detail scooped out a shallow grave; officers gathered up the scattered bits of mail; guides searched for clues to the murderers' trail. The culprits had taken precautions to throw off pursuers. But the Uchee guide, checking every twig, every blade of grass, every soft spot in the soil, discovered a lone moccasin track. Then others. Soon the trail became well marked and the detachment followed it at a lope.

Night dropped quickly. It was moonless and the trail became hard to trace. The dragoons worked their way through the scrub, marching with caution. They fell upon a small clearing where campfires still smoldered, but the savages had moved on.

After resting, the command remounted at dawn and began slogging through broad, marshy plains blanketed by man-high grass, which brushed mosquitoes and sandflies into their faces. It was late afternoon before they emerged from the morass and entered a pine barren. Up ahead lay a freshly killed deer, still warm and quivering, blood trickling from parts where the Seminole had severed the flesh for their evening meal.

Picking their way to high ground, they sighted a lake through the open pines, beyond which lay a dense, dark hummock. In single file, the detachment edged toward the water, Beall leading, his two lieutenants a few yards to the right near the lake's rim.

Spotting the murderers' camp, Beall signaled *Charge*. Men and horses lunged forward. The Indians, like hysterical chickens, scattered through the shallow waters, crawling backward on their hands and knees, splashing forward and back in panic-stricken feints.

The troopers, jumping from their saddles, swung their rifles into action. Shots whined high above the savages. A couple of Indians who had plunged to the middle of the lake stood waist-deep in water and yelled defiance as they found themselves trapped. Reports from two rifles sounded simultaneously. The red men spun crazily and dropped.

The Americans dragged the bodies ashore where Beall, inspecting one of the warriors, exclaimed, "What a handsome-looking villain he is!"

"Don't fall in love with him, Captain," a lieutenant chided, "until you have seen him *skinned*. Remember your vow."

"Pshaw!" answered Beall, "the poor devil is dead now. Does any one know who he is? Where is that black rascal Tony? He ought to know."

Flushed out from the water where he'd taken refuge during the fight, Tony, a Negro guide, gazed down at the body and said, "Bress de Lord! it am Waxehadjo!"

Chief Waxehadjo had butchered at least seven express riders. From his body the Yankees recovered watches, guard chains, gold pencils, rings, and pins. Rounding up captives, they returned to Tampa Bay.

Later that same year, 1840, Colonel William S. Harney, with ninety men from the Second Dragoons and Third Artillery, marched out to seize Chief Chekika who had mutilated Sergeant Simmons and his comrades at Charlotte Harbor. In canoes borrowed from the Navy, led by John, a Negro guide, the command entered the Everglades—marshy stretches of water dotted with myriads of islands. Reedlike grass of greenish-yellow stood chest high. Small highways, dark of color, laced their way through the tropical panorama. Along the shores of the islands, alligators stretched their scabby lengths in the sun, snapping at the dragoons' approach before waddling away. Moccasins cruised through the shallows, their heads lifted inches above the water. Tall cranes fished in the grass. The days were hot and the nights were filled with strange and horrifying sounds.

The marks of travel were upon the troopers. Harney's uniform was torn and stained, mud-spattered and faded. The days spent forcing their way through almost limitless stretches of thick grass had honed the men to a tough resilience. One dragoon wondered if the settlers of the territory, who were crying for action against the aborigines, had any idea of the country in which the soldiers had to operate. Properly armed, a band of Seminole could surprise and exterminate whole companies in the isolated swamps.

Horse soldiers and artillerymen canoed from island to island, clawing their way ashore, searching. On the fifth day out John, the guide, pointed to yet another island in the distance. Harney and his men, paddling silently, beached their dugouts in the grass.

Moving with wariness, they darted from one cover to the next. Their movements drew no fire as they pounced catlike out of the foliage upon an Indian village, clubbing with their muskets, wielding their knives. Harney discharged his gun full into a face and jumped to dodge the blow of a hatchet.

Corporal Lewellin and Private Hall waded into the high grass, hard on the heels of the fleeing chief. Chekika stopped abruptly and turned. Smiling and unarmed, he walked toward the Americans, hands up in token of surrender. But Private Hall, remembering the disemboweled Sergeant Simmons, coolly leveled his rifle and fired. Surprise and bewilderment flooded Chekika's eyes. His body sagged, his knees buckled, as a rush of crimson appeared with suddenness at his temple. He pitched forward, dead.

The detachment hunted down and captured the rest of the band. Troopers went from hut to hut, gathering evidence of the brutal massacre at the trading station—$2,000 worth of goods and thirteen Colt's revolvers. Harney wasted no time over formalities.

Over the cross limbs of trees, ropes were flung. The loose ends were held firm by a half-dozen dragoons. Twelve Indians, blindfolded, their arms tied behind them, were led beneath the crude gallows where soldiers adjusted the nooses about their necks.

Harney gave the order. Troopers pulled on the ropes. Their victims were drawn upward, struggling until their twisted heads were less than two feet beneath the limbs. Then the ends of the ropes were looped around and fastened securely to the trunks. For minutes the wretches spun, knees up, elbows out as far as the knots permitted. All at once, their knees sagged, their bodies hung limp. The massacre of Sergeant Simmons and his comrades was avenged.

In other parts of Florida, Seminole ranged the country in small bands, raiding isolated cabins, butchering, raping, scalping. Poorly guarded trading posts were broken into, their goods pilfered or burned. Throughout the short days of winter and the long humid hours of summer, expeditions and patrols searched for the enemy. Groups of white settlers banded together as vigilantes to track down or bushwhack lone Indians or small units, but the war during 1841 lacked the drama of great actions

Peace appeared as remote as ever. Recruits, who had excitedly volunteered on the promise of high adventure, swore with frustration and headed for home once their enlistments were up. They had a multitude of complaints. The food was nauseating. Supplies were slow in arriving. They were debilitated by fevers and prostrated by sunstroke. Changes in command had failed to improve the situation. Official Washington was concerned and the War Department pressed the Army to push the campaign with vigor.

Colonel William J. Worth, commanding the Florida Army in 1842, learned of an enemy concentration in Wahoo Swamp. Dragoons, infantry, and artillery, the whole expedition commanded by Worth himself, got in motion for the Pilaklikaha Hummock, twenty miles from Tampa Creek.

Encamped at Abraham's old town, the command prepared to move at dawn, guided by the aging Chief Holartooche. At 1:00 A.M. the chief threw back the flaps of Colonel Worth's tent, entered and, privately displaying deep emotion, pleaded for the lives of women and children in the approaching battle. If men were captured, he urged Worth not to hang them. The colonel nodded his head in assent. The old warrior walked out into the night.

Sunrise. The columns rolled out through a thinly wooded section of stunted, spindly trees, palmetto scrub, and tall grass. Troopers and foot soldiers loaded their rifles, carefully patching the balls, priming and pricking the vents, removing coverings from the locks, examining the quantity of powder in their horns, arranging extra bullets and patches. The steady tread of the soldiers shook the heavy dew from the foliage.

Holartooche excitedly reported to the colonel, "An Indian just passed here."

"How do you know?"

"This blade of grass," the Indian replied, holding it up, "was trod upon this morning; you see it is crushed; the sun nor the light of day has not shone upon it—had either, it would have wilted— you see it is green, but crushed. Here are more—there is the print of a foot!"

The columns halted. More tracks were examined.

"He is running to make known the approach of the troops," said the chief.

Three miles farther on the command sighted a hummock—a mass of dark green foliage and entwined grapevines surrounded by water. They pushed forward slowly through black scum, over sunken roots and logs. Here and there the sunlight was shut away. Cypress trees shot upward. Thick creepers hung down and Spanish moss dangled motionless from the branches.

Suddenly, dark figures erupted from the green tangle. Naked, smeared a hideous scarlet, emitting barbaric cries, the Seminole turned a barrage of fire on the advancing infantry. The forward section stumbled on toward the hummock. Yells and screams echoed and reechoed. The whoops became louder and louder, until they mingled in the shouts of the Yankees.

Above the rattle of gunfire, the Seminole heard the screams of Chief Halleck Tustenugge. His band, confused, exhausted, the wounded half-maddened with pain, saw their retreat cut off. They gave ground. The Americans advanced relentlessly. Suddenly, the savages broke for safety and swarmed past the dragoons, dodging, scattering into the swamps. The soldiers chased them in all directions, but the warriors were lost in the vastness of water and foliage.

Back at the clearing, the dragoons buried a downy-faced private, Augustus R. Wandell, K Company. They dug a hole with their hands and tin cups, wrapped the body in a dirty blanket, and deposited it in its lonely resting place. Wandell's requiem was the distant yelp of the savage and the sporadic blast of a rifle.

Colonel Worth and the command in Florida were slowly beating back the Seminole on all fronts. The Army was applying the pressure. Escape routes were squeezed into narrow corridors. Most of the Seminole villages lay blackened and smoldering. Fields were charred, herds driven away.

By the spring of 1842 the Americans had either killed most of the Indians or deported them to the wilds of Indian Territory. There lingered in Florida a handful of bands, but these remained in the swamps, remote, no longer a threat to the pioneer.

In Washington President John Tyler recommended to Congress that hostilities cease in Florida. As the 2nd Dragoons departed from the territory for Baton Rouge, Louisiana, they sang "The Dragoon Bold," written by one of the officers, a song which became traditional in the regiment.

> Oh! the dragoon bold he knows no care,
> As he rides along with his uncropp'd hair;
> Himself in the saddle he lightly throws,
> And on the weekly scout he goes.
>
> At night he camps in the old pine wood,
> He lights his fire and cooks his food;
> His saddle-blanket around him throws,
> And on the ground he seeks repose.
>
> If an anxious care should cross his mind,
> 'Tis of the girl he's left behind,
> When he parted from her in sorrow and woe,
> And went to the wars a long time ago.
>
> Then cheer, boys, cheer for the girls afar,
> We'll all go home at the close of the war;
> And, sadly tanned by a Southern sun,
> We'll spin long yarns of the deeds we've done.

chapter 3.

"The other side of the mountain."

COLONEL STEPHEN WATTS KEARNY ROLLED OUT OF HIS
blankets at the first challenge of the bugle and was on his
feet, putting on his uniform as the notes of *Reveille* still
hung in the damp air. It was dark in the tent, and when he
pushed back the flaps and glanced outside, the movements of the
troopers already about their labors were still indistinct. To the east
he could see faint streaks of light.

The First Dragoon Regiment broke camp quickly on that day,
May 19, 1845. Kearny's trumpeter walked back to his saddle and
mounted, waiting until the colonel had stepped into his saddle before placing the bugle to his lips, giving forth *Prepare to Mount*.
Other trumpets blared. Each dragoon grasped the reins with his
left hand and put his left foot into the stirrup. The single note of
Mount brought them all swinging upward into their saddles.

Kearny raised his hand and brought it down sharply. The
earth rumbled as 250 armed dragoons moved westward on that first
day out from Fort Leavenworth. Ahead rode Thomas Fitzpatrick,
famous "Broken Hand," the guide.

This expedition was far different from that early ordeal of
suffering, the Dodge expedition of 1834. Trained in prairie marches,
veteran of many western campaigns, Colonel Kearny had stripped
his command of all except essentials in preparation for this mission.
Riding ramrod-straight in the saddle, he glanced back at the cavalcade. He was trailed by his orderly and chief bugler; then came the
staff officers; then a division mounted on gray horses, cantering by
twos; then another division on black mounts, another on bays, another on sorrels, and a fifth of grays; then the howitzers and the
wagons carrying only flour, coffee, sugar, salt meat, guns, and am-

munition. Behind, guarded by a detail of nine men, thundered a drove of cattle and sheep and, beyond, the main guard under a lieutenant brought up the extreme rear.

During the 1830's and 1840's frontiersmen, driven by land hunger, wrestled against the heat of summer, the numbing blasts of winter, and attacks of marauding Indians. Primarily the duty of the First Dragoons was to defend more than 1,000 miles of frontier with a force of 600, a mere fraction of their potential enemies. During the regiment's formative years its colonel, Stephen Watts Kearny, who had replaced Henry Dodge, was pleased that fierce Indian warfare had been avoided.

The trooper's life on the plains was one of monotony and training, of constant patrols and scouting. The officers and men of the First had revolutionized the regiment by hard work, drill, and discipline. Under Kearny's watchful eye the troopers had been schooled in the proper care of their horses, and men spent hours grooming their animals, rehearsing treatments for various sicknesses and injuries. The colonel made them repeat almost endlessly the acts of bridling, saddling, mounting, dismounting, unsaddling, unbridling.

Out on the western frontier during these years the First Dragoons were gradually and painfully forging an efficient, if unreasoned, school of tactics for keeping the peace on the border. Summer patrols galloped across the lines of communication between Indian tribes and wrought confusion among the warriors. Savages could still pillage and plunder, but their retreat would be halted by the troopers' fast forming across the trails of retirement.

Although constant duty in the summer months was admirable training, acute tactical problems remained. General Winfield Scott in 1829 had translated French Army manuals into English. These fundamentals were employed by the Army in the Mexican War and were to serve indirectly as a basis for Hardee's *Tactics* of Civil War renown. The matter of organization received attention in 1835 when the War Department established a cavalry school at Carlisle Barracks, Pennsylvania—a school which was to become the clearing house for cavalry affairs.

European influence was again injected into the dragoons when a military commission returned from a tour of the Continent. One of the American officers, Philip Kearny, nephew of Stephen Watts

Kearny, had studied six months at the Royal Cavalry School at Saumur, France, and later served with the *Chasseurs d' Afrique* in the Algerian campaign. The most important result of this experience was Kearny's report to the Secretary of War and the attached supplement, *Applied Cavalry Tactics Illustrated in the French Campaign.* Published by the War Department in 1841, it became the accepted guide for cavalry tactics of the United States Army and until the Civil War was regarded by cavalrymen as the best work available on the subject.

Across the width and breadth of America in 1845 men were talking about Oregon country. An armed clash with the British seemed imminent. In ever-increasing numbers American settlers' wagons were rolling westward on the Oregon Trail, rumbling through regions occupied by hostile bands of savages. Garrisoned on the edge of the plains at Fort Leavenworth, the First Regiment of Dragoons was trained to meet whatever crisis might arise. The War Department had ordered five companies of troopers to march as far as South Pass to warn the Indians that bloodshed or violence would be severely punished.

In the first week after leaving Fort Leavenworth, Kearny and his horse soldiers had covered 120 miles, following the northwesterly trails of other marches. They moved through the picturesque landscape of the Missouri River, reached the open prairies and, crossing the plain between the two branches of the Blue River, struck the Oregon Trail.

On May 24, 1845, a stiff wind sprang up an hour before sunset shoving angry clouds into the west where they massed crimson and gray. Kearny reined in his horse and raised his hand as a signal for the columns to halt. Rising in his stirrups, he squinted at the rolling country before him. Off in the distance were undefined dark spots. A lieutenant, peering through his spyglass, exclaimed, "It's a company of Emigrants!"

"We felt the same interest and excitement," reported Lieutenant James H. Carleton, an erstwhile sailor from the state of Maine, "which a passenger, who has been long at sea, would experience as the cry 'Sail ho!' would greet his ears from the look-out aloft."

Kearny could soon discern the great swaying hoods of canvas. The line seemed endless. Spurring their horses and trotting toward the white-topped caravan, the dragoons were no longer moving on a carpet of grass. The grass had been crushed, broken into small bits, ground into the soil by thousands of hooves, shod and unshod, sliding, shuffling, stamping without letup, and by hundreds of wagon wheels, many of them the most ponderous in use anywhere. It was small wonder that the wheels and hooves were churning up a cloud of dust, a spiraling column which resembled a tornado in the offing.

The loads of the wagons were as varied as the folks who drove them. It was astonishing what restless men and women picked to lug halfway across America: parlor organs, stiff portraits of Grandma and Grandpa, plows, bedsteads, full-length mirrors, accordions, stoves, kettles, clocks, bedding, washtubs, rocking chairs—in short anything and everything that might be found in a secondhand store.

At sunset the wagons groaned to a halt. Many of the troopers had never before seen a wagon camp. It was laid out in a slipshod circle. There was the usual quota of children crying, playing, most of them old enough to be afoot. Scattered on the ground were items of household gear and here and there lay garbage and other debris, flung outside the ring of vehicles and left unburied. Altogether it was a sorry sight.

Morning came bright with a clear sky. The army columns were in motion early, marching up the valley of the Little Blue River, passing other caravans headed for Oregon. They splashed across the shallow waters and quicksands of creeks, whose banks were blanketed with cottonwoods, oaks, and pea vines. They cantered across spreading prairies and overtook more emigrants who reported increasing numbers of Pawnee and Sioux. Kearny and his staff gave sound advice to the settlers, whose guards were ill-equipped and poorly trained for the arduous journey.

The regiment camped on the shores of the Platte River on May 29. It had marched 300 miles. As the sun dropped down, the dragoons pitched their shelter tents in a solid line, company by company, on the river bank and then sat cross-legged on the ground before little fires, smoking and conversing, waiting for mess call. Hundreds of horses fed upon the plain and sentries strolled in a circle outside. Beyond was the circular village of another wagon train, nestled near an oasis of timber.

The command lolled and rested on May 30, but took up the line of march the following day. The weather was threatening. The wind moaned and the mutter of thunder accompanied vivid zigzag streaks of lightning. Then the storm burst. A gale-force wind bent and twisted trees, dumped water over the men in bucketfuls, and brought frequent blasts of whipping hailstones. Darkness increased rapidly and night fell before the fury of the tempest eased into a steady drizzle. By midnight the storm had ended.

The dawn came early on Sunday, June 1. For three hours the expedition filed along the south bank of the Platte River. Suddenly the column leaders halted. Up ahead on a gentle rise were the men, women, and children of a wagon train clustered together in a circle. Soon all but two men trudged down the slope and separated for their wagons. In a few minutes the entire train was jolting forward again, winding back to the main trace.

Kearny's scouts galloped up to the leader of the company, a hulking, stern man of forty. They asked why he had ordered his party up the hill.

"Strangers," he said, his voice trembling, "the cause were a funeral, and them men thar are covering up the body of my own pretty boy. Last night he left me for a better world than this—did the poor little fellow—but 'twas hard to give him up and to leave him thar in such a lonesome place."

The scouts expressed their sorrow and tried to console him. He replied sadly, "I should have felt better if the poor little thing had died nearer home, so I could have buried it in a grave-yard whar other children lie; but then again, strangers . . . my dear child sleeps as near the angels here as thar—so it matters but little whar I laid him. He had suffered a good deal—my little boy had."

Solitary graves such as this, sometimes covered with wolf tracks, marked the Oregon Trail. That night a dragoon lieutenant noted: "There they solemnly consign to the unblessed earth—to the howling wilderness—the father's hope—the mother's love and her pride. Pity her! It is no common loss!"

After riding along the South Fork of the Platte River for a day, the regiment started across. The divisions plunged in by twos, the lead companies failing to reach the far shore before the rear guard had shoved off into the water. On the banks wagoners screamed obscenities at the mules when the iron tires of the wagon wheels chewed into the sand. Ungreased axles squealed high notes of protest at each slow turning of the hubs. The mules, wagons, and howitzers finally lumbered out on the other bank. The cattle crossed easily, but the sheep almost perished in the swiftly churning channels.

Kearny and his troopers loped along the trail on June 7. Without warning, the horses came to a sudden, snorting halt on the brink of what appeared to be a strange lost world. The ground dropped away, and there, extending for three miles, was a violent sea of stone, rocks, precipices, and chasms—a fantastic kaleidoscope of forms. Kearny dismounted, tossed his reins to his orderly, and stood scrutinizing the panorama. The dragoons sat silent on their horses, groping to orient themselves amid this conglomeration of rock—upflung, chewed out, twisted in an endless variety of shapes and colors.

Groups of emigrant trains were waiting, their leaders searching for a pass, a trail, a way through to the valley of the North Fork. The army columns turned sharply and marched two miles before coming to the head of a deep gorge.

The guide, Fitzpatrick, wheeled and kicked his horse into a slow walk and started down to see if he had the correct passage. He returned within the hour and reported that they were at the head of Ash Hollow—a famous defile with which he was well acquainted— through which he could lead the columns without much difficulty.

Slowly, warily, in single file the regiment trailed the guide through the labyrinth of towering rocks, winding around jutting points, inching down steep hillsides. The troopers appraised this rock and multicolored stone not as a natural wonder, but for the potential work it represented. Everything on wheels, they realized, was going to have to be worked down the worst grades by ropes.

The wagons began the hazardous descent. Suddenly the command started at a series of crashing sounds mingled with mule cries as an ordnance wagon rolled and bounced downward dragging its mules to kingdom come. It hit a massive rock and exploded, flinging debris back high up the trail. Miraculously no one was injured.

Crag after crag was negotiated until the dragoons reached the bottom, where they turned and twisted through a crooked canyon, only yards wide and walled in by soaring perpendiculars hundreds of feet above. Around them lay the dry and sandy bed of a wet-weather creek. Abruptly the soldiers entered a lush grove of ash, where a cool stream gushed from the sand, the first water they had seen since early morning. The sun was dropping in the west as the troopers plodded forward into the region where the width of the canyon increased.

Finally, they came to a spot of grass large enough to supply half of the expedition's horses. Kearny ordered one division to dismount and camp nearby; while he and the other squadrons moved a mile farther on to the bank of the North Fork.

That night the dragoons could hear the echoes of neighing horses, the cracking of whips, the tinkling of innumerable bells, and the profanity of the drivers cursing their cattle forward. The emigrant trains were having their troubles in the tortuous passage.

The expedition pressed westward on June 9. Travel-stained and weary, Colonel Kearny rode in the Army's regulation dark-blue flannel shirt, light-blue kersey pants, and black boots. His staff officers were similarly dressed. Their uniforms were dusty and unkempt, even here and there coming out at the elbows. To the rear the main body of the regiment stretched out raising a high, curling spiral of dust which drifted eastward. The dust, rolling from under the hooves of the first division, became progressively heavier and thicker as it moved toward the rear, blanketing the other divisions. There was no shade anywhere except in the lee of the canvas-topped wagons and sometimes, depending on the angle of the sun, even these could hardly shade horse and dragoon.

Toward noon on June 14, men began to catch glimpses far ahead of the buildings of Fort Laramie, the trading post owned by the American Fur Company, stopover for thousands of pioneers before they jumped off for Oregon. Roads linked the fort with the branches of the Missouri River and, to the south, with the Spanish settlements in New Mexico. Wilderness traces blazed by fur trappers, savages, and mountain men crisscrossed here.

Despite the heat of the afternoon, the place had an air of activity. High on a pole the national colors hung bright against the cloudless sky. Fort Laramie was a gusty, teeming center. Men, women, and children from the wagon trains passed through in a continuous file. Pioneer faces, Mexican faces, renegade faces, faces of half-breeds, Indian faces—the venturesome of a hemisphere paused here. Denizens of the fort gaped at Kearny and the regiment, the first American troops ever to be seen in this locality. "Here," wrote Captain Philip St. George Cooke, "barbarism and a traditional or half-civilization meet on neutral ground; but as a struggle, it is certain that the former has the best of it."

The colonel wisely selected a camp sight in an area well-removed from Fort Laramie, ensuring better grass for the horses and safeguarding his men from the pollution of trading-post life. Runners cantered off in all directions to notify the neighboring Teton Sioux of a council meeting intended, Kearny hoped, to insure the peaceful passage of the emigrants.

Officers of the regiment rode out from camp on June 16 for an open plain where 1,200 Indians—men, women, and children—were grouped beneath two American ensigns and an Indian banner. The Americans dismounted, strode over to the multitude, and sat down on canvas stools. Indians chiefs squatted cross-legged in a gigantic semicircle before the officers, while women and children shuffled about behind in a wider arc.

The proceedings were spectacular. Colonel Kearny, with an interpreter, addressed the silent crowd:

> Sioux: I am glad to see you. Your Great Father has learned much of his red children and has sent me with a few braves to visit you. I am going to the waters which flow to the setting sun. . . . I am opening a road for the white people and your Great Father directs that his red children shall not attempt to close it.
>
> There are many whites now coming on the road, moving to the other side of the mountains. They take with them their women, children and cattle. They all go to bury their bones there and never return. You must not disturb them in their persons or molest their property. Should you do so your Great Father would be very angry with you and cause you to be punished.
>
> Sioux: You have enemies about you but the greatest of them all is whiskey. I learn that some bad white men bring it here from Taos and sell it to you. Open your ears and listen to me. It is contrary to the wishes of your Great Father that whiskey be brought here and I advise you whenever you find it in your country, no matter in whose possession, to spill it on the ground. . . .

"The other side . . ."

> Your Great Father is the friend of his red children and as
> long as they behave themselves properly will continue to be so.
> I have not come among you to bring you presents but your
> Great Father has sent a few things that you may remember
> what I have said to you.

The principal chief of the Teton Sioux, Bull Tail, arose and replied: "If my people will be good to the whites, they will find that presents they are about to receive will come often. Father, this does very well and pleases me. What you have told me, I am glad of from my very heart. All you have told me is very good. . . . I remember the words you have spoken. My people will do as I say."

Americans distributed blankets, beads, mirrors, and trinkets and, to impress the Sioux, fired off howitzers. That night troopers shot off fireworks to inform the Great Spirit of the Indians' pledge of peace.

At dawn the next day the regiment moved out in a cold drizzle, leaving behind Company A to watch the Sioux concentrated in that region. Back in the saddle it was the old routine. The plains stretched away perfectly level and featureless. Each day the sun swept across the huge archway of heaven, and by noon it was beating down. There was nothing to see except an occasional rattlesnake or grizzly. Captain John Henry K. Burgwin almost broke a leg when he fell from his mount chasing a bear. In another accident Private Smith shot himself in the arm while carelessly pulling his rifle from some bushes. Surgeon Samuel G. I. DeCamp crudely amputated and Smith, swung into a litter, was lugged back to the relative ease of Fort Laramie.

After days of exhausting travel, the regiment reached Deer Creek, waded through the shallow streams of the North Platte, and emerged on its northern bank. They filed around the bluffs of the Red Buttes and over parched wastelands pocked with stones and sagebrush. Dropping off a detail of troopers with the weakest horses, the command swerved off in a new direction and left the Platte. The columns struck out over the alkaline *jornada* to the Sweetwater, turning into a gently rising valley, then clawing their way up a natural ramp.

On June 30 the dragoons left the source of the Sweetwater and, wending their way for six miles, fell upon a westward flowing stream, a branch of the Green River. Neither Kearny nor his men had been aware of crossing the Continental Divide and all were amazed and a little disappointed to discover that South Pass was just a rolling plain, not a breathtaking mountain gate.

Here in the Rockies, 280 miles from Fort Laramie, 850 from Leavenworth, the regiment paraded, celebrating the first time American soldiers had ever mustered on a Pacific watershed. The eyes of the men turned and stared at the snow-covered ranges. Through this historic pass Kit Carson, John C. Frémont, and thousands of settlers had traveled from the Mississippi Valley. Gazing at the wagon trains jolting their way down the trace toward Oregon, Kearny roughly calculated that he had already encountered 850 men, 475 women, 1,000 children, 7,000 cattle, 400 horses and mules, 460 wagons.

The command, fully rested, began the return trek to Fort Laramie, saddlebags and pockets bulging with horned toads, rock specimens, skins, hides, and other curiosities. On the night of July 3, a wagon-train master asked Kearny to fire one of "the big guns" at sunrise on the Fourth.

"Do it," he bellowed, "and I will treat you all!" The colonel assented, but hastened to assure the pioneer that he drank nothing stronger than "Sweet Water." On Independence Day howitzers erupted. The entire adult male population of the emigrant train was rip-roaring drunk by noon.

Retracing their steps, the columns made Fort Laramie on July 13 after a journey plagued by an epidemic of fever, known as "Tyler Grippe." The regiment moved out again the next day, heading toward the south fork of the Platte River, 130 miles due south. Along the banks of the Chugwater, the dragoons discovered a Cheyenne village. Here, dismounting, they heard the colonel address the savages and helped dole out a liberal supply of trinkets.

Saddling up and filing southward, troopers crossed tortuous wastes and sighted Long's Peak far off, dwarfing the other mountains. They marched past graves marked only by piles of buffalo bones or horse skulls. Moving down the Cache la Poudre, they crossed the south fork of the Platte, spurred their tiring mounts past the desolate ruins of an adobe trading station. The dreary landscape finally melted into grassy slopes and shrubbery beside Cherry Creek. Here in the shade of firs and oaks they eased back and relaxed from the ardors of the trail. On July 25 the command marched thirty-one miles over the highland between the Arkansas and the South Platte Rivers to Fountain Creek.

The daily routine never varied. Trumpets blasted *Reveille* at four in the morning. Inspection followed, then buglers blew *Stable Call*, feed time for the horses. Before sunup troopers hastily downed steaming cups of coffee, cakes baked overnight and, occasionally, fried buffalo meat. They hoisted the baggage into the wagons, re-packed it, then saddled the horses.

Departure from camp was at 6:30 A.M. Kearny called a stop for "nooning," the exact time depending on the availability of grass and water. On the march companies continually changed positions in the columns. The colonel called no halts on Sundays and, in the expedition's official correspondence, no one recorded a single religious service.

Toward evening the dragoons halted, dismounted, unsaddled their horses, and unpacked the wagons. Lighting the fires, butchering the buffalo killed by the hunters, cooks prepared the evening meal. The soldiers, after gulping their coarse food, lounged about the fires, smoking their pipes, admiring the sunset, joking. They crawled into their tents and fell fast asleep to be startled suddenly at 4:00 by the clang of *Reveille*.

Under a broiling sun on the 27th, the regiment loped along the banks of the Arkansas River near the northern boundary of Mexico. Since the United States had annexed Texas in March, 1845, relations between the two countries had been taut. The War Department had planned that the Kearny expedition return via the Santa Fe Trail to display American might along the southwestern frontier.

The dragoons sighted the Stars and Stripes at Bent's Fort on July 29. Salutes from a swivel cannon welcomed the troopers, the first military caravan to stop at this desolate trading station on the Santa Fe Trail. Founded in 1829, this renowned post received hardwares, calicoes, and dry goods from Missouri, 600 miles eastward; sugar, flour, bread, and beans from the Mexican city of Taos, 150 miles distant; pelts and buffalo robes from the plains, brought in by roving bands of Comanche and Cheyenne.

Kearny delayed only briefly and the next morning the soldiers were in the saddle, homeward bound. Within forty-eight hours, they were camped at Jackson Grove (Big Timbers). Landmarks were becoming familiar as they passed Council Grove, Round Grove, and Stranger River, and sighted in the distance the "Knob," the prominent feature of the Fort Leavenworth reservation.

At twilight the expedition approached the post. Ahead the brilliant vision of the national flag leaped into view in all its color, illumined by the last rays of the sun. The troopers watched it wave in the sundown breeze.

The sentries saluted and moved aside for the colonel who led his men through the main gate. Once inside, on the spick-and-span parade, Kearny dismounted and gave his reins to an orderly, who led his mount away to the corral. The colonel braced up to his full height, clasped his hands behind him, and spoke a few words of commendation to his weary soldiers, words that the men scarcely heard. The colonel then walked quickly to headquarters, up the steps, and into the hall.

In his official report he described the country through which the cavalcade had marched and the problems involved in its administration. Opposing the establishment of military posts beyond the frontier, he favored sending out expeditions to impress the Indian mind with the regiment's mobility and firepower. He denounced the traders who roamed between Bent's Fort and Fort Laramie, selling whiskey to the savages and causing much difficulty and harm.

The 99-day, 2,200-mile march was over, a march that was an epic in the annals of the United States Cavalry. Every man returned alive and well, a distinct contrast to the Dodge Expedition. The only serious casualty had been Private Smith. The experience and confidence gained on this march were to pay dividends the following year, 1846, when friction with Mexico flared into war.

chapter *4.*

"Charge, captain! Charge."

♞ ♞ ♞

ORTH OF THE RIO GRANDE RIVER ON THE PRAIRIE AT Palto Alto, Mexican General Manuel Arista was moving his army before sunrise on May 9, 1846. By 6:00 A.M. all his columns were rumbling southward on the road toward Matamoros. To the northwest, General Zachary Taylor called in his pickets and ordered the horses fed and saddled. The morning was spent arranging for the protection of the Yankee supply train. To secure its position, soldiers mounted heavy cannon and a regiment of artillerymen was detailed to guard it, which reduced Taylor's striking force to 17,000. Only toward early afternoon was the American army ready to move forward in search of Arista.

Regimental bands struck up "Yankee Doodle." Columns squeezed into the roadway, made narrow by the scrub growth on both sides. Apart from a company of Texas Rangers, the only mounted unit in the command was seven troops of the Second Dragoons, veterans of the Seminole campaign in Florida, armed with musketoons on sling belts, heavy Prussian sabers, and horse pistols.

Up ahead of the advancing army Taylor, slumped on "Old Whitey," one leg hiked over his pummel, was chewing tobacco and grimly surveying the countryside. The results of the previous day's battle were everywhere. Dead Mexicans, dead horses, jumbled ammunition boxes, mangled vehicles, abandoned artillery. Now and then Taylor heard a man groan.

Mixed detachments of rangers, infantry, and a platoon of dragoons pushed ahead of Taylor to locate the enemy. At three in the afternoon the report trickled back that the Mexicans were four miles down the pike, drawn up to take advantage of the protection afforded by Resaca de Guerrero, an extensive, shallow ravine, which curved across the road. Here Arista had established the key point of his defense. Batteries of artillery, totaling seven guns, were mounted to sweep the approaches along the Matamoros road. The terrain for miles on either side of the Resaca was covered with an almost impenetrable growth of mesquite and chapparal. General Arista posted his infantry in the undergrowth and threw out skirmishers.

Covered by Captain Charles May's dragoon squadron and supported by regiments of Yankee infantry, light artillery sneaked down the road toward Arista. When half a mile from the Mexicans, a courier galloped up to May with orders to halt and await instructions.

Taylor's artillery opened fire, and under cover of the barrage, infantry inched and hacked their way forward to the very edge of the Resaca, but were stopped short by enemy cannon.

General Taylor personally went to the front to reconnoiter. There on the far side of the ravine, backed by lines of riflemen, the Mexican artillery, commanding the Matamoros road, belched steadily as the men serving the guns went about their business.

Faced with the necessity of forcing the Mexicans from their position, Taylor sent for May and his dragoons. The horse soldiers with drawn sabers trotted down the road in columns of four. May halted his men and cantered forward to get instructions. Taylor growled orders: "Charge, Captain! Charge, *nolens volens*."

Captain May nodded in assent, wheeled his horse, and rode back to his men. Sitting upright in the saddle, May surveyed them, then said simply, "Remember your regiment and follow your officers."

His upraised arm snapped down. Trumpets blasted. The command pounded forward at a gallop, May's black beard streaming in the wind. Dust, rising in clouds among the thickets, blinded and choked all but the leading horsemen.

Suddenly, the dragoons came to a plunging halt several hundred yards short of the ravine, barred by their own batteries. Here at the American advanced position gunners, engulfed in a pall of smoke, were pounding away at the enemy. Poor visibility and dense undergrowth obstructed movement around the cannon.

"Where are they?" bellowed May. "I am going to charge."

ABOVE: Coat of the 1st Dragoon, Mexican War period (1846).
BELOW: Unidentified Cavalry Guidon.

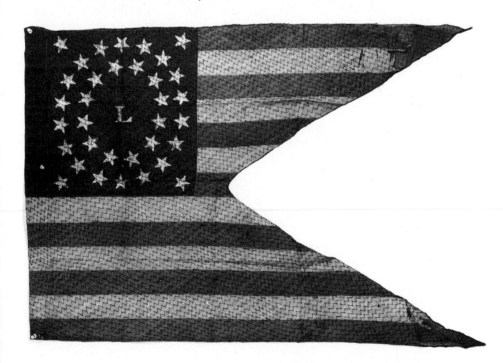

Begrimed with dust and powder, Randolph Ridgely, the artillery captain, pointed down the road and hollered: "Hold on a minute, Charley, till I draw their fire!"

Cannon crashed. Ridgely's men shoved their guns off the road. The horsemen hesitated. As the smoke lifted, the dragoons spotted the muzzles of the Mexican artillery, 300 yards away on the far side of the Resaca, protected by breastworks of timber and swarms of infantrymen.

May ordered *Charge*. He set his spurs hard. The squadron broke into a gallop. The lead horsemen, shouting orders, tried vainly to reform the line. In the excitement and confusion an orderly advance was impossible.

Lieutenant Sackett raced past May into the lead.

"No fair," roared May, "You took the jump on me."

May looked up. Sackett's horse, shot through the head, fell dead, pitching the rider into a pool of stagnant water.

Mexican gunners poured in volleys of canister. One horse plunged madly across the plain straight at the Mexicans, its dead rider's foot caught in the stirrup. Lieutenant Ingle tumbled from his mount, a slug in his throat. A dozen other horses were riderless.

May met the enemy at a dead run. Attacker and attacked came together. In the haze of battle it was almost impossible to tell what was happening. Even as May was seeking a target, a dragoon within a foot of him reeled in his saddle without a sound and fell over against him.

May shook him off and lunged for the right hand breastwork. A few troopers crashed through behind. Sabers flashed.

Most of the horses reared back and refused to follow May. Led by Sergeant Milton, who was soon cut down, horses and men wheeled and skirted the guns to gain the Mexican rear. D company swerved left and dashed for another battery, riding down the enemy, pursuing them into the chapparal. Mexican riflemen, hidden in the underbrush, recovered from their momentary shock and their guns chattered like strings of giant firecrackers exploding in sequence.

The dragoons were now scattered. Behind to the left, May heard the screams of wounded horses and men, American and Mexican. Urgently, he tried to rally his men, but could only muster six troopers.

Company D recrossed the ravine. Corporal McCaulley and his men headed down the road on the dead run, straight through a platoon of surprised Mexican lancers. May and his six dragoons veered and turned back up the road. They smashed through the Mexican battery again, captured General of Brigade de la Vega and regained American lines. Arista's men quickly reoccupied their cannon.

Ridgely's guns went into action again. But the battle of Resaca de la Palma was almost over. Grimly the 8th and part of the 5th Infantry regiments stormed into enemy positions. The Mexican wings were crumbling. General Arista hurriedly decamped, leaving behind portfolios and personal baggage. It took Captain May three hours to round up and reassemble his dragoons.

This charge was later depicted upon the Second's coat of arms— the shield emblazoned with a dragoon on a white horse brandishing a saber and charging a Mexican field gun, defended by a gunner armed with a rammer. It came to represent the spirit of the regiment.

A month after the Second had made its historic charge, the First Regiment of Dragoons, the nucleus of Colonel Stephen Watts Kearny's Army of the West, marched along the Santa Fe Trail intent upon the invasion of New Mexico. Except for the dragoons and a party of United States Army Topographical Engineers, Kearny's command was a motley outfit of recruits—860 Missouri Mounted Volunteers; a St. Louis company of horsemen bearing the name of Laclede Rangers; two companies of infantry, men who had tried to enlist as cavalry but failed to get in under the quota and insisted on going along on foot; two companies of artillery from St. Louis, one "German," and one "American"; fifty Delaware and Shawnee Indian scouts. Total force was 1,700, mostly mounted, and 16 small cannon. Rounding out the expedition, the Quartermaster Department listed 1,556 wagons, 3,658 draft mules, and 516 pack mules to transport equipment and supplies for the regulars and volunteers.

A year before the Mexican government had virtually pulled out of northern New Mexico, a region which it could no longer protect from the raids of the hostile Indians. The area was ready for conquest. Santa Fe traders had brought back stories that an American army would meet only slight resistance from the tyrannical Governor Manuel Armijo. Beyond Santa Fe was the richest prize of all, the Mexican province of California. Seize New Mexico, move westward, and grab California, such was the vision of American statesmen, especially President James K. Polk.

Marching miles in advance of the main body of troops, dragoon contingents passed familiar stations on the trail to Santa Fe. Behind in the columns the buoyant hopes of the soldiers were fast being dissipated by the hardship and toil of the campaign.

Many a volunteer company already lagged far behind. Recruits faced personal crises. Corporal McFarland suffered a severe attack of "cramp colic"; Private Ferguson was bitten by a rattlesnake; Corporal Craig came down with measles. Men of the rifle corps developed blisters and sore feet. Company commissaries became separated from their outfits. Fortunately for Kearny the enemy was far off.

As the army plodded along in this remote country where communications were nonexistent, the colonel had no idea of what was happening to Taylor's army in Mexico. He did not know that Commodore John D. Sloat on July 7 had landed a force at Monterey, California, raised the Stars and Stripes over the customhouse, and taken possession of the province for the United States.

The Army of the West straggled up to the Arkansas River, 253 miles from Fort Leavenworth, and then settled into the humdrum of a cross-country march.

The sun saturated earth and sky. Men rode drooping in their saddles, their horses near the limit of their endurance. Sometimes they dismounted and led their animals to preserve their strength. Lieutenant James W. Abert thought he had known fatigue before, but nothing to equal this. "This day," he wrote, "we made a march of thirty-one and a half miles, passing along the top of a barren ridge, between one and two miles from the river. Nothing was to be seen but the curly buffalo grass, now parched by the summer's heat. The sun poured down his rays most lavishly; the men all dismounted and walked, in order to rest and to relieve themselves from the singular sensation produced by the heat. First one and then another of the party became ill, several were seized with a severe vomiting."

The troops groused about the hardships. Swarms of flies, mosquitoes, and other insects tormented them. Frank Edwards and his comrades killed twenty rattlesnakes one morning, after their major had awakened to find one nestled by his leg for warmth.

One afternoon the wind sprang up, filling the sky from rim to rim with flying dust. It choked the troopers' nostrils and mouths and rimmed their eyes with mud. Soldier and horse struggled forward with heads down. The columns halted for a meal. The mounts looked away from the driving dust, the men huddled with their backs to it.

The afternoon turned dark. The sky boomed with thunder. With a sudden pounding the rain blasted down as a cloudburst moved across the plains. Regular and volunteer let go with yells of excitement and thankfulness.

The monotony of the march was relieved when scouts captured three Mexican spies nosing about. After the wide-eyed culprits were conducted through the entire camp, the leader exclaimed: "My God! What is to become of our republic?" Kearny purposely let them escape to spread tales of American strength.

Tom Fitzpatrick, the frontier guide, galloped in from Bent's Fort to report that Governor Armijo was conferring with the leading men of New Mexico about the defense of Santa Fe. The Mexicans were preparing to meet the invader.

The army closed to within ten miles of Bent's Fort, where it paused to rest and recuperate from the march. Fearing a scarcity of supplies on the trail to Santa Fe, Kearny slashed the trooper's daily ration to half a pound of flour and three-eighths of a pound of pork. "This," complained a horseman, "deprived us of coffee, sugar, salt, rice, &c., which had previously helped to make our provisions palatable. Now our meals consist of dough, if a simple mixture of flour and water deserves that name, fried in grease, or else what we used to call flapjacks, this being a thin variation of the aforesaid dough, poured into a hot frying-pan."

During the stopover at Bent's Fort, Kearny issued a proclamation to the citizens of New Mexico, assuring them that he was entering their country as a friend, seeking their support, and promising to ameliorate their condition. In a special dispatch to Governor Manuel Armijo, Kearny cautioned that he was coming with an overwhelming force to take possession. Harsh treatment, the colonel promised, would be meted out to all who resisted.

Captain Philip St. George Cooke of the Dragoons galloped out of Bent's Fort with the message for Armijo. Riding with Cooke was James W. Magoffin, who had made a fortune in the Santa Fe trade and had married into a Mexican family. Magoffin now lived in Independence, Missouri, and a month earlier had visited Washington to advise President Polk on Mexican matters.

The Army of the West left Bent's Fort on August 2 and marched into the desert, a "dreary, sultry, desolate" wasteland of "boundless solitude . . . heat, thirst, and driven sand." The ninety mile march from Bent's Fort to Purgatoire River was the roughest of the campaign. "Almost every day," a private wrote, "some dragoon or volunteer, trader, teamster or amateur, who had set out upon the expedition buoyant with life and flattered with hopes of future usefulness, actuated by a laudable desire to serve his country, found a grave on the solitary plains."

Horses and oxen perished. John T. Hughes, First Regiment of Missouri Cavalry, lamented: "A man 600 miles from the nearest civilized settlements in a desert country feels a kind of friendship and sympathy for his horse when he abandons him on the plains to be devoured by wolves or captured by Comanches that almost makes him shed tears. He feels as though he were abandoning his best friend to perish in a desolate land."

The command, still on half rations, labored to the foot of Raton Pass—"The Mouse" as the Mexicans called this mountain spur, which separated the waters of the Arkansas from those of its Canadian fork. For days the men wound up and down through the Pass.

The Yankees gaped at the first settlement in New Mexico, the first, other than Bent's Fort, which they had seen in 775 miles. To the troopers gazing at the red earth mesas and cliffs, the new land seemed strange, out of place. The color of the landscape amazed them; some of the mountains were reddish rock, others took on every shade of purple at odd times of day. Patterns of red earth alternated with patches of white.

An American trader, bursting with information, galloped up

to the columns. The whole territory of New Mexico was under martial law. Three hundred Mexican dragoons had hastened into Santa Fe. Twelve hundred more were momentarily expected. The Mexicans, 10,000 strong, were determined to fight it out fifteen miles from Santa Fe at a deep ravine which they were fortifying.

Geared for action the soldiers expected a clash at any moment. They had marched nearly 1,000 miles. Up ahead the lead company glimpsed a towering cloud of dust in the distance. As it settled they saw a party of Mexican lancers, wearing huge sombreros, trotting forward in a friendly manner. They handed Kearny a dispatch from Governor Armijo, a message so ambiguously worded that the colonel found it difficult to determine whether the governor wanted to meet him in council or on the battlefield.

Kearny looked up after reading the dispatch and spoke casually to the Mexican lieutenant: "The road to Santa Fe is now as free to you as to myself. Say to General Armijo I shall soon meet him, and I hope it will be as friends."

After profusely embracing the colonel, the lieutenant spurred his mount and veered off down the trail followed by his men. Lieutenant Emory remembered that this had been the first "man hug" he'd ever seen, and said to a friend, "if God spares me, it shall be the last."

That evening the Army of the West was in sight of Las Vegas, the first sizable town they had seen in New Mexico. During that night, August 14–15, staff officers woke Kearny and quietly told him that 600 Mexican soldiers were guarding the town, ready to oppose the American advance.

At dawn Kearny issued his orders. Along the picket lines, horses stamped and snorted, their shadows grotesquely elongated by the horizontal rays of the sun. The Missouri Volunteers assumed formation. Colonel C. F. Ruff, second in command, strode over to Company D and inspected them minutely. He said calmly: "You are the only mounted company under my command today and the only one designated for a charge of the regiment. The enemy is near at hand; your position is in front. Show them that you can ride them down."

Demonstrating how to make a saber wristband from his handkerchief, Ruff instructed the men of Company D to draw their sabers and let them swing from the wrist. "Before entering into action, [and] as soon as you are commanded to charge," he said, "discard your rifles and use your sabers."

Within minutes the Army of the West was in motion for Las Vegas. By common impulse, everyone held silence. Major Thomas Swords and two officers came plunging up to the advancing columns, having ridden all the way from Bent's Fort. Hearing rumors of an impending clash, they had traveled sixty miles in a night to be there. In their saddlebags was Kearny's commission as brigadier general.

Las Vegas offered no resistance. Kearny clattered into town, shook hands with the alcalde, assembled the inhabitants in the plaza, and proclaimed New Mexico a part of the United States. "Those who remain peaceably at home attending to their crops and their herds," Kearny declared, "shall be protected by me in their property, their persons, and their religion; and not a pepper, nor an onion, shall be disturbed or taken by my troops without pay, or without the consent of the owner. But listen! He who promises to be quiet and is found in arms against me, I will hang."

The general finished. He stepped down, mounted his command, and ordered the guidons unfurled for the first time. The army rode out of Las Vegas toward a gorge, where it was rumored the Mexican force was waiting.

With sabers drawn the columns passed from trot to gallop, heading straight for the defile. Still not a blow was struck. The command charged through the gorge, but the enemy was nowhere to be found. The men were bitterly disappointed.

Once the columns had reformed, they moved westward into the village of Tecolote, where Kearny repeated his speech. Twenty-four hours later he raised the American flag over the red adobe town of San Miguel and addressed its citizens. Hesitant to recognize the authority of the United States, its alcalde temporized, seeking to avoid capitulation.

"It is enough for you to know, sir," snapped the general, "that I have captured your town."

Returning from his and Magoffin's meeting with Governor Armijo in Santa Fe, Captain Cooke rejoined the command at San Miguel. He informed Kearny that Mexican officers, intimidated by the size of the American army, had dismissed their troops. The governor himself and sixty dragoons were already riding southward, escaping to the town of El Manzano, over eighty miles from Santa Fe. Nothing barred the American advance.

On the 17th of August, the Army of the West skirted the ruins of an ancient Pecos pueblo where the men from the First Missouri scattered to carve their names into the crumbling adobe. That afternoon a pompous Mexican, an alcalde from a nearby settlement, mounted on a mule, rode up to Kearny, shook hands, and tittered, "Armijo and his troops have gone to hell and the Canon is all clear."

It drizzled all day on the 18th. By midafternoon Kearny and his staff, slightly in advance of the main columns, glimpsed the buildings of Santa Fe in the distance. The rain stopped and the sun burst from beneath threatening clouds as the general turned into San Miguel Street and marched toward the plaza. With every flag and banner of the expedition fluttering in the afternoon breeze, the general and his dragoons led the infantry and the Missourians through the narrow, crowded streets. All along the line of march, children elbowed past their elders to gaze in wonder at the prancing cavalcade. Women peered through latticed wondows, many sobbing aloud.

The general and his staff dismounted, clattered into the Palace of the Governors and down the hallway into a huge room. Here Kearny met the Acting Governor of New Mexico and the prominent citizens of Santa Fe. Over glasses of brandy and wine, the general casually declared his purpose, reciting again the speech delivered at Las Vegas and the other towns.

Outside, troopers unfurled the Stars and Stripes over the Palace and artillerymen fired a thirteen gun salute. Drums beat. Trumpets resounded. Infantry presented arms. General Kearny stepped from the doorway of the Palace, raised his hand for silence, and spoke to the inhabitants of Santa Fe: "There," he said, pointing, "my guns proclaim that the flag of the United States floats over this capital."

Kearny turned from the crowd, satisfied, and walked off with his staff to accept the hospitality of a Mexican gentleman. The supper that night, reported a lieutenant, "was served very much after the manner of a French dinner, one dish succeeding another in endless succession. A bottle of good wine from the Passo del Norte, and a loaf of bread were placed near each plate. We had been from five in the morning without eating, and endless as were the dishes, more endless still were our appetites."

As officers were introduced to *haute cuisine*, enlisted men discovered chili. "The first mouthful," grumbled a soldier, "brought tears trickling down my cheeks, very much to the amusement of the spectators with their leather-lined throats." The dragoons picked up a smattering of Spanish, words like *senoritas, muchacha, adios*. Vendors hawked *tortillas* and *hojas*. Mexicans taught the Americans *Monte*, "a kind of short-hand faro played with cards," and introduced them to the saloons about town.

As the novelty and glamour wore off, Santa Fe became a disappointment. It was really just an adobe village; "mudtown" the troopers called it. In the saloons swarms of buzzing flies swirled in restless clouds over the heads of the customers or drowned themselves in pools of whiskey on the bar. "The people," described an American lieutenant, "lack that neatness and show of wealth, that taste and refinement which we left in 'the States'. . . . The women are bold and not overloaded with modesty; nor are there at this time many pretty ones to be seen."

The officers were amazed and pleased, too, that the dragoons and volunteers behaved themselves. "Considering our distance from home and all restraining influences," noted Lieutenant Richard Smith Elliott, "the fact that no shooting or cutting scrapes tarnished our record is creditable to the Army of the West and to the State of Missouri."

Kearny was busy with the usual myriad of military details: inspections, troop returns, complaints, reports, and receipts to sign and forward in triplicate. He issued a multitude of proclamations setting up a military government which, for its moderation and efficiency, has seldom been excelled.

In the midst of administrative minutia, the general grasped the success of his mission. Without firing a shot his Army of the West after a fifty day march of almost 900 miles had gained a southwestern empire, a province containing more than 100,000 people. New Mexico's importance was immediately recognized. After returning to Santa Fe from one of his mapping trips, First Lieutenant William Hensley Emory of the Topographical Engineers wrote in his journal:

ABOVE: U.S. Cavalry Officer on campaign.
BELOW: Cavalry Dragoon, 47

This country, although poor and barren . . . is of great interest to the United States, and all important to her to possess. The road from here to Fort Leavenworth presents no obstacle for a railway, and if it continues as good to the Pacific, will be the route over which the U. States will pass immense quantities of merchandise into what will, at one day become the rich and populous state of Sonora, Durango, and Southern California.

chapter 5.

"For God's sake, men, come up!"

A CALENDAR ON THE WALL TOLD GENERAL KEARNY THE date: September 25, 1846. Across the plaza of Santa Fe horses and mules were saddled and packed. Troopers inspected bundles and straps, canteens and arms. Everything was in order.

The trumpeter at a word from Kearny sounded assembly. Citizens of Santa Fe appeared in the doorways. They shaded their eyes with their forearms against the sun as they listened to the series of commands and watched the columns move out at a nodding walk. General Kearny's objective was California. He set out ignorant of General Zachary Taylor's occupation of Monterrey in Mexico and of the military government instituted in California by the United States Navy.

Before leaving, Kearny detached Colonel Donophin, commanding the Mounted Missouri Volunteers, to ride to Chihuahua and report to General Wool and his command. Colonel Sterling Price, who was then marching toward Santa Fe with a second contingent of Missourians, had not yet arrived. Also rolling westward for New Mexico was a battalion of Mormon recruits from Council Bluffs, Iowa. Unable to predict the arrival date of these reinforcements, but aware that President Polk was anxious that he reach California promptly, Kearny left instructions for the Mormon battalion to follow his trail.

The dragoons headed out of Santa Fe along the road to Albuquerque. Most were mounted on mules. The 1,000-mile trek that lay ahead was to make foot-soldiers out of most of the command. Horses and mules were scarce in the Southwest and, as the United States government was niggardly in supplying funds to the Quartermaster, the Army of the West was destined to arrive in California fatigued and ill-equipped for a rough campaign.

The expedition swept down the Rio Grande Valley. On the first day out, Dr. John Strother Griffen, assistant surgeon, United States Army, scrawled in his diary: "Left camp early & had a hard days march through a perfectly barren country, one that would not feed a single goose to an acre. . . . men are mounted on mules —some of them devlish poor at that. One or two gave out to day. This is a bad prospect for California to have animals giving out the first day. It is said that there is gold in the sands, and that a man can make a living washing dirt, it is well this can be done, for I am damned if any one could make a living ploughing."

Moving past Albuquerque the dragoons marched south. On October 6 as they followed the twisting Rio Grande, they saw a huge boll of dust floating above the western horizon like a solitary cloud. Horsemen emerged riding all out. They reined in beside the command.

Kit Carson, the legendary mountain man, leaned forward on his saddle pommel. Twenty-six days earlier he had ridden out of Los Angeles with dispatches for Washington. Kearny learned that Navy bluejackets under Commodore Stockton and a volunteer battalion of soldiers under Major John C. Frémont had conquered California. Since California was in American hands, the general sent 200 of his 300 horse soldiers back to Santa Fe.

In the desolate wastes of New Mexico comrades parted. Kearny dispatched the mail eastward by dragoon and ordered a reluctant Carson to wheel about and act as guide for the Army of the West. One hundred troopers accompanied by the Topographical Engineers set out into the arid emptiness.

The dragoons labored across the valley of the Rio Grande, turning westward on October 15. Skirting abandoned copper mines, they filed across the Continental Divide, camped on the headwaters of the Gila, then began toiling down that river valley. Of the westward advance, Captain Henry Turner noted in his journal:

What difficulties do we have to encounter, we who perform marches in such a country—how little do those who sit in their easy chairs in Washington think or know of the privations, the difficulties we are daily, hourly subjected to. Even our anxious friends at home can form no idea of the trials and fatigue that we undergo each hour in the day—wading streams, clambering over rocks and precipitous mountains or laboring through the valleys of streams where the loose earth or sand cause our animals to sink up to their knees at almost every step. Then our frugal meals, hard bed and perhaps wet blankets. This is the soldier's fare but I am sick of it and have no longer to endure it willingly, particularly when we get no credit for it. Unless we are fortunate enough to get into a fight before reaching California, and be successful in it too, our laborious service in marching over this country will never be appreciated.

Captain Turner's assessment is corroborated by Dr. Griffen's diary:

the only consolation a man has is that his mule is feeding and may be able to carry him another day farther on the journey—our pack animals are getting in a most pitiable condition—their backs are cut all to pieces—and so poor and weak that they can hardly be goaded along. Then the beef—poor and tender-footed—When they get into camp, and one of them has to be butchered—he meets his death—lying down, or can the poor devil be made to stand up long enough to be decently disposed of—every bush in the country is full of thorns—and every piece of grass so soon as it is broken becomes a thorn at both ends—every rock you turn over has a trantula or centipede under it, and Carson says in the summer—the most beautiful specimens of rattle snakes are scattered around in the greatest profusion. The fact is take the country all together, and I defy any man who has not seen it—or one as utterly worthless—even to imagine any so barren—The cactus is the only thing that does grow.

The ragged bluecoats veered north of the settlement of Tucson through the lands of the Pima and Maricopa, peaceful Indians with whom the soldiers bartered for food and animals. On November 22 the Americans encamped near the mouth of the Gila River, where it tumbles into the Colorado.

Night fell swiftly. Off to the east across the bottom of the Gila, dragoons glimpsed other campfires. Twenty volunteers reconnoitered and discovered a party of Californians, who were driving 400 horses towards Sonora in Mexico. Letters carried by the Californians contained recent news. Instead of marching toward a tranquil province, Kearny's reduced command was heading into the midst of a counterrevolution. Only San Diego in southern California, guarded by a frigate and a sloop-of-war, remained in American hands. Sensing that a bitter conflict lay ahead, the general commandeered the half-wild horses from the Californians and mounted his troopers. But these unseasoned animals quickly broke down in the desert sun.

The army forded the broad Colorado River, entering California near today's international boundary and, swinging north and west, struck out across the waterless waste. Of all the God-forsaken sections the dragoons had soldiered in, this seemed the worst. The country faded and swam in the heat. Dust rose from every hoof. Kearny's face was a dusty mask; his shirt, drenched with sweat on which the dust had settled, was stiff with mud. There was no escape from the heat. The horses and mules had gone miles without water and were feeling it. Seeing a horse or mule suffer was worse than seeing a man or dog suffer, for horses or mules didn't protest, they just collapsed. Some were saved by tugging at their halters, while other troopers pushed against the animals' buttocks.

Friendly Californians had advised that there was a lake ahead, but the water was too slimy and salty to drink. As the command shuffled toward the lake, the stench of decaying animals confirmed the report. The lake had receded to a pool, diminished to half its original size and the water was unfit for man or beast. Officers prodded their mounts away, but two men, staggering in late, flopped face down into the pool before discovering their error. Fortunately the water was not poisonous.

The troopers, their rations exhausted, finally emerged from the desert on November 28 and started up a mountain where they hit chill winds blowing down from the snow-covered peak. They were now 1,800 miles from Fort Leavenworth.

"Our men were inspected to-day," lamented Captain Abraham R. Johnston, "Poor fellows! they are well nigh naked—some of them are barefoot—a sorry looking set."

High in the mountains, the dragoons encountered Mexicans fleeing for Sonora. They reported war in California. Pumping them for information, Kearny learned that guerrilla warfare had flared up with the ranchers.

On December 3 the weary command trooped into Warner's Ranch, sixty miles from San Diego. The pudgy, red-faced man-in-charge confirmed the news—Mexico controlled all California except the ports of San Francisco, Monterey, and San Diego. That night an English settler, E. Stokes, left Warner's Ranch for San Diego with dispatches from Kearny.

The dragoons relaxed the following day, December 4. During the evening an informant materialized out of the darkness and whispered to Kearny that a contingent of eighty Mexicans were encamped some distance away to the east.

The next morning the Army of the West moved out through a driving rain. It halted temporarily at rancheria Santa Maria. Here Captain Archibald H. Gillespie, U.S. Marine Corps, Lieutenant Edward F. Beale, U.S. Navy, and a detail of thirty-five men reached Kearny with letters from Commodore Stockton in San Diego. The general learned that a huge enemy force lay in wait nine miles distant. Prodding his dragoons, Kearny marched two more miles before pitching camp in a mountain canyon. Darkness fell without a moon. It rained steadily. It was a night none was ever likely to forget, a night of tension, of dampness, of sheer misery.

Sent forward to scout enemy positions, Lieutenant Thomas C. Hammond's detail aroused a stray dog. Its yelping alerted the Mexican camp but, despite patrol reports of interlopers, General Andres Pico flatly refused to believe they were Americans until another patrol brought in a blanket stamped "U.S." and a blue jacket. Finally convinced, Pico belatedly ordered his men to round up their horses.

Lieutenant Hammond's outfit returned about midnight. A silent Kearny strode back to his tent after hearing that the enemy was alerted. An hour later he ordered an immediate advance. The mountain chill was so intense that the trumpeter couldn't blow *Reveille*. The horse soldiers tumbled out at the noncom's shouts. One by one the men unwound themselves from frozen blankets and stamped woodenly out of the tents. It was still drizzling. Firearms were wet and useless.

The dragoons, some on broken down mules and horses, others

on foot, descended the trail by twos and moved out of the canyon into a valley. A dozen men under Captain Johnston, mounted on the pick of the horses, separated from the advancing columns and nudged out ahead. Behind in the main body, Kearny gave a hand signal and the troopers broke into a trot. Misunderstanding the command, Johnston drew his sword and waved his men into a gallop. Overeager and undercautious Johnston began a frontal attack. Leading fifty dragoons, Captain Benjamin D. Moore spurred his mount into a gallop and followed at Johnston's heels.

Pico's men waited in the gully before the village of San Pascual. They were Californians raised in the saddle, mounted on well-trained, fresh horses, armed with muskets and lances. The drumming of the approaching horses and the accompanying yells of the Americans grew louder.

The Mexicans fired. The reports tore the morning apart. A Yankee toppled from his saddle, forage cap falling from his head, his hands clawing at his blue shirt. Leandro Osuna hesitated. For a moment the blue outline of Captain Johnston was in Osuna's sights. Gently the Mexican squeezed the trigger. The smoke cleared. The American's saddle was empty. Two dragoons spurred their mounts into a thicket of mesquite and reined up. Looking down they saw Captain Johnston, dead, a bullet hole in his right temple.

Waving their sabers, the Americans plunged on. Kit Carson's horse was shot from under him. "When we were within 100 yards of their camp," Carson recalled, "my horse fell, threw me and my rifle was broken into two pieces. I came very near being trodden to death. Being in advance the whole command had to pass over me. I finally saved myself by crawling from under them. I then ran on about 100 yards to where the fire had commenced. A Dragoon had been killed, I took his gun and cartridge box and joined the mêlée."

Suddenly the Californians broke and charged westward seeming to disappear as through a trap door, moving around the bend of a knoll, temporarily out of sight. Bewildered by this feint, Captain Moore sounded a charge. His fifty dragoons galloped in pursuit, riding irregularly. They were soon strung out in an overextended skirmish line, the riders as much as fifty yards apart.

The Mexicans, lances poised for attack, emerged, fanned out

over the more open ground, and outflanked the oncharging Americans. Moore could see them plainly. He looked around for help. Thirty yards away a hatless trooper lay prone on the ground. Just ahead General Pico halted. Whipping out his pistol, Moore fired and missed. He lunged with his saber.

Parrying the blow and brandishing his sword, Pico executed a counterthrust. Simultaneously from the rear, two Mexican lances gouged Moore's body. He fell from his saddle. Another Californian, Thomas Sanchez, leveled his pistol at the limp form and fired.

Lieutenant Hammond, Moore's brother-in-law, roared to his dragoons, "For God's sake, men, come up!" A hard charging Mexican thrust his lance deep into Hammond's side. The lieutenant pitched forward, convulsed in agony. His stubbled face a mask of dirt, the right sleeve and side of his shirt wet with blood, Hammond suffered for two hours before dying.

Americans struggled across the flats to join the fight. Fast riding Californians lassoed and jerked them from their saddles. Shouts in Spanish were answered in profane English. Their guns water-soaked and ineffective, troopers charged with sabers and gun butts, but Mexican lances outreached American swords.

Kearny with the main columns, hearing the clamor of battle, drove home his spurs and rushed headlong into the free-for-all. In the whirlpool of men and horses, the general fired his pistol until it was empty, then used his saber. He fell upon a Mexican and began fencing. Something struck him. His knees buckled. Lieutenant Emory, running up, beat off his attackers. Kearny lay wounded.

The battle ended abruptly. The Mexican lancers galloped off. As the smoke cleared the fullness of the American failure was plain —eighteen dead, thirteen wounded, among whom was Kearny.

The dragoons quickly bivouacked. Their camp was no camp at all, but a jumble of arms, animals, and soldiers. The dead were identified, their meager personal effects gathered up and delivered to the proper officers. Beneath a willow tree, the burial detail worked mostly in silence. "Thus," said Lieutenant Emory, "were put to rest together, and forever, a band of brave and heroic men." To the rear of the camp, several depressed troopers, bitter over the outcome of the battle, belabored General Kearny for ordering them into action on half-starved mounts and with water-soaked weapons.

The American attack had been unnecessary, poorly conceived,

badly executed. The bloodiest engagement of the entire conquest of California, San Pascual, was a Mexican victory. Although the Army of the West had kept the field of battle, it had no strategic value. The entire responsibility for the blunder rested with Kearny.

The seventh of December dawned, noted Lieutenant Emory, on the "most tattered and ill-fed detachment of men that ever the United States mustered under her colors." More haggard, more tired than they could ever remember, the dragoons marched out of camp with the hope that by some miracle they might reach San Diego. At San Bernardino ranch they watered their horses and caught and killed stray chickens to feed the wounded.

Two miles from the ranch, after making contact with probing parties of Mexicans, Kearny, his wounds much improved, growled orders to pitch camp. He was surrounded and further progress toward San Diego appeared futile.

To procure reinforcements, Kit Carson, Lieutenant Beale, and an Indian volunteered to penetrate twenty-nine miles through enemy positions. "As soon as dark we started on our mission," remembered Carson. "In crawling over the rocks and bush our shoes making noise we took them off; fastened them under our belts. We had to crawl about two miles. We could see three rows of sentinels, all ahorseback, we would often have to pass within 20 yards of one. We got through, but had the misfortune to have lost our shoes, had to travel over a country, covered with prickly pear and rocks, barefoot. Got to San Diego the next night."

While Carson and his volunteers sought help, the Army of the West grimly held its position. More of the wounded died. "Last night," recorded Emory, "the brave Sergeant Cox died, and was buried to-day deep in the ground, and covered with heavy stones, to prevent the wolves from tearing him up. This was a gallant fellow, who had, just before leaving Fort Leavenworth, married a pretty wife."

Gaunt and depressed, Kearny doubted that Carson could reach San Diego. Worried that the Navy might withhold reinforcements, even if informed of the situation, troopers kept their vigil and prepared for the worst.

At 3:00 A.M. on December 11, sentries sounded the challenge: "Who goes there?"

"Americans." Eighty marines and 120 sailors slogged up the

ABOVE: Charge of Captain May and 2nd Dragoons against Mexicans at Resaca, 1846. BELOW: Colonel Sumner and Troopers, Topeka, Kansas, July 4, 1856.

slope, met by hails which swelled to cheers and excited hellos.

The reinforced dragoons marched out and before evening glimpsed the mighty Pacific Ocean. Weary and begrimed the Army of the West—the merest remnant of the force that had bravely set out from Santa Fe—trudged into San Diego. Out in the harbor the U.S. frigate *Congress* and sloop-of-war *Portsmouth* rode at anchor. Here ended one of the longest and most grueling marches of American history. The First Dragoons had conquered a treacherous wilderness, hunger, thirst, heat, cold to be defeated at San Pascual. But courage and determination had brought Kearny's command through to journey's end.

Rapidly recovering from his wounds, the general wrote to his wife, Mary, a week later: "I know my dear wife that you may be uneasy about me. . . . Let me therefore in the first place tell you that I am moving about as if nothing had happened to me, that my appetite is perfectly good & that I feel but little inconvenience from my wounds. . . . I expect in less than a week to be on my horse & as active as I ever was."

He finished the letter, then added, "Kiss all my dear little ones for me. I hope William and Charles are learning fast. Harriet, I am certain is improving & Mary and Louis no doubt, also Puddy [Ellen], Clarence and the youngest [Henry] must occupy your time. I hope that you have some good woman in your nursery to take care of them. Take care of yourself and the young ones."

The troopers' job was not finished. They were to participate in an overland advance on foot against Mexican-held Los Angeles. Early on the morning of December 29, the march began—57 dragoons, 442 sailors and marines acting as artillery and infantry, 60 volunteers, and a wagon train of one carriage and 10 oxcarts. At the head of the columns rode General Kearny, who was in direct command of this force which, at the San Gabriel River, twelve miles from Los Angeles, met and defeated the Californians. On January 10, 1847, Kearney's men ran up the American flag in Los Angeles.

During the Mexican War, American generals failed to exploit the full potential of the mounted arm. At the outbreak of the war, the cavalry consisted of two regiments of dragoons. Under the pressure of war, Congress raised a regiment of Mounted Rifles and added a third regiment of dragoons.

The War Department scattered horse units all over the West, from Missouri to California, from Oregon to Mexico, violating the principle of concentration of force. The role of the troopers under Generals Taylor and Scott was a bootless venture. Through ignorance or indifference, these commanders made slight use of the mounted arm except for reconnaissance. In battle even where the terrain was excellent, neither Scott nor Taylor committed the horse soldiers to a major action. Junior officers in Mexico, who later took commanding positions in the Civil War, learned few positive lessons about cavalry. So minor were the troopers' contributions that Congress disbanded the Third Dragoons soon after Kearny rode into Los Angeles.

chapter 6.

"I wish you could see me in my scouting costume."

♞ ♞ ♞

OLLOWING THE MILITARY OCCUPATION OF CALIFORNIA, THE discovery of gold and the desire for land lured hordes of canvas-topped wagons westward. Trails widened into roads, roads into highways. The United States Army's prime concern was to police these thoroughfares to Utah, Oregon, and California with a force of slightly more than 10,000 men. While the acquisition of a western empire from Mexico expanded the frontier and complicated its defense, the strength of the military was reduced to its prewar size.

The West of the 1850's gobbled up the Army's manpower. Of the 166 companies distributed among the three military-geographical divisions—Eastern, Western, and Pacific—126 were garrisoned west of the Mississippi River. The mounted arm, three regiments of horsemen, contained the First and Second Dragoons and the Regiment of Mounted Rifles.

Mounted and infantry commands were often overextended in their efforts to control the Indians and hunt down roving bands of renegades and thieves who preyed upon the westward moving caravans. Settlers and military officers berated the government for not increasing the size of the Army. Infantry, they asserted, was no match against the fast riding redman. Westerners implored Congress for more horse soldiers. The *Daily Missouri Democrat* sneered: "As well might we send boys into a cornfield to catch marauding crows with hopes of success as to start foot-soldiers in pursuit of Indians."

Embroiled with the explosive issue of Negro slavery, Congress was unresponsive. Finally in 1855 the legislators authorized four new regiments—two infantry and two cavalry—which increased the

76

military establishment from 10,000 to 15,000. To avoid the appearance of a permanent increase, the two new regiments of horse were called "cavalry" and the War Department organized and maintained them as a separate entity, distinct from dragoons and mounted rifles. This permitted Jefferson Davis, Secretary of War, to influence promotion within the cavalry.

The fundamental difference between dragoons, rifles, and cavalry was in name and dress, not in function. The trimming of the dragoons' jacket was orange; the rifles', green; the cavalrys', yellow. Out on the plains each regiment, on paper at least, carried a different set of weapons. All horse regiments in the American army were light cavalry. Unlike European armies it maintained no heavy units. Giants laden with defensive armor, mounted on powerful horses could have served no practical tactical function on the American frontier. Immobility rendered such outfits incapable of performing patrol duties as heavily encumbered men and horses could not endure long marches.

The United States Army divided each regiment of dragoons, rifles, or cavalry into three squadrons or battalions of four troops or companies. Each regiment's commanding officer was a colonel; its second in command, a lieutenant colonel. Majors commanded squadrons. A captain and a first and second lieutenant officered each troop. Such organization varied on the trail depending upon the strength present for duty.

Squadrons were numbered 1st, 2nd, 3rd; the troops, lettered A through M, the letter J being omitted because in the day of handwritten orders and correspondence, I and J were easily confused. Veterans referred to the 3rd Squadron as the "Milk" Squadron, since the letters of the four troops composing it could be arranged to spell that acrostic. From each troop fluttered a guidon, swallow-tail in design, the top half of which was red with the troop letter in white, the bottom half white, with the regimental number in red.

Jefferson Davis selected Colonel Edwin V. Sumner to command the First Cavalry and made Joseph E. Johnston its lieutenant colonel. During the summer of 1855 Sumner drilled his recruits at Fort Leavenworth and in the autumn pushed toward the open plains.

Back at Jefferson Barracks, St. Louis, officers began arriving to organize the 2nd Cavalry. Of the twenty-five who held commissions, seventeen were Southerners, twelve of whom were later to wear general's stars in the Confederate armies. Davis picked Albert Sidney Johnston to command and appointed Robert E. Lee lieutenant colonel. Two of the regiment's majors were William H. Emory and William J. Hardee; two of its captains, Earl Van Dorn and E. Kirby Smith. Fitzhugh Lee and John B. Hood were listed among the lieutenants. During its first years of active service, the 2nd Cavalry patrolled New Mexico and western Texas, where companies were scattered in small detachments on garrison and scouting duty.

From every section and circumstance men enlisted in the mounted arm of the service. Newly arrived immigrants, unemployed Irish and Germans, were lured by generous bounties. Suffering financial reverses or social disappointment, native Americans volunteered for distant army stations. Opportunists enlisted to get "comfortably transported to California at the expense of the government." For the venturesome, "whose imagination inflamed them with thoughts of scouring the prairies on fine horses, amid buffalo and strange Indians," frontier duty held a glamorous appeal.

They fought with an appalling variety of weapons. European officers and American weapon makers had already demonstrated the effectiveness of the rifled barrel and elongated ball, which gave greater accuracy and range than smoothbores with round shot. American officers agreed uniformly on the practicability of Sharps' carbines and Colt's repeating pistols. But the United States government, tediously slow in adopting wholesale substitutions, ignored the revolution in firearms. Its armories were stuffed with a half million antiquated and obsolete muskets and it balked at the cost of replacing such equipment with modern weapons.

When the dragoons were first organized in the 1830's, they toted breechloading, smoothbore Hall carbines, a weapon designed especially for mounted men. An innovation which distinguished the Hall carbine, Model 1833, was its percussion system, the first cap-and-ball to be adopted by the War Department. Riding fast across the prairies, the dragoon carried this gun alongside his right thigh, muzzle down, supported in a leather cup close to his hand. By 1846, however, arsenals and shops were turning out cavalry-type musketoons in ever-increasing quantities to meet the needs

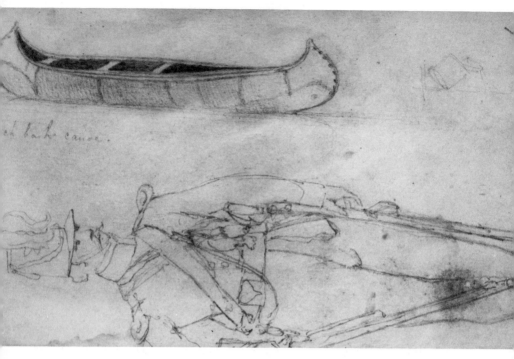

1st Dragoon and equipment, Fort Snelling, 1851. Sketch by Frank Mayer.

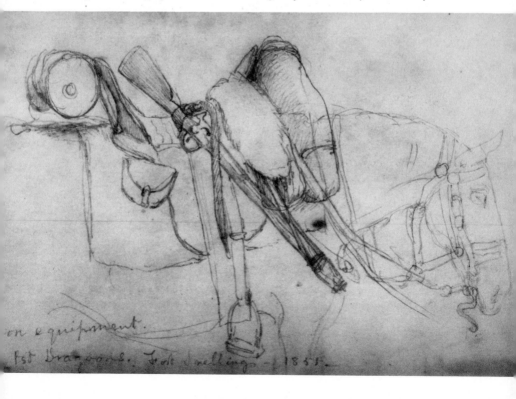

of the Mexican War and discontinued the manufacture of the Hall carbine. A few officers experimented with Sharps' breechloading carbine, which was destined to win fame in the Civil War.

Prior to the Mexican conflict, the dragoons had also ridden with flintlock, single shot "horse pistols," heavy, solid, and well-built which fired with limited range and accuracy. Troopers saved these for the last blow at close quarters. Numbers of American officers and Texas Rangers carried a new weapon during the Mexican War, a gun which was to revolutionize warfare on the plains, the U.S. Repeating Pistol, Model 1847. Samuel Colt in collaboration with Sam Walker of the Texas Rangers had devised this rugged .44 caliber six shot pistol, nicknamed "The Second Dragoon" after the troopers who had experimented with it in the Seminole War.

Although regulations in the 1850's called for Sharps' carbines and Colt revolvers, the trooper in actual practice fought with a heterogeneous assortment of horse pistols, Colt revolvers, Harpers Ferry rifles, Hall breechloaders, Sharps' carbines, musketoons, and ancient flintlocks—anything and everything. Captain Ewell's company stationed at Fort Buchanan in New Mexico Territory bore firearms described as no better than "old rattletraps," antique museum pieces.

Mounted men bitterly criticized their other weapon, the saber, a noisy encumbrance. The saber's advantage, a few argued, was in the cavalry charge when row upon row of plunging steel blades struck terror in the uninitiated. The impulse was to turn and run. But against Indians the only chance a trooper had to wield the saber was when his adversary had engaged another opponent. The mounted red man was too shifty and quick to be caught by a blow from a swinging blade. The cavalry's use of the lance was limited by the Army's principle of employing mounted troops capable of dismounted action. As cavalry tactics developed, the Army emphasized the use of rapidly concentrated firepower and discovered that mounted riflemen were far superior to lancers.

Dress on the frontier differed as much among the troopers as did their weapons. From a Texas post, Lieutenant E. Kirby Smith, 1st Cavalry, scrawled a letter to his mother:

I wish you could see me in my scouting costume. Mounted on

my mule—the dearest, gentlest, and most intelligent brute
. . . corduroy pants; a hickory or blue flannel shirt, cut down
in front, studded with pickets and worn outside; a slouched
hat and long beard, cavalry boots worn over the pants, knife
and revolver belted to the side and a double barrel gun across
the pommel, complete the costume as truly serviceable as it
is unmilitary.

Snooping through Texas on an inspection tour, a captain
gaped in disbelief at the ridiculous-looking soldiers. Coats were
too short. Jackets, intended to fit the fattest men, were cut larger
around the waist than the chest. Trousers were so tight that big feet
could barely squeeze through the legs, yet were immense in the
seat. During the blistering heat of summer dragoons usually wore
nonregulation broad-brimmed sombreros, white trousers, hickory
shirts, and Navajo-type leggings. In winter on the northern plains
they served in wolfskin caps, deerskin coats, trousers of buffalo-
calf leather, and wrapped themselves in anything they could find
or steal. Sometimes the horse soldiers affected brass rings in their
ears and fraternal emblems, bear claws, and other oddities on their
buckskin fronts.

These makeshift uniforms deviated drastically from War Department regulations. Officially, the dragoons wore blue fatigue
jackets trimmed with orange, a flat forage cap with wide orange
band—a poor imitation of the French *kepi*—sky blue trousers
reinforced with a "saddle piece" and trimmed with two orange
stripes down the outside seam. Originally the insignia was a gilt
star pinned on the forage cap but in 1850 the War Department
substituted crossed sabers to be worn edges up with the number of
the regiment in the angle above.

Throughout the early years the Army specified troopers employ the standard flat saddle, almost identical with today's English
saddle. In 1847 a board of officers recommended the adoption of
the Grimsley saddle and described it as "Combining strength,
durability, peculiar fitness to the horse's back and convenience for
military fixtures, this pattern, more than any other yet furnished
for Dragoon service, gives an erect posture and easy seat to the
rider, at the same time that little or no injury is done to the
horse's back on the longest marches."

The Grimsley pattern persisted for ten years and it made friends and created enemies. Captain Earl Van Dorn, 2nd Cavalry, declared: "In every scout or march . . . in which the Grimsley saddle was used, I never failed to have sore backed horses (withers generally) in proportion to the distance I have marched over, or the kind of weather I had to encounter." Colonel Albert Sidney Johnston, 2nd Cavalry differed. "Have to observe with regard to the remark in the report that 'with the Grimsley saddle a large proportion of the horses' backs were made sore,' the sore backs might rather have been produced by the ignorance of the soldiers of the proper method of adjustment, than from any fault of the saddle."

The famous McClellan saddle replaced the Grimsley and became standard equipment just prior to the Civil War. While serving as a military attache in Europe, Captain George B. McClellan visited Crimean battlefields and came away impressed with the Prussian cavalry's "horse furniture." "With certain modification," he wrote in 1856, "it would be a better equipment than any we have yet had in our service." Differing from any previous saddle, the 1858 McClellan or Civil War model was basically a rawhide covered tree, with black leather skirts, D-shaped quarter strap rings of round stock, no quarter safes, and fenders, which were issued but not always used. This saddle was to remain in use with only minor changes until the horse cavalry was abolished in 1942.

At the outbreak of the Civil War, regulations specified a saddle blanket of indigo blue and a saddle equipped with a single girth of blue woolen webbing. On active duty a man usually slung a pair of holsters, occasionally with leopard-skin flaps, from his pommel. In one he stuffed his pistol, in the other, an extra horseshoe, nails, curry comb, and brush.

The army occupied a variety of western stations. On the most desolate frontier, where posts were temporary, troops camped in Sibley tents, while those who patrolled regions near older settlements lived at permanent garrisons.

In a typical fort located in the more settled areas of the plains, officers' quarters, a row of small cottages containing three or four rooms, lined one side of the parade ground. Enlisted men's barracks—low, long, solid-looking buildings—marched down the opposite side and, behind, were the mess huts. In the center of the

ABOVE: U.S. Troops entering
Salt Lake City, 1858.
RIGHT: Albert Sidney Johnston.
BELOW: Government train
en route to Utah, 1857–58.

parade stood the post commander's imposing house. Placed on the third side of the fort was the neat, trim administrative building flanked by the quartermaster's warehouse. The sombre-looking guardhouse, small but strong, stood on the fort's fourth side. In space between this structure and the end of the officers' quarters, a field piece pointed at the horizon.

Off, sitting by itself, was the post hospital and, likewise, apart from the fort was the sutler's store, the favorite lounging place of the soldier. Situated conveniently close were the stables and wagon sheds.

Much less elaborate, resembling the crude forts of an earlier day, the typical post on the farthest frontier, was a collection of rough adobe or log huts which served as quarters for both officers and enlisted men. Sun, wind, rain, snow penetrated the badly heated and poorly ventilated rooms with their canvas or dirt floors. Men battled fleas and bedbugs, mice and snakes which slipped through the walls of the congested huts. In the treeless areas of the west, even bunks, tables, and benches were luxuries.

On the more permanent posts the men quickly adjusted to the daily routine.

5:55   Reveille. Mad dash to latrine. Dark and cold. Shave.
6:00   Roll Call. Make up bunks, police up area.
6:15   Mess Call. Run to mess huts.
7:00   Stable Call
7:05   Sick, lame, and lazy call. A straggling line of sick and imagined sick. Their stories fall on unsympathetic ears. Quick knife and back to duty for a blister.
         Details to clean latrines. Fall in to be inspected.
8:00   Fatigue Call
8:05   Drill Call
12:00   Dinner
         Fatigue Call, Drill Call, Stable Call.
         Retreat at sunset
5:00   Supper. The walk back is slower this time of day. Personal gear to be shined, mended.
9:00   Tattoo. Rest for troops, except sentries.

Across the parade ground, beginning at the guard house, the sentry sang out: "Number One. Ha-alf pa-as-st ten o'clock." And beyond, toward the corrals, responded Number Two: "A-all's we-ell!" The watch call went the rounds, echoing and reechoing over the parade until it again reached Number One.

On the frontier, engulfed in loneliness, troopers craved social life and companionship. Since post commanders paid scant heed to the recreational needs of the men, soldiers cooped up in the dead of winter created their own amusements. Singers, comics, tellers of tall tales enlivened barracks life. Although the pay was meager and orders read, "No Gambling," horse soldiers whooped it up at cockfights and played endless games of monte and chuck-a-luck. Hangovers from "lightning whiskey"—a mixture of alcohol, tobacco, and other narcotics—undermined the soldier's physical and mental health. Naïvely troopers justified their drinking by proclaiming it eased the nervous disorders of the bowels in summer and warded off chills in winter.

Although the horse soldier led an active, outdoor life, he was constant prey to disease, a victim of colds, rheumatism, abscesses, and ulcers. Surgeons listed disorders of the digestive system as the most common complaint, ailments caused by improper diet, impure water, and bad whiskey. At Fort Yuma, "the hottest post in the United States," men suffered from sunstroke and mental breakdowns. Amputations tried the courage and stamina of the bravest since surgeons, lacking chloroform, administered a no more effective anesthetic than a concoction of ice and salt.

Social diseases claimed many. Camp followers tried the patience of officers. In the spring of 1853 when strumpets were debauching the men at Fort Union, New Mexico, the commanding officer threw an eight mile off-limits cordon around the post and ordered the arrest of any civilian loitering in the area. The New Mexico legislature clamped down on vice by passing a law punishing all prostitutes with thirty stripes and three months at hard labor.

Throughout the 1850's commands reported that losses from desertion were greater than from any other single cause. Gold was the magnet which lured many soldiers from their desolate frontier posts. During 1849, 40 percent of the men garrisoned in California headed for the mines. At Fort Laramie sixteen riflemen overpowered the sentries, jumped on their horses, and raced for California.

Some troopers had concrete grievances for deserting. For

minor violations of discipline soldiers faced severe and ingenious punishments, as in the case of a habitual drunkard sentenced to traipse around the camp for a week encased in a barrel. Soldiers shaved one culprit's head, stripped him to the waist before forcing him to walk around the parade ground three times as a fifer and two drummers played "The Poor Soldier, I Hope the Devil Won't Catch You." For deserters courts-martial reserved more brutal punishment—flogging and branding. Corporals bound the luckless victim to a post and administered fifty lashes with the cat o' nine tails. Senseless, the deserter was then carted off to the hospital where they applied salt and water to his open wounds. Once he recovered his faculties, the culprit was indelibly branded on the left hip with the letter "D" and drummed out of the service.

The trooper in the trans-Mississippi West endured hardship, suffered from intense cold and heat, pocketed beggarly pay, and carefully maintained a neutral posture as friction mounted between extremists. Two crises in the 1850's displayed the cavalry's versatility in helping to subdue civilian unrest which almost led to bloody strife—first in Kansas, then in Utah.

chapter 7.

"This is the most disagreeable
duty in my whole life."

🐎 🐎 🐎

TOWARD EVENING HEAVY CLOUDS BEGAN PILING UP IN
the west as Lieutenant James McIntosh and a detachment of 1st Cavalry trotted into Lawrence, Kansas, in April, 1856, accompanied by Sheriff Sam Jones of Douglas County. They were to arrest six Kansans who had defied the sheriff's posse.

Lieutenant McIntosh was slim and wiry, weighing perhaps 140 pounds. In place of the regulation pistol belt and holster, he wore, slanting across his hips, crossed belts with loops containing cartridges and open holsters carrying .44 caliber Colt pistols. Along the main street the detail reined in their horses and dismounted, the men checking their carbines to see if they were loaded and capped. Far off thunder rumbled as the troopers started off down the street to arrest the six Kansans. Up the street behind them surged a club-swinging mob.

By sundown Lieutenant McIntosh had seized and locked up the culprits in a clapboard shack. Two troopers guarded the prisoners while the soldiers pitched tents at the rear of the makeshift jail. Public excitement in Lawrence rose to a hysterical pitch. Baiting and denouncing Sheriff Jones, but refraining from violence, the angry crowd glowered at the horse soldiers. Silhouetted in the torchlight, McIntosh turned to Jones and cautioned the sheriff to sleep inside the shack where he could be protected by the guards. Undeterred by the danger, Jones refused and, paying no heed to the gesticulating mob, strolled back to the tent with McIntosh.

An hour later, bored with chitchat, Jones and McIntosh threw open the flaps of the tent and headed toward the water barrel for a drink. A carbine crashed. Jones whipped around. "That was intended for me," he screamed at McIntosh, "here is the hole in my pants."

Incensed by the mob's action, the lieutenant strode up to the roughnecks. McIntosh stood there with fists on hips, staring into the row of stubborn, hostile faces. Just as he started to warn them, a shot exploded. From the darkness, a trooper's voice cried out, "Lieutenant, the sheriff is dead!"

McIntosh ran to the tent. Jones lay kicking and bounding about on the ground until, after a mighty shudder, he died. In seconds the soldiers formed, ready to assault the mob. Faced with carbines and pistols, the citizens of Lawrence grudgingly dispersed and retired to their homes.

Apprehensive that the rowdies would muster again, McIntosh dispatched a civilian, E. T. Yates, and a trooper to overhaul a detachment under Lieutenant Stockton. Promptly obeying the call for assistance instead of continuing to Fort Leavenworth Stockton wheeled his outfit around and cantered into Lawrence two hours later. Again on top of the situation, McIntosh scribbled off a report and sent an express to Colonel Edwin Sumner, commanding the 1st Cavalry at Fort Leavenworth.

Colonel Sumner was determined to keep the lid on an explosive situation. Kansas teetered on the brink of civil war. Since Congress had created the territory in 1854, Northerners and Southerners contested the region, each side bent upon making Kansas either a free or slave state. Newcomers venturing into the troubled region were a motley crowd. Most Northerners were ordinary westward moving settlers in search of fertile land. But a segment of the inflow was armed and financed by Northern abolitionists, who wanted to forestall the Southerners and also earn a profit.

Quickly responding to the challenge, Southern agitators aided small groups of slaveowners in the territory. Tension mounted. On election day in 1855 pro-Southerners streamed across the border from Missouri and stuffed the ballot boxes to elect a majority of slaveholders to the first territorial legislature.

Disorders multiplied. Secretary of War Jefferson Davis alerted regiments of the 1st Cavalry and 2nd Dragoons to stand ready to quash insurrections and aid the territorial governor.

On May 21, 1856, one month after the murder of Sheriff Jones in the abolitionist stronghold of Lawrence, bands of proslavery Missourians galloped in and sacked the town. This atrocity enraged the fanatical abolitionist John Brown. With four sons and two other disciples and with "letters of God" in his pockets, John Brown grimly rode for Pottawatomie River where he dragged five allegedly proslavery men from their bunks and systematically butchered them. This outrage, which was the work of a deranged mind, brought vicious retaliation from the proslavery men.

"War! War!" cried the Westport, Missouri, *Border Times*, "pro-slavery men murdered by the Abolitionists in Franklin County. . . . LET SLIP THE DOGS OF WAR!" The editor appealed to the South for men, guns, and money. Newspapers throughout Missouri reprinted the *Western Dispatch's* description of the crime and its editorial assertion that "for every southern man thus butchered, a . . . (dozen) of these poltroons should bite the dust." The tragic episode at Pottawatomie touched off a four-month reign of terror throughout Kansas.

In Westport, Missouri, "Captain" H. C. Pate boasted he'd take John Brown dead or alive. He organized the Westport Sharpshooters and scoured the countryside, plundering, terrorizing Free Staters. Near Osawatomie, Pate and his gang encamped at a place called Black Jack. Rumors of their presence had already filtered into Brown's headquarters. Joining forces with a Free State unit, Brown searched the prairies. As a June dawn approached, his force crept close to Pate's camp and commenced firing. The battle blazed. The Westport Sharpshooters, their position gradually deteriorating, surrendered after three hours.

At Fort Leavenworth bugles shrilled the advance. In spite of mild confusion Colonel Sumner and his command were in motion at a little after 6:30 A.M. With Sumner pacing them, the horse soldiers drove across the prairie to pacify the belligerents.

John Brown spied them near Middle Ottawa Creek. Calculating the odds, shrinking from battle with United States Cavalry, the old warrior decided to parley. Sumner refused. He demanded the release of Pate and his Missourians. Brown complied. The colonel turned and tramped to and fro gazing at Pate.

"What business have you here?" snapped the colonel.

"I am here by orders of Governor Shannon," replied Pate.

"I saw Governor Shannon yesterday, and your case was specially considered; and he asserted you were not here by his orders."

Sumner's eyes bored into the line of sharpshooters. "You are Missourians, all of you," he snarled, "and when you crossed your state line you trampled on state sovereignty. Now, go, sirs, in the direction whence you came." The colonel waved his hand dismissing Pate and his party.

Sumner wheeled back to Brown. He'd come, he informed Brown, to serve him with a warrant for the murder of the five men at Pottowatomie. As if by signal, a United States deputy marshal fumbled among his papers. He found no warrant. Deeply chagrined, Sumner pointed his finger at the deputy marshal and chided him for being afraid to serve the warrant even in the presence of the United States Cavalry.

An atmosphere of distrust and uneasy peace brooded over Kansas. On orders from Governor Wilson Shannon, Colonel Sumner headed for Topeka with five troops of cavalry and two pieces of artillery to prevent the free-state legislature from assembling. Shannon recognized the legality of the proslavery legislature, which was already convened and enacting laws. If the free-state lawmakers were to meet, declared the governor, it would "produce an outbreak more fearful by far in its consequences than any which we have heretofore witnessed. . . . Two governments cannot exist at one and the same time in this Territory in practical operation; one or the other must be overthrown." Colonel Sumner shared his opinion.

Topeka sweltered on Independence Day, 1856. The brutal heat didn't abate and the sky remained cloudless. On the outskirts of town squads of free staters cradled muskets in their arms, alert for a possible raid by the Missourians. Inside a shack serving as the legislative chamber, Assistant Chief Clerk Samuel Tappan called the roll. Outside Sumner's troopers surrounded the building. A sweating, disheveled crowd listened to a lieutenant reading the official proclamation: "All persons are forbidden from assembling, organizing, or attempting to organize or act in any legislative capacity." His voice droned on.

On the steps of the shack Sumner could hear the hubbub within. He pushed open the door and gloomily surveyed the assembly.

"Gentlemen," he said, calmly, "this is the most disagreeable duty of my whole life. My orders are to disperse the Legislature and I am here to tell you that it must not meet, and to see it dispersed. God knows I have no partisan feelings in the matter, and I will have none so long as I hold my present position in Kansas."

Nobody ventured to interrupt him.

"I have just returned from the border," Sumner continued, "where I have been driving out bands of Missourians, and now I am ordered here to disperse you. You must disperse. This body cannot be permitted to meet—Disperse. Let me again assure you that this is the most disagreeable duty of my whole life."

Digesting these remarks, the free staters shoved back their chairs and walked out peaceably.

Throughout July and August troops of 1st Cavalry and 2nd Dragoons crisscrossed the prairies stamping out brigandage. The chronic state of political turmoil acted as a magnet upon the riff-raff of America. "The disorders in the Territory have, in fact, changed their character," remarked Lieutenant Colonel Philip St. George Cooke, "and consist now of robberies and assassinations, by a set of bandits whom the excitement of the times has attracted hither." Lieutenant James McIntosh, 1st Cavalry, reported an ever-increasing number of robberies along the roads leading to Palmyra and, at Cedar Creek, his detachment discovered three murdered men lying face down in the mud.

While the cavalry and dragoons guarded the borders, the tension between the proslave and free-soil parties grew ominous. Reports reached Fort Riley early in September that a small army of free-soilers, lead by Sam Walker, was marching for the pro-slavery capital of Lecompton intent upon wiping out the Missouri militia, releasing prisoners, and having "their rights." A squadron of 2nd Dragoons galloped out of Fort Riley. Lieutenant Colonel Philip St. George Cooke spotted 360 men marching toward Lecompton. The dragoons reined in on a little rise. Leaving them behind, Cooke rode alone at walk toward the advancing lines of free-soilers. Grasping his carbine he dismounted and shouldered his way through them toward Sam Walker, dropping a sharp word here and there.

"You have made a most unfortunate move for yourselves," he barked, "the Missourians, you know, have gone, and the militia here are nearly gone, having commenced crossing the river yesterday, to my knowledge. As to the prisoners, whilst I will make no terms with you, I can inform you that they were promised to be released yesterday morning . . . and that it apparently would be so if they would restrain entirely from reprisals or any outrages, return to their occupations, and show moderation."

The free-soilers drew back. Stepping forward, Walker apologized for the show of force and departed. An explosion had been averted, narrowly.

"Lecompton and its defenders," recalled Cooke, "were outnumbered. . . . Americans stood face to face in hostile array. . . . I rejoiced that I had stayed the madness of the hour and prevented, on almost any terms, the fratricidal onslaught of countrymen and fellow citizen."

After watching the free-soilers disperse, Cooke mounted his horse and trotted back to secure the release of the abolitionist prisoners. But acting governor Woodson, who had replaced Shannon, hedged. Angrily Cooke dispatched an armed patrol to the governor's headquarters, where that hesitant official, awed by the force outside, reluctantly signed the papers unlocking the doors of the town jail.

When John W. Geary, the newly appointed governor, arrived in Kansas to assume his responsibilities, the cavalry's problems multiplied. Two thousand armed Missouri Ruffians, uniformed and drilled, began a march on the free-state capital, Lawrence. Abolitionists armed themselves and waited. From a dry goods box in the streets John Brown piously advised on killing proslavers.

"If they should come up and attack us," Brown sermonized, "don't yell and make a great noise, but remain perfectly silent and still. Wait till they get within twenty-five yards of you, get a good object, be sure you can see the hindsight of your gun, then fire. A great deal of powder and lead and very precious time is wasted by shooting too high. You had better aim at their legs than at their heads. In either case, be sure of the hind sight of your gun."

Cooke and his patrols rode into Lawrence, hoping to avert open collision. After inspecting the 300 free-soilers and their ridiculous attempts at defense, Cooke ordered Lieutenant Colonel Joseph E. Johnston and the command to form battle lines on the outskirts of town.

As September 15, 1856, dawned bright, Cooke and Governor

Geary double-checked the dragoons' entrenchments before trotting out on the Franklin Road. Up ahead they saw the Missourians, 2,500 strong, their "cannon-matches lighted." Mounted militiamen charged up to the colonel and Geary and escorted them to the main columns. Cooke jumped to the ground. Reins draped over his arms, he walked toward the Missouri leaders and introduced himself as "an old resident of Kansas and a friend of the Missourians." Then he spelled out his terms. They must return home. If they resisted, Cooke promised to sustain Governor Geary with cannon fire. He threatened and cajoled until the Missourians agreed to disband. Cooke's persuasiveness ended the last organized invasion of Kansas by the Border Ruffians.

After turning back the Missourians, cavalry and dragoons relentlessly pursued and intercepted bands of free staters roaming the trail from Nebraska. Captain Thomas Wood's patrol surprised a gang celebrating their successful shoot out at Hickory Point. Business-like, the dragoons confiscated 47 Sharps' rifles, 38 muskets, 20 revolvers, and one cannon. Another dragoon squadron, acting on a tip, halted and systematically searched an emigrant train. Disregarding the denials of the wagon master, soldiers uncovered quantities of "household goods"—242 breechloading rifles, 62 sabers, and 50 revolvers.

By October, 1856, warfare in Kansas subsided. Cold weather and the impartial actions of the mounted regiments cooled the spirits of both factions. General Persifor Smith, commanding the Western Department, concluded that peace had returned to the troubled land. Save for two companies, detailed to remain with Governor Geary, officers and men of the 2nd Dragoons and 1st Cavalry took up winter quarters at Forts Riley and Leavenworth.

♞ ♞ ♞

The Utah Expedition was one of the strangest episodes in American history. After the United States won the western empire from Mexico, the Mormon colony in present day Utah was automatically brought under federal control. The previous year, 1847, the Saints, leaving the confines of the United States, had toiled across the Great American Desert to establish a sovereign nation. When the Mexican War ended, the Mormons, again under the aegis of the United States government, viewed the situation with genuine alarm. Brigham Young, the Mormon leader, demanded immediate statehood. In this way the Saints hoped to govern themselves, worship unmolested, and guard their policy of polygamy.

From almost every pulpit and platform in America, men and women protested vehemently. Assured that Congress would refuse to grant them statehood, the Mormons requested and received territorial status. President Millard Fillmore named Young governor of the Territory of Utah and appointed three "gentiles" and three Saints to territorial posts.

Before the year had closed, discord rocked Salt Lake City. The "gentiles," outvoted on every issue, treated contemptuously by the Mormons, became disgruntled. Two resigned and returned East. They lashed out at the Mormons and denounced them for plotting to establish an independent nation within the United States. Their charges triggered a storm of protest against Brigham Young and his disciples. Propaganda flooding the East, branded the Mormons as "lewd, lawless, sinful, and immoral."

In the spring of 1857, the new president, James Buchanan, and his Secretary of War decided to appoint new administrators to the territory. Their authority was to be upheld by 2,500 troopers and infantrymen. The secrecy which shrouded Buchanan's efforts to bulwark the government's position was interpreted by the Mormons as a declaration of war.

Organizing the Utah Expedition, the War Department appointed Colonel Albert Sidney Johnston, 2nd Cavalry, to replace Colonel William S. Harney, veteran dragoon officer, as commander. When Johnston assumed leadership in September, 1857, the expedition was already underway for Utah under Colonel E. B. Alexander.

In Salt Lake City Brigham Young learned of an American army pouring across the plains toward Utah. Suppressing the news, Young waited until the celebration of the tenth anniversary of the Saint's arrival in Salt Lake City. Amid the frivolity of this holiday, a carefully coached courier stormed into the city yelling "Invasion! War!" Young's oratory that day suddenly but smoothly changed to a diatribe. He cried: "Woe, woe to that man who comes here to unlawfully interfere with my affairs. Woe, woe to those men who come here to unlawfully meddle with me and this people."

Speaking the same day, Heber C. Kimball, First Counsellor to Young, bellowed: "Sending a man here with 2,500 troops!—they have no design in God Almighty's world only to raise a rookery with this people and bring us into collision with the United States, and when they come here, the first job will be to take br. Brigham Young, and Heber C. Kimball and others and they will slay us, Utah their design."

A voice yelled out: "They can't come it."

"No," stormed Kimball, "they can't come it."

Young called out the Nauvoo Legion (Mormon Militia).

> *Old squaw-killer Harney is on the way*
> *The Mormon people for to slay;*
> *Now, if he comes, the truth I'll tell,*
> *Our boys will drive him down to hell.*

Young estimated the American army's timetable of invasion. He was pleased. The expedition, he reasoned, could never reach Utah that autumn. It must winter in the Rockies. With food and forage scarce in a hostile land, the army would be vulnerable. Cutting its extremely tenuous supply line from Fort Leavenworth would be more effective than bloody battle. Young wanted to debilitate the army, not destroy it. He was anxious to avoid outright war, fearing reprisals might undermine the Mormon movement.

Galloping out of Fort Bridger, their base of operations, Mormon cavalry watched the American expedition as it trudged over the Oregon trail. Colonel Alexander's position was precarious. Winter was approaching. He had received Brigham Young's proclamation forbidding the entry of armed soldiers into Utah. It stipulated, however, that the Army might winter along Black's Fork or the Green River, unmolested, if the soldiers deposited their arms with Utah's Quartermaster and promised to withdraw by spring.

Suddenly the Saints struck. Mounted Mormons, assured that the dragoons were far behind, sneaked past the 10th Infantry and pounced upon two supply trains camped along the Green River. The next day, October 5, they surprised and destroyed another wagon train near the Big Sandy. The raiders vanished as abruptly as they appeared. Flames ignited by the Mormons consumed 72 wagons, 300,000 pounds of flour and bacon, enough to feed the entire contingent for two months.

Far behind Alexander's columns of infantry rode Lieutenant Colonel Philip St. George Cooke and his six troops of 2nd Dragoons who, assigned to the expedition at a late date, were trying desperately to catch up. Soon after they left the shabby military post, Fort Kearny, the troopers hit rain and frosts. Difficulties multiplied. Alexander's command had depleted the grass. Horses died of hunger. Mules collapsed. One soldier died of lockjaw.

Snow fell on October 17. The dragoons staggered into Fort Laramie where Cooke condemned 53 of the 331 horses. Receiving news of the Army's desperate need, the command pressed on from Laramie. On their approach to South Pass they struck north winds and drifting snow. The air turned to frozen fog. The men could see nothing. They marched into the frozen cloud, struggling through the snow-blocked mountain passes.

The going got so hazardous that Cooke ordered the troopers to dismount and lead their horses. Snow had drifted into the canyons and in some places the men sank to their waists. The booming wind reverberated like cannon from the mountain peaks. Veterans had seen blizzards on the plains, but they had never before heard the wind make such a racket. Sergeants went down the lines, ordering men to keep their hands and faces covered.

A black cloud closed about them. The wind almost jerked them off their feet. The whole column halted momentarily. They stood without moving while the sleet stung their faces and the wind hammered against them, piling up snow on their shoulders. One trooper recalled that his joints ached unbearably with the cold and that all feeling had left his hands.

Soldiers lost track of time. Too stunned to complain, they began swinging their arms. They slapped their faces and shook their heads. The command plowed forward. The trail turned and wound through a heap of icy rocks. A fresh rush of snow came from above. The hysterical heehawing of the mules was swallowed up in the storm. Cooke's dragoons stood in imminent peril.

As night drew on, the strain became intensified. Guides led the struggling columns behind a giant rock, but it proved too small to provide much shelter. The regiment huddled there in the deep snow. The storm kept on pounding.

When Cooke woke the next morning it was still snowing. His thermometer registered 44 degrees below zero. His bottle of wine froze in the trunk. "Morning light had nothing to reveal," Cooke reported later, "the air still filled with driven snow. The animals soon came, driven in, and, mingled in confusion with men, went crunching the snow in the confined and wretched camp, trampling all things in their way. It was not a time to dwell on the fact that from that mountain desert there was no retreat nor any shelter near, but a time for action. No murmurs, not a complaint was heard."

Cooke had lost fifty mules in thirty-six hours. The ravenous animals that survived gnawed on ropes, wagon tongues, and covers. It was hard that morning to get the men on the move. Aching and bruised they all suffered from frostbite and from the same hunger that crippled the animals. They marched out leaving behind nine horses freezing in the snow. Cooke came across the frozen bodies of three unknown men and carcasses of animals blocking the trail. The beasts lay as they had fallen—oxen yoked together. "At all events," said a trooper, "there they remained until thawed out the next spring, when, I was told, the stench was intolerable."

As Cooke was inching forward to make contact, the Army of Utah had gone into winter quarters at Fort Bridger, located on the emigrant road. The Mormons had already deserted the bastion. Fort Bridger, a stone structure which was to serve as the nucleus of the entrenched camp, was built and owned by Jim Bridger. This colorful mountain man had directed the Mormons to Salt Lake City and now, accepting a major's commission, he was serving as the army's principal guide.

The weather moderated slightly. The troopers, leaving behind a trail of abandoned animals and equipment, pressed on for Fort Bridger. When Cooke stumbled into camp on November 19, he realized his command couldn't have covered many more miles. Of the 144 horses in his original contingent, 130 lay scattered on the plains. With the arrival of the cavalry, Johnston's Army of Utah was now united on the banks of Black's Fork.

Details of soldiers started unloading the supply wagons which had been carelessly thrown together in Kansas. The Quartermaster at Fort Leavenworth, too lazy to assign each wagon train a proportionate quantity of all the articles to be transported, had haphazardly packed one after another with what was conveniently at hand. Wagons, burned by the Mormons, had been loaded with flour, bacon, all the mechanics' tools, stationery, and horse medicines. Had the Saints razed the next three trains, flames would have consumed all the expedition's clothing. When work details unpacked the wagons at Fort Bridger, they gaped in disbelief. They found only 150 pairs of boots and shoes and 600 pairs of stockings for an army of 2,500 men. Already soldiers walked about camp shod in moccasins with the temperature registering 16 degrees below zero. The wagons contained an abundance of bed sacks, 3,000 of them, articles totally worthless at Fort Bridger. Fortunately, the command had rescued enough cattle and supplies to assure subsistence for the winter months ahead.

The soldiers, bored, cooped up in frigid monotony, brawled, scrapped, and drank. Trouble started when teamsters opened up gambling on the banks of Black's Fork, where they systematically fleeced the army. In the barracks the restless, irritable men got drunk, stole government property, attacked one another, and twice broke up officers' parties. Privates whose terms of service had expired refused to reenlist. Ten soldiers deserted, several defecting to the Mormons, spreading stories of evil conditions at Fort Bridger.

Typical of the low morale was Private Henry Evans, who elbowed his way into an officer's tent searching for a drink. When ordered out, Evans announced that "he would be damned if he would go till he got ready and further that he did not care a damn for Lieut. Dudley or any other cursed sergeant in the company." In another instance of insubordination, Bugler John Burns, drinking heavily, started to abuse Judge D. R. Eckels, a civilian official with the expedition. When a lieutenant tried to calm him, Bugler Burns punched him in the nose, yelling, "God damn you, Thompson, I won't obey you, you son of a bitch."

Colonel Johnston ordered Cooke and his dragoons to patrol the distant valleys and guard the army's horses, oxen and mules, a grueling and thankless task. Angrily, the colonel and his horsemen reported to the herd camp at Henry's Fork. Cooke continued requesting assistance from the infantry. Grudgingly, Johnston sent help but refused to relieve the weary and worn-out dragoons. Mormons fired upon the guards occasionally, once hitting a sergeant, whose life was saved by the ball flattening itself against his waist plates. In an unprecedented step, the incensed Cooke ordered his men to pillage, "to help themselves to anything they wanted that has been left behind by the Mormons."

While Johnston and his army fought boredom in the mountains of Utah, the nation vigorously denounced President Buchanan for launching a force so late in the season and decried the mismanagement of the expedition. Philadelphia philanthropist and friend of the Saints, Thomas Leiper Kane arrived in Washington and offered his services to Buchanan as a conciliator. Kane promptly secured semiofficial recognition. Obstructed by the snow and ice in the mountains, the Philadelphian sailed to Panama, crossed the isthmus, and went northward by steamship. After huddling with Brigham Young at Salt Lake City, Kane rode east through the Rockies to Johnston's headquarters. At Fort Bridger, Andrew Cumming, whom Buchanan had appointed territorial governor, agreed to accompany Kane to Salt Lake City without a military escort. The Mormons peacefully accepted the new governor and, with diplomatic skill, Cumming won their confidence.

Kane and Cumming retraced their steps to Fort Bridger where they advised Johnston—now a general—that peace existed in Utah. The general remonstrated. His orders were explicit. The army would march to Salt Lake City. Johnston, however, consented to issue a proclamation, reassuring the Mormons that they had nothing to fear from the Army of Utah.

Two thousand miles away in Washington, President Buchanan, unaware of Kane's success, dispatched a Commission of Reconciliation to the territory with a signed pardon for all Mormons if they would obey and reaffirm the laws of the land. At Fort Bridger in late May these commissioners talked with Johnston and Cumming, then rode on for Salt Lake City. After talks with Brigham Young, the commissioners reported that all differences between the United States and Utah had been settled peacefully. They suggested that Johnston proceed to Salt Lake City at his convenience.

On June 15, 1858, Colonel Cooke, his new silver eagles glistening in the sunshine, moved out from Fort Bridger with his dragoons, along with the infantry and artillery. He was now colonel of the regiment. Neither Cooke nor his dragoons glanced back as they rode out of the shadowed valley and left behind the relics and debris of a deserted camp. The trail ahead lay through two canyons.

The troopers brought up the rear behind the infantry, supply trains, cattle, and sheep. They damned the God-awful dust of the dry creek bottom, which settled and caked on their sweating horses. In the ranks the men rode with chins tucked low, a bandanna or other oddment of cloth secured to shield their nostrils, making them resemble a gang of highwaymen.

The Army of Utah pitched camp one mile outside of Salt Lake City on June 25. Beside their worn and stained tents, officers rested on their canvas stools, comfortably weary, warm, and well fed. Tomorrow would see their triumphal entry.

Early on the 26th the peaks and canyons echoed to *Reveille*. The men tumbled out at the noncoms' shouts, munched breakfast, struck tents, packed wagons, and marched toward the City of the Saints. From old habit the dragoons moved into three-column formation with a minimum of confusion.

The sky was dotted here and there with high clouds as General Johnston's army spilled out of the last gorge onto a broad plateau. The first files topped a rise—Salt Lake City, neat, orderly, impressive, lay before them. Its buildings, almost entirely adobe, stood well apart surrounded by green luxuriant trees and shrubbery. From the heights the dragoons noticed the streets ran straight and wide, crossing each other at right angles. Beyond was the Jordan River and beyond it the gray, eternal desert, rimmed by peaks and mountains.

Regimental colors snapped in the wind. With bands blaring the Army of Utah entered Salt Lake City. The soldiers were shocked. Men, women, and children had abandoned their homes. Windows were boarded up, nailed shut. Doors were bolted. Gates closed. From a few houses, all the woodwork had been removed, leaving nothing except adobe walls. Mormon leaders had decided not to resist the United States soldiers but, instead, to retreat southward. If pushed by Johnston and his hordes, they planned to adopt a scorched-earth policy.

Hour after hour the troops and trains poured into the city, the silence broken by the music of the bands and the noise of marching feet. Here and there in the streets half-naked Indian

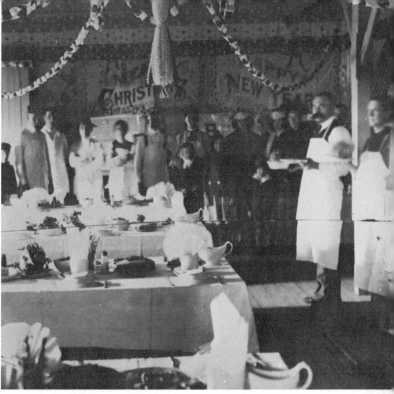

ABOVE LEFT: *Newly arrived cavalry recruit.*
RIGHT: *Christmas dinner table in mess hall at Fort Yates.*
BELOW: *Interior of 8th Cavalry trooper's quarters at Fort Yates.*

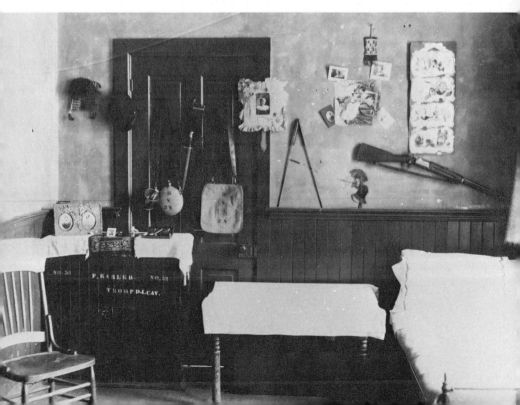

boys paddled in the gutters, pausing to stare at the passing columns. The silence was so appalling during the intervals between companies, dragoons could hear the gurgling of City Creek. "It was substantially a city of the dead," recalled an officer.

To break the monotony of the regular marches, bands struck up "One Eyed Riley," and men began to sing the coarse ditty long treasured in the barracks.

> *As I was strolling round and round,*
> *A-huntin' fun in every quarter,*
> *I stopped meself at the little Dutch inn*
> *And ordered me up Gin and Warter*

> CHORUS: *One Eye Riley, Two Eye Riley,*
> *Ho! for the land with one eye, Riley!*

Johnston did not stop but moved the army out of the city westward, across the bridge of the Jordan, then southward along its banks for three miles before pitching camp. Here the Army of Utah ended its march. The general learned that Brigham Young had sent the Saints to Provo. Finally convinced of their safety, the Mormons returned to their former residences at Salt Lake City. The "Mormon War" was over.

chapter 8.

"*Bugler, sound the advance.*"

🐴 🐴 🐴

OBERT PECK HAD RUN AWAY FROM HOME TO JOIN THE
cavalry. In 1857, along with 300 other recruits, he was
crammed on board a steamboat which chugged up the
Missouri River for Fort Leavenworth, dodging snags and
huge chunks of ice. The river seemed to stretch endlessly before
and after them, always and everywhere twisting and turning back
on itself. In many places it was a mile-wide expanse of naked
sandbars, reefs, and mud flats.

As the paddle-wheeler neared a miserable, dirty village, the
new troopers surged up to the hurricane deck and anxiously
scanned the Kansas shore. Instead of seeing a solid and mighty
bastion, they stared in disbelief at the dilapidated business houses
which fronted the steamboat landing. Before a warehouse, a guard,
his bayonet glistening in the winter sun, paced stiffly back and forth.

Peck hollered: "Where's the fort?"

Directing his gaze up over the hill, the sentry pointed to the
Stars and Stripes floating from atop a flagpole. "That's the fort,"
he cried, "about three quarters of a mile back."

Three hundred greenhorns poured off the decks and climbed
to the top of the hill. The fort was a conglomeration of stone,
brick, log, and frame buildings, which resembled a country village.

Corporals quickly corralled the recruits and formed them into
makeshift lines. They assigned Peck to E Company, 1st Cavalry.
That afternoon Private Peck made an informal inspection of his
barracks' area. Each man's cot was properly opened up for the day
with mattress doubled back and bedding folded edge by edge
inside. At the head of his bunk each trooper had three wooden
pegs driven into the wall where he hung his saber, forage cap, and

uniforms. Near the door was a rack nailed to the wall from which dangled two brass bugles with faded yellow cords, braided and tassled. Here in the barracks Private Peck learned that Fort Leavenworth was bulging with soldiers—the entire 1st Cavalry and 6th Infantry and several companies from the 2nd Dragoons and 4th Artillery. Old-timers filled the new cavalrymen with stories about their commanding officer, Colonel Edwin V. Sumner. He was "the greatest martinet in the service," a "chief devil." "Old Sumner," someone growled, "had had one good effect on us—he has taught some of us to pray who never prayed before, for we all put up daily petitions to get rid of him."

The silver-haired, iron-willed colonel cared little what the troopers thought. His energies were being expended in organizing and equipping an expedition to chastise the western Indians. The Cheyennes, emboldened by the cavalry's preoccupation in Kansas the summer before, had hit the warpath.

The expedition of 1857 was divided into two commands; Major John Sedgwick and four troops of 1st Cavalry were to march along the Santa Fe Trail and the upper Arkansas River to the foot of the Rockies, searching for Cheyennes. From there Sedgwick was to hike to the South Platte River and down that stream to meet Sumner. The colonel's columns—two troops of cavalry and four companies of 6th Infantry—after marching to Fort Laramie on the Oregon Trail were to strike back toward the South Platte.

On May 18, 1857, Major Sedgwick's command rolled out from Fort Leavenworth. Private Peck, Company E, Captain Sturgis', rode in the mass of men and horses. Later he recorded the events of that march across the plains:

> After passing Council Grove we were fairly on the plains and saw little more of timber, consequently had to depend mostly on buffalo-chips for fuel; and the prairie chickens, which were so numerous in the Kansas settlements that they were a great nuisance to the farmers, were seen no more after we struck the plains.
>
> At Cottonwood creek, about fifty miles west of the Grove, we saw the first buffalo, a few scattering small bands appearing at a distance; but from there on their numbers increased amazingly, and, when in the thick of their range, we were

often in great danger from the stampeding of the vast swarms of these animals that covered the prairie in every direction, for when those immense herds started on a run it was impossible either to stop or turn them out of their course. . . .

As we were approaching the Big Bend, crossing the level stretch of eight miles between the Plum Buttes and the Arkansas river, with our beef herd and a train of about fifty six-mule teams strung out behind us, we had an exciting bit of experience in a buffalo stampede. . . . This stampede might have resulted in a direful calamity to us but for the prompt action of Captain Sturgis, who, having been in such a predicament before many times, knew just what to do and how to do it.

Sedgwick, though an old officer in the service, had never had much experience on the plains, having been in the artillery for nearly twenty years, and the sight of that brown mass of animals—so vast in extent that we could see no end in flank or depth—thundering towards us in an irresistible torrent, made him turn pale, as he appealed to Sturgis: "Sturgis, what'll we do?"

"Time is too precious for explanations now, major," replied the captain; "better turn the command over to me for a little while—I'll steer you through it."

"Take command, captain, take command, and give your orders," replied Sedgwick, eagerly.

Before the last word was out of Sedgwick's mouth Sturgis was giving his commands: "Orderly bugler, give my compliments to company commanders and say that Captain Sturgis is in command. Then hurry on back to the train as fast as you can go, and give my compliments to the quartermaster and tell him to corral his wagons quickly, in as small a space as possible, teams heading south, with the beef cattle inside the corral."

The buffalo were coming from the north. In another moment Sturgis had us headed about and going back to the train on a gallop. At the start of the stampede the buffalo had been probably two miles or more from us. On reaching the train, which was being hurriedly formed in corral, with the beef herd on the inside, as ordered, Sturgis halted us and commanded: "Dismount, to fight on foot!" This leaves each No. 4 holding the horses of the other three men of his set. We quickly "formed ranks," after dismounting, and were then marched out, on "double quick," about a hundred yards to meet the buffalo. Our flanks were then thrown back, forming us in the shape of a huge V, with the point towards the coming herd, and the open ends of the V enclosing our horses and train.

The stampede was now coming near, driving right at us, making the earth tremble, presenting a solid front as far as we could see, right and left. To me it was a fearful sight, for I thought, "What will be left of us when that dense avalanche of horns and hoofs sweeps over us?" I had been told that we were to split the herd by firing into them, but could not see how they could find room to divide, they were crowded so closely together. However, when the command was given, "Commence firing," we poured into their faces such a sheet of fire and lead from our Sharp's rifles that they did the impossible, splitting, but crowding savagely to the right and left, actually climbing over each other in their frantic efforts to avoid our withering fire, thus making an opening that cleared our train and horses; but that torrent of brown wool went right on without any perceptible check in its speed.

We stood there loading and firing as fast as we could work our pieces, boxes of cartridges being brought up from the ammunition wagons and placed in rear of each company to keep us supplied, and it seemed at times that in spite of our efforts we were doomed to be overwhelmed by that living tornado; the dust they kicked up was often blinding to us, as well as to the buffalo, and we had been crowded back, inch by inch, till we were closely packed about our horses and wagons, when we were greatly relieved to perceive a thinning and straggling in the threatening mass, and were glad to hear the command to "Cease firing." The danger, with the buffalo, had passed, leaving the ground around us covered with dead and badly crippled buffalo, while many wounded ones went limping on after the stampeders. I heard one of the officers say, as he looked at his watch, that it lacked but a few minutes of half an hour from the command "Commence firing" to "Cease firing," with the buffalo going on a steady lope all the time.

We cut up and stowed away in our wagons the choicest meat from some of the young and tender buffalo, and leaving the rest of the killed and crippled for a grand feast for the wolves, we moved on to the Big Bend, camping on the bank of the river. . . .

Our road from the Big Bend westward lay along the north bank of the Arkansas river, sometimes several miles off, sometimes close in. . . .

About fifteen or eighteen miles west of the ruins of old Fort Atkinson was the Santa Fe crossing of the Arkansas. The crossing was opposite—almost under—a high bluff, that overlooked the ford and surrounding country for some distance. . . .

At the Santa Fe crossing, of course, we parted company with that famous old trail, and traveled along the north bank of the river on a well-worn road, then called the California trail.

The Santa Fe road, from the Arkansas to the Cimarron, then ran about due north and south on the sixty-mile stretch, without water, called the "journeda," for I remember to have noticed, in traveling it afterwards by night, coming from the Cimarron to the Arkansas, that we were going towards the north star all night.

All the freight for the western country was then transported across the plains in wagon trains, sometimes of mule teams, sometimes oxen. We had met several of these outfits from New Mexico, going into the states for goods, their wagons being usually empty, but sometimes carrying light loads of wool in huge sacks, that being about the only commodity that New Mexico exported. We had also overtaken and passed some freight trains going out loaded, and several emigrant outfits en route to California. The teamsters employed in the New Mexico trains were mostly Mexicans.

Frequent graves were to be seen along the roadside, many of them being marked by rude wooden crosses. Such almost invariably indicated the last resting place of some Mexican, who is always a Catholic. I had noticed, too, but thought it the result of carelessness in placing the crosses on the graves, that nearly all these cross-pieces were in a slanting position, but on mentioning this peculiarity to one of the old soldiers, he informed me that when the horizontal piece was slanted it meant, "died with his boots on," or a violent death—usually killed by Indians—and that where the cross-piece was fastened at right angles to the upright (and these were few, for people seldom die of disease on the plains), it signified, "died on the square," or a natural death.

Major Sedgwick had employed at Leavenworth, as guides, scouts and trailers for the expedition, a half-dozen Delaware Indians from their reservation on the Kaw River, near Lawrence. They were under the command of old Fall Leaf, a noted chief of their tribe. The Delawares had then adopted white men's garb and ways to a great extent, and were far superior to the plains Indians. They did us excellent service throughout the trip.

The Arkansas river, from where we first struck it, at Big Bend, to some distance west of the Santa Fe crossing, was a broad, shallow stream, showing many sand-bars and islands, but no timber except a few scattering trees now and then on some of the islands, but as we approached the mountains we found more timber along the river banks, and the stream grew narrower and deeper.

Bent's Fort, on the upper Arkansas, was the second white man's habitation we struck after leaving Council Grove. . . .

Shortly after passing Bent's Fort, following the California trail up the river, we got our first sight of the snow-covered summit of Pike's Peak, resting on the western horizon like a small white cloud, which many of us thought it really was; but day after day, as we marched towards it, the white cloud grew larger, higher, and plainer, other mountains on each side of it coming into view, till in a few days it seemed like we were running up against the whole Rocky Mountain range.

Near the mouth of a creek called Fountain que Bouille, we turned off from the Arkansas and struck over the divide for the head of Cherry creek, passing through some fine bodies of pine timber. . . .

Soon after reaching Cherry creek, while marching down

it, we met a party of six or eight men—Missourians, and all afoot—with a little old wagon drawn by a single yoke of steers. . . . These men were the first discoverers of gold in the Pike's Peak region. I have always been sorry that I did not ascertain their names, and more about them, in order to give them the credit to which they are entitled, for giving to the country so important a discovery. The honor of this discovery has been claimed by others, but I am satisfied that those Missourians were the first to make known to the public the presence of gold in that part of the country. . . .

Those men had a wounded comrade lying in their wagon who had accidentally shot himself through the hand. In pulling his rifle out of the wagon muzzle foremost, a day or so before we met them; the wound had reached the gangrene stage, and they halted to ask surgical aid from our doctor. Our surgeon decided that it would be necessary to take the man along with us, and while halting to bring up a wagon and transfer the man, we got a chance to talk to them a little, and they told us their troubles. I think they had been in the mountains between the mouth of Cherry creek and Pike's Peak all winter and spring prospecting, and had found plenty of gold, some of which they showed us, put up in bottles and little buckskin bags.

They had originally intended to keep the discovery of gold a secret, but the Indians had run off all their stock except the yoke of steers, and had otherwise made life such a burden to them that they finally concluded the only way to make mining safe and profitable was to go back to Missouri, proclaim their discovery, make up a strong party that would be able to hold their own against the Indians, and return determined to have "the dust."

We parted company with them—they continuing on towards the States, and we moving on down to the mouth of Cherry creek, where Denver now stands, and camped, on the 29th of June, 1857. . . .

The California trail, which we had been following, crosses the South Platte here, just below (north of) the mouth of Cherry creek, and seems to take through the mountains, while we leave it and follow down the right bank of the river on a dim wagon-trail that did not appear to be used much.

This part of Kansas Territory was literally a "howling wilderness," with little indication of its having been occupied or traversed by white men, except the old wagon-road we had been traveling, with here and there a stump and a few chips by the roadside, as the mark of some California emigrant. Game was very abundant, and comparatively tame. Herds of elk, antelope, and deer were frequently seen from the trail as we marched along, and occasionally a bear. . . .

We had one or two desertions shortly after leaving Cherry creek, and our officers seemed to fear that the reported gold discovery had caused these men to abscond for the purpose of going into the mountains prospecting. For fear of others being led to desert to go gold hunting they caused to be circulated through the camp reports that the rumored gold discovery was a fake, and instructed the wounded prospector to contradict his first statements and deny the discovery of gold in paying quantities. . . .

On the Fourth of July we laid over on the bank of the Platte, and, with our two howitzers, fired our national salute of thirty-two guns in honor of the day.

We had now got clear of the foot-hills and timbered country and were back again on the plains. We had expected to form a junction with Colonel Sumner's command somewhere in this part of the country, but had not heard a word from them since leaving Fort Leavenworth. As the echo of our last gun died away we were cheered by the answering boom of cannon from down the river, and distinctly counted thirty-two guns. Of course, we understood that this must be from Colonel Sumner, and Major Sedgwick immediately dispatched one of Fall Leaf's young Delawares to the colonel's camp, which was found to be about fifteen miles down and on the opposite side of the river, near the mouth of Crow creek.

Next day we moved down opposite the colonel's camp, and in fording the river to join him got a lot of our horses and mule teams mired in the quicksands, but finally got over without the loss of an animal. . . .

On the 13th of July, with twenty days' rations on our pack-mules and otherwise lightly equipped, we crossed the river, leaving our trains of six-mule teams under charge of P. G. Lowe, chief wagon-master, escorted by a company of the Sixth infantry, to return to Fort Laramie for a supply of rations and forage, and then again to come back to the South Platte, about the old Salt Lake crossing, and there await orders from Sumner.

The wounded gold prospector . . . was left with our train and I never heard of him again, but suppose he recovered and returned to his home in Missouri.

I think most of the officers and soldiers of our pack-mule outfit fully expected that we would find and clean out the Cheyennes and get back to our supply-train within the twenty days for which we were rationed. But I doubt whether Colonel Sumner and the more experienced men anticipated such an easy job, for it was said of the "old bull o' the woods" that whenever he started on such a trip he never expected to get back in twice the time of his rations, and during the last half after rations had run out, his command was liable to have to subsist on their pack-mules or horses, if he struck a warm trail.

We left all extra luggage with our wagons, such as tents, blankets, and overcoats, taking no clothing but what we wore, and no bedding but our saddle-blankets, lightening ourselves and our horses of every pound that could possibly be dispensed with. We took no wheeled vehicles except one two-mule ambulance for the use of the sick, and the four mountain howitzers, which were united in a four-gun battery under command of Second Lieut. Geo. D. Bayard, of G. company. We were entirely without shelter. The colonel took along a tent-fly, to use for headquarters and adjutant's office, and one fly was allowed for the hospital.

After crossing the river we followed down the south bank of the South Platte, eastward, for three or four days, and then bore away in a southeast direction. Our guides seemed to have ascertained or guessed something of the whereabouts of the Cheyenne village, and led us as though they knew where they were going; though the old lodge-pole trail we were following was by no means fresh—apparently not having been used for a year or more.

On the sixteenth day from the time of leaving our train,

on the 29th of July, traveling generally in a southeast course, we found the Cheyennes, and thought for awhile that we had "found more Indians than we had lost." During the previous day our Delaware scouts, who usually kept the country explored for ten or twelve miles in advance and on each flank, had found some fresh signs. The country being somewhat broken in many places, for we were near the headwaters of Solomon river, Colonel Sumner had taken the precaution to march the command in three columns, "en echelon" (a sort of stair-step formation), from which they could be brought quickly into line, to meet an attack from the front, rear, or either flank. Our pack-mules were kept close to our rear. The three infantry companies, and sometimes the battery, would unavoidably drop to the rear in rough ground, but we made frequent short halts to allow them to close up. Be it remembered that this was all a treeless prairie, with seldom even a bush to be seen.

On this day (July 29), about ten o'clock A.M., old Fall Leaf sent one of his Delawares galloping back from the front to report to Colonel Sumner that his trailers had sighted a small party of Indians, some distance ahead, who seemed to be retreating as our scouts advanced. This proved to be a reconnoitering party of Cheyennes who had been sent out to watch us, and were falling back on the main body as we approached. Colonel Sumner seemed to fear that the Cheyennes were all on the retreat and might escape us; so he determined to push on with the six companies of cavalry, and try to bring the enemy to a fight, even if he had to leave the infantry and artillery behind. And it is probable that the Indians had planned to draw us out in a rapid pursuit of that decoy party, and after getting us well strung out to fall on us with their whole force and clean us up in detail; for, as we afterwards learned, they had no notion of running from us. Instead, they had come out fifteen miles from their village, selected their ground to fight on, and were coolly awaiting our approach apparently so confident of defeating us that they had made no preparations for moving their village, a precaution they seldom neglect when they are about to have a fight near their camps.

"Bugler, sound the advance."

As soon as the colonel got the word that the Indians had been sighted, he halted the command and sent orders to all company commanders to see that their men were prepared for action. At the command, we dismounted, tightened up saddle-girths, and examined arms and equipments to see that everything was in fighting order. Little preparation was necessary for we had frequently been admonished on the trip to keep our "kits" in good shape, and were always ready for a call.

As soon as the captains remounted their companies and reported ready for action, the "old man" rode out in front of the center column and made a little speech. He had a very loud, strong voice, and I think this, together with his well-known fighting proclivities, had probably earned for him the name "Bull o' the Woods," by which sobriquet his men were fond of speaking of their old white-headed, white-bearded fighting colonel. His speech on this occasion was about as follows: "My men! the enemy is at last in sight. I don't know how many warriors the Cheyennes can bring against us, but I do know that if officers and men obey orders promptly, and all pull together, we can whip the whole tribe. I have the utmost confidence in my officers and soldiers. Bugler, sound the advance!"

As the clear notes of the bugle rang out, followed by the captains' "Column forward! march!" we again struck the trail, and all seemed encouraged by the colonel's confidence. This was the first bugle-call we had heard for several days, Sumner having dispensed with those signals lately, lest the sound might be borne to the ears of some scouting Cheyenne; but now there was no longer any use for such precaution. A few minutes after we had resumed the march, the notes of "Trot!" reached us from the colonel's orderly-bugler, and each captain commanded: "Trot! March!" Our pack-mules were also put in a trot, and kept close in our rear. The infantry, of course, now dropped behind. Lieutenant Bayard's battery kept up with us for a little while, but soon, in crossing a miry little creek, some of his mules bogged down, and we left them floundering in the mud, with Bayard swearing a blue streak at the unfortunate detention. We saw no more of the infantry or battery until after the fight.

It seemed a little reckless of the colonel to scatter his command this way, and attack an enemy of unknown numbers on their chosen ground with only a part of his force, but he had probably estimated all the chances and was so much afraid that the Indians would get away from us that he decided to try to bring them to a fight and take the risk of either whipping them or holding them till our reenforcements came up. Deducting the "sick, lame, and lazy," who had been left behind with the train, and the men on detail manning the battery and attending to the pack-mules, we had scarcely an average of fifty fighting men in the ranks of each company of cavalry—a little less than 300 men all told—ready to go into action.

As we came down a hollow from the upland prairie, debouching onto the Solomon river bottom, and rounded a bluff-point that had obstructed our view to the eastward, before us and extending down along the north bank of the river, was an almost level valley of several miles, at the lower end of which stood a few scattering cottonwood trees. About these trees we could see a dense mass of moving animals that at first looked like a distant herd of buffalo. But we had been told by our guides that we were more than two days' march west of the buffalo range. Several of the officers halted long enough to take a look through their field glasses, and promptly announced: "They are Indians, all right, and a swarm of them, but no sign of lodges; they seem to have been halted about those trees, and are now mounting and moving this way."

Soon we began to see the glint of a rifle barrel or lance point here and there, reflecting the rays of the sun. We afterwards discovered that the Cheyennes had been awaiting our arrival several hours, in the vicinity of the trees, had coolly unsaddled and turned their horses out to graze, and they and their mounts were well-rested and fresh when the fight began, while we and our horses were quite jaded. We found near those trees, after the fight, a number of their saddles, blankets, and other impedimenta that they had discarded; for, on going into battle, the Indian warrior wants the free use of every limb and muscle, usually dispensing with everything in the way of clothing but his "gee-string," leggings, and moccasins, often doffing even his leggings, many times throwing off his saddle and riding barebacked, to give his horse more freedom of action.

When the Indians had approached near enough that we could make a rough estimate of their numbers we saw that they greatly outnumbered us, and noticed that they were advancing in a well-formed line of battle, but differing from our formation in being several ranks deep, and preserving sufficient intervals between the men to give each perfect freedom of action. And all the time they were yelling. . . .

Just when we were nearly in rifle range of the enemy we saw our old Delaware chief, Fall Leaf, dash out from our line till he got about midway between the two bodies, when he suddenly halted his horse, raised his rifle, and fired at the Cheyennes. As he turned and rode back, followed by several shots from the enemy, we heard Colonel Sumner say in a loud voice to Lieut. David Stanley, who was beside him: "Bear witness, Lieutenant Stanley, that an Indian fired the first shot!"

It is probable that he had been hampered by one of those milk-and-water orders from Washington, to "first exhaust all means to conciliate the Indians before beginning hostilities," and he seemed relieved to be able to establish the fact that an Indian fired the first shot, pretending not to have noticed that said first shot was fired by one of his own Indian scouts and not by a Cheyenne. Up to this time the colonel was possibly expecting that the Cheyennes might halt, display a white flag and request a "pow-wow," but now that he could establish the fact that an Indian begun hostilities, he was under no obligations to wait longer for peaceful overtures from them to satisfy the demands of the weak-kneed sentimentalists of the East.

When the Cheyennes were almost in rifle-shot they were outflanking us both right and left. Our right was moving along the bank of the river. A large party of the Indians had crossed the river, and, after passing our right, was about to recross and come in our pack-train in the rear. They were also turning our left, all the while keeping up that infernal yelling. Noticing that the Cheyennes were turning our left, the colo-

nel ordered Captain Beall (the left company) to deploy his
company to the left and head them off. He seemed to have
determined to offset the disparity of numbers by a bold dash
that would create a panic in the enemy's ranks, and roared
out, "Sling—carbine!" then immediately, "Draw—saber!" and
we knew the old man was going to try a saber charge on them.

I noticed with some surprise that when the command
"Draw—saber" was given (which I then thought was a serious
mistake in the colonel) and our three hundred bright blades
flashed out of their scabbards, the Cheyennes, who were coming on at a lope, checked up. The sight of so much cold steel
seemed to cool their ardor. The party that had started to cross
the river after passing our right also hesitated, and Captain
Beall, with his company deployed to the left, easily turned
back those that were turning our left flank. I then said to myself, "I guess 'Old Bull' knows what he is doing; after all;
he knows the Indians will not stand a saber charge." And
so it proved.

At their first checking of speed, a fine-looking warrior
mounted on a spirited horse, probably their chief, dashed up
and down in front of their line, with the tail of his war-bonnet
flowing behind, brandishing his lance, shouting to his warriors, and gesticulating wildly, evidently urging his men to
stand their ground, when he saw symptoms of a panic among
them. Many of us found time to admire his superb horseman-
ship, for he presented a splendid sight as he wheeled his horse,
charging back and forth, twirling the long lance over his head
now and then.

The Indians had almost ceased their yelling, had slowed
down almost to a walk and were wavering. We had kept a
steady trot, but now came the command in the well-known
roar of "Old Bull," "Gallop—march!" and then immediately
"CHARGE!" and with a wild yell we brought our sabers to a
"tierce point" and dashed at them.

All their chief's fiery pleading could not hold them then,
for every redskin seemed suddenly to remember that he had
urgent business in the other direction, but as they wheeled
to run they sent a shower of arrows toward us, by way of a
"parting shot" as it were. Few of the missiles, however, took

effect. They scattered as they ran, some going to the north, some east, but by far the greater number struck across the river and went south; and these, as we afterwards discovered, were heading for their village, which was about fifteen miles south of the Solomon, on the next creek.

Our men, of course, became much scattered in following them, fighting occasionally, when a party of the Indians could be overtaken and brought to bay, but their horses were fresh and well rested, while ours were jaded. It was a running fight, mostly a chase, for about seven miles, when the colonel had "recall" sounded, calling us back to the Solomon where the fight began. Our pack-mules had been ordered halted there when the charge was made to await the result.

It was estimated that about thirty Cheyennes were killed, though they were scattered over the country so far and wide that it was almost impossible to count the dead correctly. If it had not been for the fact that a number of their horses had stuck in the quicksands while crossing the river, we would have got but few of them. Some ten or twelve Indians who had been compelled to abandon their mired horses in the river, and who had reached the further side afoot, were soon overtaken and killed on the slope of the hill after crossing. They fought like devils as long as there was breath in them, never seeming to entertain the idea of surrendering, for they generally believed that if taken alive they would be tortured to death the same as they would have served us if taken prisoner by them. It was here on the slope of the hill, after crossing the river, that most of their casualties occurred. Quite a number of the dismounted Indians escaped by being taken up behind others of their comrades who had got through with their horses, but many of these were overtaken on account of the double load.

Besides the dread of torture, Indians consider it a great disgrace to surrender while yet able to fight. As a rare instance of disregard of this rule, one strapping big Cheyenne, who had lost his horse, but was not wounded at all, surrendered to a party of our men, without offering any resistance, seeing that there was no chance of escape.

When I got back to the Solomon river, after the "recall"

had been sounded, I found the colonel establishing camp on the south bank, about opposite the ground where we made the charge. The three companies of the Sixth infantry and Lieutenant Bayard's battery were just crossing the river, coming into camp, all cursing their luck at being left behind. The hospital tent-fly had been hastily put up to shelter the wounded from the hot sun, and I went there immediately after finding my company's camp and unsaddling and picketing out my horse, anxious to learn who had been killed or wounded. At the corner of the hospital tent my attention was first drawn to two still forms, side by side, covered by a saddle-blanket, and on turning back the blanket I was shocked to meet the dead face of an intimate comrade, Private George Cade, of G company, and alongside of him Private Lynch, of A company. A small hole in Cade's breast, over the heart, showed where a Cheyenne's arrow had gone through him, which must have killed him instantly.

Lynch had been shot several times with arrows and twice with his own pistol, and a cut around the edge of his hair, with the edge of the scalp turned back, showed that the Indians had also attempted to scalp him. He had been detailed to lead his company's pack-mules for the day, and was so occupied just before we came into line to make the charge. Seeing his first sergeant passing near, Lynch called to him to ask if he couldn't send another man to relieve him, as he wanted to go into the fight. The sergeant replied: "No time for any change now, Lynch; you'll have to stay and hold the mules," and then rode on to join his company. Just then the charge was ordered. Lynch was heard to exclaim, indignantly: "Hold hell in a fight! Does he suppose I've come all this way out in the wilderness to hold pack-mules when there's a fight going on?" And with that he dropped his leading strap, drew his saber and charged with his company. After crossing the river, Lynch's horse—a fiery, hard-mouthed thing—took the bit in his teeth and ran away with him, outrunning his company, overtaking a party of the Indians who shot him with arrows until he fell off his horse; then, halting and dismounting quickly, they drew Lynch's pistol out of its scabbard, shot him twice with it, and one Cheyenne had boldly begun scalping him when our men overtook them and killed several near where he lay. His revolver was found in the hand of one of the dead Indians, but his horse had continued running with the fleeing Cheyennes, and we never saw it again.

Cade and Lynch were all the killed, but under the tent-fly were twelve wounded. Among the number, First-lieut. James Ewell Brown Stuart had received a pistol ball in the shoulder from an unhorsed Cheyenne whose life Stuart was trying to save; it is possible that the Indian had misunderstood his intentions. . . .

It was estimated that there were about 900 or 1,000 of the Cheyenne warriors. If Colonel Sumner had known that we were almost in sight of their village when he gave up the pursuit, it is probable that he would have gathered his men and followed them right on, but we did not discover that their camp was so near in time to take advantage of the opportunity to inflict further punishment on them. The fact was we were all pretty well tuckered out, as were our horses, also; and probably our Delaware scouts were in a similar condition, and, on that account, had failed to penetrate the country far enough in advance to detect the Cheyenne village.

Old Fall Leaf and his Delawares went into the fight with us, and did good service, but the cowardly Pawnees, that Colonel Sumner had brought with him from Fort Kearney, only followed in our wake, scalping the dead Cheyennes, and gathering up their abandoned ponies, of which they had collected about sixty head, which the colonel agreed to let them keep as part pay for their services.

As I have before mentioned, some of our men had taken one Cheyenne prisoner. On hearing of this, after the fight, the Pawnees went in a body to Sumner's headquarters and tried to buy the prisoner of him, in order to have a grand scalp-dance over him, and put him to death by torture, offering to surrender to the colonel the sixty captured ponies, and also to forfeit the money that was to be paid them on their return to Fort Kearney, if he would only give them that Cheyenne, and they seemed fairly wild with a fiendish desire to get him into their possession. Of course, the old man would not listen to any such a barbarous proposition, and promptly

ordered them back to their own camp, on the outskirts of
ours. They went away, very angry at his refusal. The "Old
Bull" was so disgusted with the conduct of the skulking Pawnees this day that he immediately discharged them, and they
started next morning back to their village, near Fort Kearney. . . .

I have an unpleasant remembrance of our experience for
the next twenty-three days after the battle; of long and exhaustive marches in the hottest and driest part of the season,
and almost at the point of starvation. Our miserable pittance
of three-fourths of a pound of fresh beef to the man, of the
poorest quality, issued each afternoon after camping (and in
a day or so after the fight we hadn't a bit of anything else in
the way of food, not even a grain of salt), was sometimes eked
out by using the meat of a horse or mule that chanced to give
out and would be shot to prevent its falling into the hands
of the enemy.

We found frequently along the trail freshly made graves,
showing that a number of the Cheyenne had succumbed from
their wounds after the fight. It soon became evident that there
was little prospect of our catching them again, for the trail
showed that several parties had split off from the main body
since leaving their village; and by the time we reached the
Arkansas river the band we were following was small, and
well in the lead of us.

While elements of Sumner's command headed either for
Fort Kearny or Fort Leavenworth, other horse regiments secured
the peace in remote regions of the American West during the
years immediately prior to the Civil War.

1858: Captain Earl Van Dorn and four companies of 2nd Cavalry moved out from the Brazos River. After marching ninety
miles in thirty-eight hours, they made contact with Comanche
near Wichita Village and defeated them decisively. At Camp
Verde in Texas troopers herded a group of dromedaries across the
countryside and organized a camel corps for work on the plains,

an experiment which failed. High in the Rockies the northern column of the Gila Expedition, commanded by Colonel Loring, Mounted Rifles, overhauled and defeated a band of savages, killing the notorious chief Chuchillo Negro. Surrounded by 1,200 redmen in Oregon country, three companies of the 1st Dragoons and Company E, 9th Infantry, fought valiantly but were overpowered and force-marched at night to safety. To discipline the savages, units of dragoons and infantry routed them at the junction of the Snake and Tucanon rivers on September 1.

1859: Earl Van Dorn, 2nd Cavalry, and his troopers fought their historic battle with the Comanche in Texas, a savage free-for-all in which Lieutenants E. Kirby Smith and Fitzhugh Lee, later to win fame in the Civil War, were severely wounded. In the autumn the Mexican bandit Cortinas, sneaked across the border near Brownsville, Texas, with a band of cutthroats and murdered several Americans. A troop of 2nd Cavalry together with infantry units stubbornly pursued the renegades and engaged them until Cortinas retreated across the Rio Grande.

1860: Cortinas continued to cross the border and harass Americans. After the city of Reynosa in Mexico refused to deliver up the culprits, backing up their stand with rifles and cannon, Colonel Robert E. Lee, commanding the 2nd Cavalry, slipped over the border to Matamoros and met with Mexican General Garcia to plot the outlaws' capture. Garcia dispatched a detail of soldiers, which pounced upon Cortinas' band near Rancho Santa Cruz. The soldiers seized and hanged one of the offenders and dispersed the others.

By the time of the Presidential election of 1860 soldiers on frontier posts had heard and read enough about slavery and secession to sense the seriousness of the national crisis. "I am a Southern man in all my feelings," wrote Captain E. Kirby Smith, "and will stand by the fireside whilst the roof tumbles about my ears,—and such I fear will be the result in the event of a violent secession." But Abraham Lincoln's election, followed by South Carolina's secession from the Union shocked even those officers and troopers who had expected it. Events rapidly crowded in upon each other. Soldiers read and discussed reports from the East, but each made up his mind alone.

chapter 9.

"What in hell are you falling astern for."

WHEN THE GUNS AT FORT SUMTER, SOUTH CAROLINA, exploded in April, 1861, and plunged the nation into bloody Civil War, Union generals neither valued nor understood the potential of the horse regiments. Despite its twenty-five years of service to the country, Americans did not look upon the mounted arm with special pride nor did little boys see it as a *corps d'elite*. The cavalry's record in the Seminole and Mexican wars was not remarkable and the regiments had never acquired numerical importance.

Whatever feeling Americans had for the cavalry centered in the border and southern states. Under the leadership of Robert E. Lee, Jeb Stuart, and other officers, the Confederacy was to organize, maintain, and employ large mounted units. In a position to secure horses immediately, its population accustomed to riding, the South could field a mass of expert horsemen. Virginia, North Carolina, and Kentucky abounded in horses of aristocratic blood, sons and daughters of such noble racers as *Sir Archie, Boston, Eclipse,* and others less famous in turf annals. Skilled in the use of firearms, Southerners shot expertly from the saddle and possessed an intimate knowledge of their countryside's topography.

After the outbreak of hostilities, President Lincoln ordered the regular army increased, called for volunteers, created a new cavalry regiment, the 3rd, and then reorganized the mounted arm of the service: all regiments would be designated "cavalry." The 1st Dragoons became the 1st Cavalry Regiment; the 2nd Dragoons, 2nd Cavalry; Mounted Rifles, 3rd Cavalry; 1st Cavalry, 4th Cavalry; 2nd Cavalry, 5th Cavalry; 3rd Cavalry, 6th Cavalry.

Union commanders had scarcely heeded the revolution in

firearms and its relation to the horse units. The increased range of rifles and the invention of breechloading and magazine guns, making continuous, long-range fire possible, destroyed the effectiveness of saber-charging horsemen against trained infantry. Experience with these improved weapons along the western plains in the 1850's had taught the cavalry officer on the spot the virtues of dismounted action and the tactical value of irregular warfare. Yet official and semiofficial works on tactics preached the orthodox doctrine with emphasis upon the shock charge. Formal military thinking had not reached the point of handing the trooper a rifle and pistol and dispatching him to the scene of action as a striking force.

Lincoln's highest ranking military officer, Winfield Scott, a veteran of the War of 1812 and Mexican conflict, was convinced that the insurrection would be of too short a duration to train mounted regiments. Undervaluing the horse soldier, Scott believed that cavalry would play no significant part in overall strategy. He decided the expense of outfitting and training horse units could not be justified. Equipment for a mounted regiment of 1,200 cost over $300,000 and the pay scale for cavalry personnel was higher than that of infantry.

Hampered by his own lack of experience with mounted troops, the general-in-chief blindly followed the European dictate that cavalry could not effectually be employed in broken or wooded countryside. His failure to realize that horse units might be adapted to such a terrain led to his flat refusal of the offer by immigrant Carl Schurz to raise a New York regiment of veteran German cavalrymen.

From state officials across the nation letters and telegrams flooded the War Department asking permission to accept volunteer mounted troops. To such requests the blundering, incompetent Secretary of War, Simon Cameron, tersely replied, "Accept no cavalry."

Official policy veered in mid-June, 1861, when Lincoln, beseiged with offers, yielded to public pressure and quietly overruled Scott and Cameron. Stampeded by an overeager public, the War Department unwisely began accepting cavalry units from everywhere without investigating their fitness for active service.

From Maine to Missouri special interest groups organized

mounted regiments. An attorney in Bethlehem, Pennsylvania, raised a company of Moravians. Brigham Young recruited a horse company of Mormons for ninety-day service. A group of Iowa temperance men established a "cold water" regiment and critics accused Frank Wolford of corralling a collection of alcoholics for the 1st Kentucky. A unit known as the Kentucky Light Cavalry was formed—its name astounded even its members who were all Pennsylvanians. "Colonel" Smockenska organized a regiment of lancers among men of Polish origin.

If an individual successfully assembled a volunteer regiment, he received a colonel's commission when his outfit was mustered into federal service. The prospective colonel acted as an entrepreneur and appointed friends and relatives to recruit battalions, companies, or platoons in return for commissions as majors, captains, or lieutenants. Brains and initiative were considered the only essential attributes for officers.

Schoolhouses and town halls in rural areas served as rallying points for enlistment drives. Prospective colonels scoured the highways and byways, rapping on farmhouse doors, placating mothers, enticing youngsters. Newspapers carried spectacular advertisements promising high adventure, fine equipment, brilliant uniforms. Recruiters mustered in men without reference to size, weight, previous occupation, or capability. The majority did not know how to fire a gun or ride a horse. Inexperienced officers commanded equally green men. "The blind led the blind," reported a private, "and often both fell into the ditch, though not always at the same time."

Northern cities teemed with Hussars, Blues, Light Horse, Mounted Rifles—for the most part uninstructed and unmounted, but bursting with enthusiasm. As enlistments increased Washington was confronted with the problem of equipping the newly created horse regiments. No aspect of building the Union cavalry was more chaotic. Horse soldiers lacked everything from bullets to suspenders. Through haste, carelessness, or criminal collusion, the government blindly accepted almost every offer and paid almost any price for commodities regardless of quality or quantity.

Early in the war the army relied heavily upon the individual states to secure mounts, but soon the federal government, states, cities, and towns were competing for horses. Certain sections were oversupplied; others were understocked. Prices spiraled.

124

Recruiting poster
Civil War

1862

$300–Bounty–$300

$200 Dollars Cash in advance,
BEFORE LEAVING THE CITY.

The men will be mounted upon splendid Chargers, and armed with fine Sabres, Sharps Rifles, and Colt's Revolvers.

☞ $100 will be paid to each man when honorably discharged.

Saddlers, Horse Shoers & Buglers, wanted.

Major H. C. SPALDING,

is to command this splendid Battalion, which, in equipment, will be equal to any in the service.

Principal Recruiting Office,
43 LIBERTY STREET, N. Y.

OPPOSITE THE POST OFFICE.

Come on Brave Boys! Now is the time to avoid the DRAFT, and secure a small fortune by enlisting.

The War Department purchased horses by contract from the main markets centered in St. Louis and Cincinnati. The dishonest palmed off unsound mounts which were passed by unscrupulous inspectors. Many horses entered the cavalry service diseased, blind, ringboned, or broken winded. A board of survey in St. Louis discovered only 76 horses out of 411 fit for duty. Five were dead, 300 undersized and overaged. These horses had each cost $11 more than the regulation maximum of $119. When ordinary profits proved insufficient, scalawags learned that beasts branded originally as cavalry mounts for $119 apiece, could be rebranded as artillery horses and sold for $150.

By 1863 officers were searching the countryside as far north as Augusta, Maine, and Madison, Wisconsin. Bidding rose in the open markets as agent vied with agent to fill his quota. Forced to go far afield for animals, the Army paid steamboat lines and railroads to ship the animals to the proper depots. The railroads charged a standard rate of $7 per carload, making shipments expensive.

To standardize quality, the War Department issued specifications. Cavalry mounts were to be "sound in all particulars," "good square trotters, bridle-wise"; colors—bay, black, sorrel. But overeager agents ignored these regulations and the quality of horses varied with the regiments. The best horses employed by the Union were the Morgan and Canadian breeds which, while not large, possessed great endurance.

Across the land in the cavalry camps recruits quickly learned that the northern states were rich in draft horses, poor in riding horses. Hastily formed outfits mounted their men on animals fresh from the plow, dray, and heavy wagon, animals as unfamiliar with cavalry work as their riders. They balked at leaping narrow ditches or low fences.

Never astride a horse before, the raw troopers—"Jockey soldiers" the infantry called them—clutched wildly at manes and saddle straps, terror shooting across their faces at the commands *Trot* and *Gallop*. Even those who had ridden before did not ride "The Army Way" and had to be retaught. Ludicrous spills and runaway horses were common sights. Cavalry drills always drew crowds; some came to admire, others to laugh.

Regiments like the 1st Pennsylvania, whose enlistees were

already efficient horsemen, were rare. More typical was the 1st Maine Cavalry. On a blustery October morning in Augusta as the regimental band thundered *Yankee Doodle* and *Hail Columbia*, Governor Washburn mounted the reviewing stand. Row upon row of horses, rearing, jumping, and neighing passed the platform in comic disarray. In the ranks Private Joseph Gatchell of K Company, a unit composed entirely of seafaring men, yanked on the reins to keep his plow horse in line. Captain Prince, troop commander and erstwhile whaling skipper, bellowed: "Come up there! what in hell are you falling astern for?"

"Why, captain," retorted Private Gatchell, "I can't get the damn thing in stays!"

"Well, give her more headway then!"

That night in the stalls where the regiment slept, a private wrote home to his dad.

> *"In a horse-stall on the*
> *Agricultural Fair Grounds*
> *Nearly Opposite the Capitol*
> *Augusta, Maine, October 4, 1861*
>
> Dear Father:—
>
> . . . *We have had a good time so far, and all are in tip-top spirits. We have a good cook, and everything for him to work with. Potatoes at every meal, so far. . . .*
>
> *I feel tip-top, and think I am going to like it. Slept well last night, and waked up this morning without being called.*
>
> *We were most all green at camping out, and it was sport for us to listen to the various remarks, good, bad, and indifferent, of the several new sojers. The partitions between the stalls are not made clean up, so we could hear all that was going on.*

Greenhorns knew no rest. They learned to Dress Up. Keep Step. Wheel into Line. Then the manual of arms: Shoulder Arms! Right Face! Forward March! Right Wheel! Left Wheel! Halt! Order Arms! Squad drill. Troop drill. Squadron drill. Regiment drill.

Once the trooper was taught to ride and maintain some semblance of formation while in motion, he still had to learn how to swing a saber without falling off, gouging his neighbor, or cutting off his mount's ears. He also had to master the manual of the pistol and carbine and care of his horse.

From the moment the average volunteer first stumbled out on the drill field, he insisted upon his rights as a soldier. He usually knew every article and every privilege he was entitled to, and he meant to have them all. He accepted everything the quartermaster issued and demanded the other goods "allowed by regulations." In the recruit's eyes both the quartermaster and army regulations were deficient, and he made further additions to his equipment by gift from home or by purchase in town. Many a trooper went forth to battle burdened by a peddler's pack of extra blankets, comforters, books, patent medicines, and bulletproof vests.

Fully equipped, the volunteer was a fearful and wonderful object. Mounted upon his powerful draft horse in the midst of all the paraphernalia and adornments of war, he was a moving arsenal and military depot as he pranced across the drill field. Upon his body he carried weapons and accouterments, the combined weight of which was over fifty pounds. His properties rose before and behind him like fortifications, and were slung over his shoulders and covered his flanks. To the uninitiated it was a mystery how he ever got into the saddle. Infantrymen snickered that this was accomplished with a derrick or by first climbing to the top of a high fence.

A troop commander in the 10th New York gives a classic description of the mounted trooper:

'The general' was sounded, 'boots and saddles' blown, and Major Falls commanded: 'SHOUN! 'AIR T'-A-O-U-N-T!'

Such a rattling, jingling, jerking, scrambling, cursing, I never before heard. Green horses—some of them never had been ridden—turned round and round, backed against each other, jumped up or stood up like trained circus-horses. Some of the boys had a pile in front, on their saddles, and one in the rear, so high and heavy it took two men to saddle one horse and two men to help the fellow in his place. The horses sheered out, going sidewise, pushing the well-disposed animals out of position, etc. Some of the boys had never rode anything since they galloped on a hobbyhorse, and clasped their legs close together, thus unconsciously sticking the spurs into their horses' sides.

128

Cartoons of Civil War
Training Camps

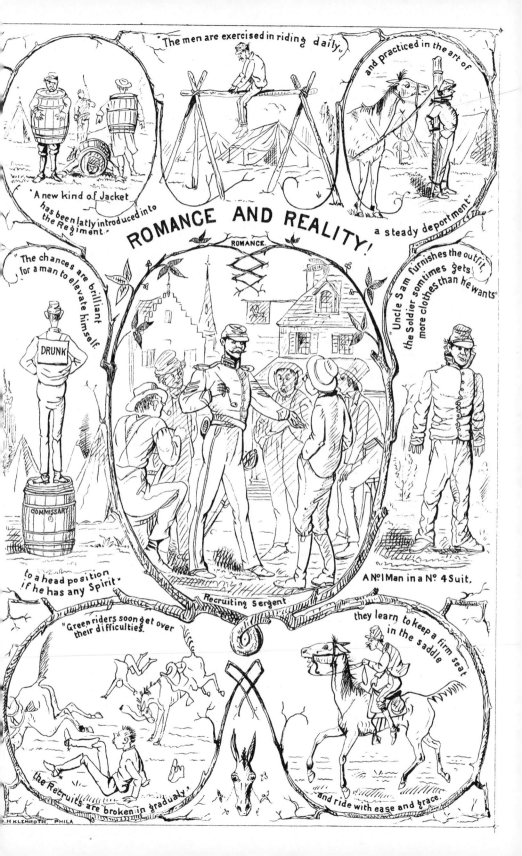

Well, this was the crowd I commanded to mount on the morning I was ordered by General Smith to follow him. We got in line near headquarters, and when he got ready to start he started all over. He left no doubt about his starting! He went like greased lightening!

As soon as I could get my breath I shouted, 'BY FOURS, FOR-D, 'A-R-C-H!' then immediately, 'G-A-L-L-O-P, 'A-R-C-H!' and away we went over the hard-frozen ground. . . .

In less than ten minutes the Tenth New York Cavalry-men might have been seen on every hill for two miles rear-ward. . . . Blankets slipped from under saddles and hung by one corner; saddles slid back until they were on the rumps of the horses; others turned and were on the under side of the animals; horses running and kicking; tin pans, mess-kettles, patent sheet-iron camp-stoves, the boys had seen advertised in the illustrated newspapers and sold by the sutlers—about as useful as a piano or folding bed—flying through the air; and all I could do was to give a hasty glance to the rear and sing out at the top of my voice: 'C-L-O-S-E U-P!'

But they couldn't 'close.' Poor boys! Their eyes stuck out like those of maniacs. We went only a few miles, but the boys didn't get up till noon.

Both men and horses suffered terribly from the weight of the extra baggage and soldiers soon learned what was actually necessary for existence. Armored vests, lariats, nose bags were conveniently lost. Clothing was reduced to an absolute minimum. A pair of blankets gave way to a single one. It became a fine art to lessen the burden of the horse, and the trooper packed so lightly that the heaviest part of the load was his carbine.

Early in the war generals employed the Union Cavalry in-effectively. They broke up regiments into small units for escort, courier, picket, and patrol duty. Although General McClellan, who succeeded Scott in November, 1861, had written an exhaus-tive study of the proper use of the cavalry, he failed as commander of the Army of the Potomac to apply an intelligent policy in the field. He parceled out his horse regiments among his infantry corps, division, and brigade commanders. The smallest infantry organization had its company of troopers. The horsemen, complained an officer, "acted as grooms and boot blacks at the various headquarters." Cavalry officers looked with despair on their shattered squadrons and submitted in disgust to the disintegration. Infantrymen held the mounted regiments in contempt. "Who ever saw a dead cavalry man?" they sneered.

Green horse units were thrust into the field. In Missouri Lieutenant Charles Dow, Company F, 1st Iowa, wrote home:

> *Dear Mother and Father, Brothers and Sisters. About ten P.M. our forces came upon the main body of the enemy in full retreat . . . the enemy not knowing of our close proximity, camped, leaving one regiment about two miles out for a strong picket guard.*
>
> *About half-past eleven o'clock P.M., a clear, moonlight night, Company F., First Iowa Cavalry, was ordered to prepare to make a charge on this outpost regiment with sabers. Immediately all our forage tied on behind us was cut loose, sabers were drawn, and with scabbards under our legs to prevent rattling or any noise, the company formed in a column of fours and moved silently forward going into the timber . . .*
>
> *The moon shone beautifully. What my thoughts were at that time is my biz; not a thought of danger or fear crossed my mind. In the meantime a small howitzer was wheeled up to the front of our column to fire the first shot, loaded almost to the muzzle with small shot, etc. Our mode of attack was, eight men on the right were to fire their carbines on the enemy (after the howitzer), at the same time the balance were to charge and cut down all who opposed.*
>
> *Soon we were within a short distance of their pickets, thus preventing an alarm. We could hear them talking, we were so close. One cuss says, 'I say Bill, ain't this a nice place to sleep?' Another, playing cards, says, 'My trick, by God.' Another 'Whoa, God damn you,' to his horse.*
>
> *The brush was very thick between us and them, and I wondered not a little how we could get through. My wonder ceased by hearing the order from Lieutenant Hursh . . . to wheel to the right and fire. Boom! went the little brass devil. Bang! bang! bang! went the carbines. 'Charge!' and we were upon them.*

And now commenced a scene it is impossible to describe. Every man there was a man. The rebs fired one volley, scattering like chaff, without arms, hats, shoes, coats, horses, saddles; nothing was taken by them. The stampede was in them, and those not cut down or shot scattered, leaving everything. . . .

In a letter home a trooper in the 1st Massachusetts Cavalry complained about conditions in camp:

If the flies will let me, I shall write you a letter, but they are so very plentiful, and so very hungry, that it would be something to accomplish worth boasting of. This long spell of dry weather has made all kinds of insects very abundant, and has made the flies madly voracious. They are everywhere. and eat everything they come in contact with. Fortunately they seem to need rest at night, but by day they neither rest themselves nor will they let anybody else rest. I have never seen them so terrible anywhere. Between them and the dust and heat our life is not exactly agreeable. . . .

At the present rates my pay don't amount to anything at all. We have calculated that in favorable times an officer will owe the government about $25 a month, instead of getting anything from it. They make us pay twenty-five cents a pound for beef, fifty-one cents for coffee, etc., etc. Beef used to cost seven cents and coffee fifteen cents.

An officer of the 1st Maine related his experience in Virginia:

Finally the rebs made a stand in some woods, and would go no further. A brigade of the Second corps was along with us, and a portion of them was sent into the woods to help our dismounted men. Lively skirmishing was kept up for a while. We were in the road, ready, if wanted, but the skirmishing began to die away, and as a battery opened on us, throwing shell rather near, we were taken back a short distance and formed a line of battle in the field, dismounting, and I made up about an hour of sleep I lost the night before.

There had been scarcely any firing for an hour when the infantry was most all called back to strengthen another part of the line, and we were ordered up again. Got most up there when the Johnnies opened on us fiercely, emptying three or four saddles and laying out two or three horses. Whew! didn't the bullets sing! We were taken out of the road lively, and formed a line in the field on the right of the road. . . . Bullets flew thick and fast. We could do nothing but sit there on our horses awaiting orders. . . .

On the left of the road was a corn-field, and we had infantry in the woods that side of the road, but they broke and ran back through the corn-field, letting the rebels down on our left, an opportunity of which they quickly took advantage. That field was just alive with rebels, yelling like demons, and pouring a cross-fire into us that was telling fearfully. . . .

Men and horses were getting laid out strangely. We were told not to fire, as we might hit our men; and in fact we could not fire to much advantage, being sideways to the enemy. But it was too good a chance, and some of the boys could not help it.

I began to get nervous. I had been under fire long enough without doing anything, and wanted to be busy. I was bound to fire, if I did no good. Was just getting a cap on my carbine when we got the order: 'Fours—RIGHT ABOUT!' which showed plainly our officers saw it was no use to stay there, as we could do nothing.

I dropped my carbine, and just as we were wheeling a bullet struck my elbow. It numbed my arm and hand so quickly, and struck so solid, I thought it was pretty well used up. I told the one next to me I was hit, and he left the field with me. When we got out of range we stopped, looked at my elbow (and I will let on I did dread to pull up my sleeve), and finding I was more scared than hurt he went back, and I kept on down to the hospital. That is all I know about the fight, only that they drove our men back to where we fought them the day before.

Two years of training and fighting transformed the Federal cavalryman into a hardened and disciplined campaigner. The practical school of the picket and skirmish line forged volunteers into soldiers. Gone were the fancy uniforms. Most troopers by 1863 wore plain infantry pants, tunics and forage caps. They managed to purchase or pilfer huge piratical boots into which they tucked their pants and pistols. The War Department substituted Spencers, Colts, and Henrys, all of which were repeating, for the cumbersome, single shot muzzle-loaders issued two years before.

Early in the spring of 1863, General Joseph Hooker, commanding the Army of the Potomac, started consolidating all the horse units within the Army into one corps. "It was then that we commenced practicing the lessons which the enemy had taught us," said cavalry officer Wesley Merritt, "pursuing his tactics to his ruin. From the day of its reorganization under Hooker the cavalry of the Army of the Potomac commenced new life."

By 1863 tactics had reached a peak of refinement in covering retreats. Units halted, dismounted, bushwhacked pursuing troops and then, remounting, repeated the process further down the line. Units demonstrated similar techniques and finesse in screening and reconnaissance operations. Both sides, Union and Confederate, excelled at these duties. A new system of strategy and tactics was developing in the United States, divorced from many of the conservative ideas which dominated European military thought.

By far the most spectacular and most sought after cavalry mission was the raid. All major raids of the war were directed against lines of communication, supply bases, and production areas. To succeed it had to be well planned, boldly and rapidly executed. Speed was essential to prevent capture or serious engagement. The strategic raid as a frequent cavalry mission was a new and far-reaching concept in the warfare of the Western world.

chapter 10.

"I'll bet my money on the Stars and Stripes."

🐎 🐎 🐎

A GENTLE BREEZE CAME IN FROM THE SOUTH ON THE morning of April 18, 1863, as 1,500 confident cavalry veterans of the 6th and 7th Illinois and 2nd Iowa moved out from Lagrange, Tennessee, and trotted southward in two columns, laughing, joking, singing.

> Are you going to march all night?
> Are you going to march all day?
> I'll bet my money on the Stars and Stripes,
> Who'll bet on the Southern Grey?

Out in front rode the brigade's commander, Colonel Benjamin H. Grierson of the 6th, an unlikely character, a former small-town music teacher and bandmaster from Illinois. Enlisting as a private in 1861, he had been commissioned major in the regiment, then promoted to its colonel.

Grierson's orders were simple: slice through the heart of Confederate Mississippi, smash railroad tracks and supply dumps, create the impression that a big move was in preparation, and continue south to Union-held Baton Rouge, 400 miles away.

Two months earlier in February, 1863, General Ulysses S. Grant had sat at his headquarters in Millikin's Bend on the Mississippi River meditating on the difficulties of the winter of 1862–63. None of the plans to maneuver his army into a good fighting position around Confederate Vicksburg had worked. Grant wanted that stronghold to open the Mississippi to Union commerce and to destroy the powerful army quartered there. As the grizzled chief smoked and reflected he hit upon a scheme of shifting his legions to the west bank of the Mississippi River, then marching them southward before recrossing to the eastern side, well below Vicksburg. He would then be in position to attack the fortifications from the south.

Grant felt that a rapid cavalry raid into the interior of Mississippi would distract General John C. Pemberton and his Rebel army. Horse units would strike Jackson, the state capital, and cut the railroad tracks, creating a diversion for the Yankee march upon Vicksburg. For the job of commanding the raid Grant picked Colonel Grierson, 6th Illinois Volunteer Cavalry. To confuse the enemy and cover Grierson's dash, Grant's subordinates prepared a series of troop movements all along the line from Memphis to Corinth.

On the night before he left, Ben Grierson wrote a letter to his wife:

> . . . my command is ordered to leave LaGrange tomorrow on the expedition I spoke to you about. We will, or part of the force, will be gone probably three weeks & perhaps longer, possibly not so long. If I have an opportunity to write to you I will do so before my return.

> But you must not be alarmed should you not hear from me inside of a month. I have a faith and hope that I will return all O.K. and you must pray for my safe return and the success of the expedition. I will endeavor to do so myself and will not neglect to use all due caution.

> If the expedition is successful it will be of great benefit to the service and will not set me back any.

Grierson and his raiders crossed the Tallahatchie near New Albany on April 18. Three days later the colonel dispatched three details to hit Mississippi training camps, feints which puzzled the Rebel command.

Confederate brass had almost stripped northern Mississippi of its cavalry and sent them into eastern Tennessee. When headquarters learned that a Federal horse brigade had crossed the river and was storming through Mississippi, Colonel C. R. Barteau, commanding all that was left of the cavalry, saddled up and raced to Chesterville, a state training depot, but failed to make contact with the Yankees and fell back to cover Okolona and Aberdeen.

Early on the 21st, when Grierson's main columns neared

Houston in Chickasaw County, the colonel ordered the 2nd Iowa, Colonel Edward Hatch commanding, to cut out and demolish the Mobile and Ohio Railroad where it crossed Okatibbehah near West Point. They were then to ride south to Macon and destroy the railroad and Confederate stores there. Once this was accomplished, they were to circle northeastward, capture Columbus if possible, and raze the railroad tracks south of Okolona.

Fooled earlier by the feint against the training camps, Colonel Barteau turned and galloped in pursuit of Grierson. The gray coats reined in at the point where the colonel and Hatch had parted company. Barteau made a guess, the wrong guess, mistaking the trail of the 2nd Iowa for Grierson's main command.

Pressing on, pursuing Hatch relentlessly, Barteau and his companies overhauled the Federals near West Point and pummeled them severely. Caught in a cross fire, Hatch's soldiers tore through Confederate lines and retreated northward. Hatch swept through Okolona, put the torch to its buildings, and fled northward to Lagrange.

Meanwhile, Grierson, freed from pursuit by the 2nd Iowa's diversion, stopped his columns and reassessed the situation. His command was well within Pemberton's line of defense, but no Rebel force worth mentioning lay between him and Baton Rouge. Unless the Rebels correctly anticipated his movements and massed troops and artillery athwart his line of march, he could continue southward. To divert the Johnnies, Grierson wanted a feint against the Mobile and Ohio Railroad. Rechecking his muster rolls, he realized the brigade could ill afford to detach another large unit. However, he ordered B Troop, 7th Illinois, under Captain Henry C. Forbes, to hit the railroad near Macon and then attempt to rejoin the command. The raiders would be charging through Mississippi so fast that chances were remote that the thirty-five men of B Troop would ever catch up.

That afternoon on a scrap of paper torn from a notebook, Grierson dashed off a note to Alice, his wife: "All well. All O.K." The brigade continued racing along the byways of Mississippi, past plantations and country crossroads, through Starkville and Louisville, demolishing a bridge across the Pearl River.

Well up ahead and on the flanks, Grierson's scouts were screening the main body of raiders. Adept at skirmishing, foraging, and marauding, they were hardened soldiers and good providers. To supplement their supply of hardtack, fat salt pork, sugar, and coffee, they caught and butchered chickens, turkeys, sheep, pigs, and cattle.

By April 23, the seventh day of the raid, Grierson's brigade trotted into Philadelphia, Neshoba County, and after an all-night ride they reached Decatur at dawn on the 24th. They struck the Meridian and Jackson Railroad at Newton Station. Sergeant Richard W. Surby describes the action:

Every blue coat was ordered to lay behind the buildings until the train was secured. On she came, puffing and blowing with the weight of twenty-five cars, loaded with railroad ties, bridge timber, and plank. In a few minutes this train was in our possession and switched on a side track.

Another train would be due in a few minutes from the West. Men were placed near the switches. The command was ordered to hide themselves from view, and everything was perfected on time as the whistle sounded. On she came, rounding the curve, her passengers unconscious of the surprise that awaited them. The engineer decreased speed. She was now nearly opposite the depot.

Springing up the steps of the locomotive and presenting my revolver at the engineer, [I] told him if he reversed the engine I would put a ball through him. He . . . obeyed. . . .

The men rush[ed] from their hiding places amid shouts and cheers. . . . 'the train is ours!' It contained twelve freight cars and one passenger car, four loaded with ammunition and arms, six with commissary and quartermasters' stores, and two with dry goods and household property belonging to families moving from Vicksburg. Several passengers . . . commenced throwing out of the windows on the opposite side their valuables, which fell into the water, it being low and swampy on the other side. . . .

This train being switched off on the side track with the other, the private property thrown out, fires were kindled in each car. The whole soon became one continuous flame. By eleven o'clock the heat had reached the shells, which began to explode and must have sounded like a sharp artillery duel.

Public buildings blazed like bonfires; flames shot high into the sky. Citizens of Newton Station stood watching, unable to tear their gaze away. When the Yankees finished, Grierson listed the damage: two trains captured and destroyed, commissary and quartermaster stores burned, hundreds of stands of arms demolished, railroad tracks torn up for four miles, and seventy-five prisoners captured and paroled.

The blow was serious. Fearful lest the supplies to his Vicksburg army be cut off, General Pemberton begged the president of the Meridian and Jackson Railroad to repair the broken track at once. A telegram reached General Joseph E. Johnston in Tennessee insisting that Mississippi was "sorely pressed on all sides," urgently requesting 2,000 cavalry. A plea went out to the commander of the Department of the Gulf: "All is lost unless you can send a regiment or two to Meridian."

Confused and uncertain, Rebel commanders shot messages off in all directions, ordering massive and complex infantry and artillery movements. They appealed to all Mississippians to arm and organize.

Grierson's grubby-looking men, their uniforms splotched with mud and dust, were often mistaken for Rebel cavalry. Clattering by a schoolhouse the Federals waved at pupils lining the roadside, hurrahing for Beauregard, Van Dorn, and the Confederacy. One tiny lass, thinking she recognized one of the men, rushed up to him, asked about "John," and if her uncle was in the unit.

At another place where the command halted for a meal, the miller grumbled when Grierson handed him a receipt for the food.

"Yes I've met your sort before," he snorted, "you always say you'll pay and you give receipts, but they ain't worth a damn. I wish the Yankees would come along and clean you out; they might give a fellow something; but you, you eat up everything in the country without keeping them out; why don't you go after Grierson instead of hanging around here."

By exploiting the situation, the colonel garnered valuable information and misled the enemy.

On one moonless night a Confederate cavalry regiment was fooled by a Yankee spy and sent charging down the Jackson road in the wrong direction. This midnight escapade convinced Grierson that his brigade stood in imminent peril. He issued orders to burn all the bridges they crossed, abandoning B Troop and Captain Forbes to their fate.

🐴 🐴 🐴

Forbes and his men sneaked up to Macon on the night of April 22. Assured after a close look they couldn't capture the town, they waited until dawn, then circled back to strike a railroad bridge over the Noxubee River. Dismounting they crept forward. Forbes' eyes narrowed against the sun's glare. There on the bridge enemy guards were patrolling the tracks.

Remounted, Forbes' command galloped off for Philadelphia in hopes of striking Grierson's trail. Riding all night they cantered into Philadelphia the next day at noon only to find that Grierson had departed twenty-one hours earlier. Without warning, angry citizens stormed the troopers, but the agile horse soldiers quickly captured and paroled them, demolishing their firearms. After helping themselves to a huge repast, Troop B struck out after Grierson.

Two men, dressed and armed like Confederates, rode in advance to collect information, signaling if they detected signs of hostile forces. Through woods and ravines and down the main highways they scoured every corner and turn in the road.

All night they rode without stopping and at dawn marched through Newton Station, which was still smoldering. Here they learned that they were still fifteen hours behind the brigade.

Guessing at Grierson's moves, Forbes decided to cut east from Newton Station, cross the Mobile and Ohio railroad at Enterprise, and rejoin the command. They hurried off on the Enterprise road and neared the town. Up ahead they spotted mounted pickets strung out on the highway.

Forbes raised a hand to his laboring troopers. Drawing out his saber, fastening a white handerchief to its point, the captain and four men rode slowly toward town. Three Rebels walked out, one carrying a white flag at the end of an infantry ramrod.

The Yankee captain sat leaning over his mount's neck, his face thrust forward, his body bent, peering intently.

"I come from Major-General Grierson to demand the surrender of Enterprise," barked Forbes.

"Will you put the demand in writing?" asked a Confederate.

"Certainly. To whom shall I address it?"

"To Colonel Edward Goodwin, commanding the post."

This was the information Forbes wanted. The Union captain scribbled off the demand, "one hour only for consideration, after which further delay will be at your peril." Handing the paper to the Johnnies, the captain remarked that he'd fall back to Grierson and the main columns and await the reply. Forbes, gleefully rejoining his men, wheeled about and they moved quickly up a slope, then, striking a gallop, charged off for safety.

Troop B halted and Forbes, checking with his lieutenants, reevaluated their position. They carefully sorted out the possibilities, then agreed to continue to follow Grierson's trail. Sleeping on the lawn of a plantation that night, they awoke early, wolfed down breakfast, then cleared the area. Forbes led them toward Raleigh, where they charged a puny company of home guards with sabers, smashing their guns and seizing their captain. Cross-examining the Mississippian, Forbes found that they were now but seven hours behind the brigade.

Saddling up they raced out of Raleigh and reached a creek swollen with the recent rains. Here the bridge had been demolished. Forbes now realized that Grierson had given them up and was razing his bridges behind him. The men managed the crossing, clinging to the bridles of their horses, holding their guns above their heads. Saddlebags had been secured high on the backs of the animals.

Forty miles beyond lay the Strong River and still farther, the Pearl, rivers too difficult to ford or swim. The margin of time was wearing dangerously thin. To rejoin Grierson before he set those bridges aflame, three volunteers mounted on the best horses raced ahead at a gallop. At sundown the trail vanished in a grassy field. Swiftly surveying the ground, the men backtracked until they stumbled upon the trail which branched off to the left.

Dusk crept upon the countryside. Mist turned into a drizzle. Through the woods the volunteers faintly heard the shuffling of columns. They set their spurs hard and drove down the road toward the blue lines.

"Halt! Who comes there?"

The three refusing to slacken speed charged past hollering, "Company B! Company B!"

Cheers thundered up and down the advancing columns.

An exhausted and begrimed sergeant darted ahead and reached Colonel Grierson just as he was preparing to cross the bridge.

The sergeant spit out the message: "Captain Forbes presents his compliments, and begs to be allowed to burn his bridges for himself."

Grierson, smiling, hastily recalled his bridge-burning detail. Thirty minutes later and the sergeant would have been too late.

On April 27, Troop B, along with the main columns, moved across the Pearl River using a ferryboat captured the evening before. Colonel Edward Prince and 200 men dashed off and seized Hazelhurst on the New Orleans and Jackson road, razing rolling stock, ammunition dumps, and railroad tracks.

Meanwhile, after crossing the Pearl River, Grierson and the remainder of his command were taken for the 1st Alabama Cavalry coming from Mobile. The colonel and his staff graciously accepted an invitation to breakfast at a fine house near the ferry landing. Smiling and rustling about in the kitchen, the women served them. Suddenly, as Grierson cut into a slice of ham, a corporal burst through the door and gave away the game. When their hostesses realized they were feeding Yankee cavalry, they ran from the house. Afraid they might give the alarm, Grierson and his officers hustled outside and mounted, leaving the breakfast half finished.

At Union Church the next day, Grierson saw the Confederate cavalry coming. Helter-skelter the Rebels streamed down the highway. They seemed in complete disorder, a mob riding hell-for-leather.

The firing did not grow in volume as Grierson had expected. There were just occasional shots and flurries of shots. Suddenly the Johnnies veered and sped off. The skirmish was over.

Grierson wanted to avoid a major engagement at all costs. By this time, he said later, "the enemy had every advantage; a knowledge of the country; of every road, public and private, every stream of water large and small, with its fords and bridges; they had forces above and below . . . and in [the rear] everywhere in all directions. Their scouts were watching; their couriers flying; their troops concentrating to capture us."

After a false start down the Natchez highway to give the impression they were going to bull their way through, the marauders wheeled and took to the back roads. By nightfall the command was well below Brookhaven on the New Orleans and Jackson road. On the 30th, Grierson wrecked the railroad track from Brookhaven to Summit.

At Confederate headquarters General Pemberton was puzzled. Was Grierson headed for Grand Gulf or Jackson? For Natchez or Baton Rouge? On the 28th telegrams reported Grierson moving toward Grand Gulf. On the 29th, they had him making for Natchez. Then came another dispatch—the raiders were approaching Brookhaven.

At Port Hudson, Confederate General Frank C. Gardner pondered his maps. If the Federals tried to fight their way to Union lines at Baton Rouge, he was to cut them off. Between Grierson and Baton Rouge lay the unfordable Amite River, which could only be crossed at Williams' Bridge, 30 miles from Gardner's army.

Near Oyska on May 1, Grierson's command sighted Tickfaw River and Wall's Bridge in the distance. Sergeant Surby and his scouts clattered across the narrow plank span. A rifle report echoed. Another. Surby heard the whine of lead. Then more shots.

Sergeant Surby reported:

> We were greeted by a loud volley of carbines and musketry, coming from some eighty . . . cavalry who lay in ambush not more than fifty yards distant. It seemed as though a flame of fire burst forth from every tree. The Colonel [Major William C. Blackburn] fell, along with his horse, both pierced by the fatal bullet. . . .
>
> When the first shots were fired it was heard by Colonel Grierson, who then occupied the advance and was the advance guard of the column. On they came . . . led by Lieutenant Styles, who charged across the bridge, followed by only twelve men. . . . they were checked by a well directed volley. They rally and charge, but it is useless—they were too few and exposed, while the enemy were protected by surrounding timber. The little band have to retreat back across the bridge, leaving one man killed and two wounded, and seven dead horses. They had no support; the column was too far behind to lend assistance in time, but just as they recrossed the bridge

143

*the column came up on the double-quick. Colonel Prince . . .
ordered companies A and D of his regiment to dismount.
They were sent to the right and left as skirmishers. One section of Captain Smith's battery was brought up, the woods
were shelled, the enemy put to flight, and our men were pursuing them, and as they pass Colonel Blackburn, who laid
mortally wounded, with one leg under his horse, cries out to
them, 'Onward! follow them, boys!' and cheers. The Sixth
now take the advance—no halt is made—the Seventh look after
the killed and wounded. . . .*

*They [the enemy] began to scatter. . . . some of them
grasping their horses' manes, while their lower extremities were
half suspended in the air; their saddle-girths have broken, and
off tumble saddle and blanket, leaving the rider bare-backed
with legs pressed close to his horse's sides, his body thrown forward, resting on his neck, and bare-headed. . . . The road is
strewn with old saddles, blankets, coats, hats, and firearms.*

There at Wall's Bridge the raiders lost three killed, two
wounded. Three of Grierson's men remained behind as volunteer
prisoners to nurse their comrades. The Yankees captured a Rebel
captain, a lieutenant, and six men, the only losses sustained by the
enemy.

Ahead of the raiders was the seventy-five-mile ride to Baton
Rouge, an arduous, nonstop ride. Off toward the Mississippi River
the men faintly heard the dull *boom boom* as Union gunboats
shelled Port Hudson.

It was still night when Grierson sighted a single Confederate
sentry by the Amite River Bridge. The gray coat was outlined
against the lights of the guard shack. A quick advance caught the
sentries unprepared. They rushed out of the shanty to hear the
muffled sound of horses' hoofs rattling across the bridge.

Safely across, the brigade, bone weary and suffering from hunger, pressed forward. An officer in the rear guard reported:

*Men by the score, and I think by fifties were riding sound
asleep in their saddles. The horses excessively tired and hungry,
would stray out of the road and thrust their noses to the earth
in hopes of finding something to eat. The men, when addressed, would remain silent and motionless until a blow across*

the thigh or shoulder should awaken them, when it would be found that each supposed himself still riding with his company, which might be perhaps a mile ahead. We found several men who had either fallen from their horses, or dismounted and dropped on the ground, dead with sleep. Nothing short of a beating with the flat of a saber would awaken some of them. . . .

Sergeant Surby and his scouts watched the slow coming of day. They were met by a Union patrol out from Baton Rouge, searching for "an important force" riding for the city. The patrol was ignorant of the raid, knew nothing of Grierson, and were slow to credit the colonel's tale. After three hours of waiting until formalities were completed at Union headquarters, the troopers, followed by a cheering crowd, wended their way through Baton Rouge.

Grierson told General Christopher C. Augur that evening, "we killed and wounded about 100 of the enemy, captured and paroled over 500 prisoners, many of them officers, destroyed between 50 and 60 miles of railroad and telegraph, captured and destroyed over 3,000 stands of arms, and other army stores and government property to an immense amount; and also captured 1,000 horses and mules. . . . We marched over 600 miles in less than sixteen days. The last twenty-eight hours we marched seventy-six miles. . . . During [which] the men and horses were without food or rest."

Several days later Grierson found time to write home:

I arrived at Baton Rouge—all O.K.—with my command. I had a very successful Expedition—beyond my own most sanguine expectations. I send you a paper today—the New Orleans Era—which has a fair account of the trip. . . .

I like Byron have had to wake up in the morning and find myself famous. Since I have been here it has been one continual adoration—last night I was serenaded and a thousand cheers greeted my ears. . . . I will endeavor not to let so much attention spoil me. I will try and keep right side up with care.

General Grant, who in two months would occupy Vicksburg, was deeply impressed with Grierson's exploits. "Colonel Grierson's raid from Lagrange through Mississippi," he reported, "has been the most successful thing of the kind since the breaking out of the Rebellion." Again Grant said, "To use the expression of my informant, 'Grierson has knocked the heart out of the state.'"

The raid was regarded as a sensational and unprecedented success, an operation in which Grierson had handled himself and his men with an assurance not often seen in Federal cavalry commanders. Although the dash through Mississippi had no extensive result on the Vicksburg campaign, it jarred Southern morale considerably. An irate citizen of Okolona complained bitterly to the military: "We all partake of the humiliation resulting from such an extensive march of the enemy, without the loss on his part of a single man. It is needless to say that such a disgraceful result invites the enemy to repeated raids on a large scale. . . ."

Buttressed by the success of Benjamin Grierson and his raiders, the Federal cavalry became increasingly aggressive during the spring and summer of 1863.

chapter 11.

"Come on, you Wolverines!"

♞ ♞ ♞

THE ATTACK BEGAN AT DAWN. YANKEE CAVALRY SPLASHED across the Rappahannock at a gallop. Careening up the bank, blue-clad troopers drove toward the open fields and knolls of Brandy Station, Virginia. Followed by the 8th New York, Colonels Benjamin F. "Grimes" Davis and George Armstrong Custer, leading General John Buford's right wing, hastened down a still-dark road through the woods.

The sharp challenge of a sentry range out: "Halt! Who goes there?"

Davis and Custer, grabbing their pistols, fired and dashed past the astonished guard toward a picket camp.

Hundreds of Rebel cavalrymen were just climbing out of their bed rolls or were warming themselves by the fires cooking breakfast. The first alarm came shortly after daylight when they heard gunfire from the picket line. Officers scattered in all directions, shouting, "To horse! To horse!" Confederates, many of them hatless, coatless, and shoeless, stumbled toward their mounts.

Two days before, June 7, 1863, General Joseph Hooker, commanding the Army of the Potomac, had sent General Alfred Pleasonton and his cavalry corps with its three divisions, supported by infantry, to the Rappahannock River with orders to disperse the Rebels concentrated at Culpepper. With 10,000 men Pleasonton crossed the river at dawn, June 9, and took General J. E. B. Stuart by surprise.

The 8th New York stormed through the disorganized Rebels. Whole regiments surrendered. Along the stone walls ahead, Colonel Davis spotted Confederate heads, thousands of them, preparing for the charge. The colonel's hand snapped down. The 8th New York reined up, wheeled, and returned to the river. Interrogating the prisoners, Yankees learned that the Confederates were part of General Stuart's 10,000 "invincibles"; the men behind the fences, the general's advanced force.

The 8th New York, 8th Illinois, and 3rd Indiana turned from the river and trotted back toward the enemy. Pointing his saber toward the fences, Davis yelled, "Come on, boys!" and surged across the field, across the Rebel line, hurdled the wall, and broke into the woods beyond.

What followed was a cavalry battle unequaled on the North American continent, a savage, chaotic engagement, in which regiment charged regiment amid clouds of dust so thick that it was difficult to tell friend from foe. The broken ground, interspersed with woods, clearings, and stone-wall fences, dictated tactics, resulting in a disorganized medley of mounted and dismounted actions. Davis and the 8th New York galloped through the woods over fences and ditches. Enemy horsemen charged. A slug tore into "Grimes" Davis. He slid from his saddle crying, "Stand firm, Eighth New York!" But the regiment, enmeshed in a withering cross fire, fell back and waited.

Beyond, at Kelly's Ford, Generals David McMurtrie Gregg's and Alfred N. Duffie's supporting cavalry divisions were crossing the river. Duffie was to push toward Culpepper via Stevensburg, while Gregg was to drive toward Brandy Station and meet Buford's advance, which was already enveloping Stuart's position. The two main columns in the pincer movement were out of communication with each other, and Gregg was slower than Buford, while Duffie was slower than both.

Surprised, operating amidst confusion in a dense cloud of dust, General Stuart at his headquarters atop Fleetwood Hill demonstrated his towering ability. His officers shouted commands and redeployed troopers. Within an hour after the first Union rush, Stuart was directing his scattered forces and had them under control.

From behind every bush, pile of stone, and log of wood carbines crashed. Dismounted troopers of the 8th Illinois fired their guns so fast that some of the weapons burst. The knolls erupted with the flash of artillery fire. The earth heaved.

Above the racket of exploding shells Major Robert Morris, 6th

Pennsylvania Cavalry, ordered: *"Trot, march! Gallop, march!*
CHARGE!" The 6th galloped across the plain toward concealed
batteries which poured forth a deadly spray. Saddles emptied. Freed
from their riders, frenzied horses dashed away erratically. The color
sergeant reeled and fell. Another sergeant caught the standard.
Through the storm the Pennsylvania line surged forward and met
the enemy. Hand to hand the fight raged. The Rebels broke and
fled. Pursuing them into the woods, the Pennsylvanians discovered
themselves surrounded. Exposed to shellfire, the 6th struggled
forward.

"The noise is like deafening thunder," described an officer,
"whistling shot and screaming shell fall all around us, or go crashing through the trees, or bury themselves in the ground, sending
a shower of limbs, twigs, bark, leaves, and earth, all over us, while
the air seems filled with wickedly-whistling Minie balls. It seems
impossible that any of us shall ever get out of this alive."

Men of the 6th rode close to their horses. Alarmed and excited,
the mounts stumbled through the woods, jamming against trees,
tripping over bushes toward safety and reinforcements.

From 11 A.M. until late afternoon, the fierce struggle seesawed.
Sergeant William F. Moyer, 1st Pennsylvania, saw Confederate
troopers emerge from the forest, halt, then charge. It was so picturesque and startling for a moment that Moyer simply stared. The
spectacle seemed almost unreal. He came to himself with a start
and hauled his carbine from its scabbard:

In an instant, a thousand glittering sabers flashed in the
sunlight, and from a thousand brave and confident spirits arose
a shout of defiance which, caught up by rank after rank,
formed one vast, strong, full-volumed battle-cry, and every
trooper rising in his stirrups leaned forward to meet the shock,
and dashed headlong at the foe.

First came the dead, heavy crash of the meeting columns,
and next the clash of saber, and the rattle of pistol and carbine,
mingled with frenzied imprecations; wild shrieks that followed
the death blow; the demand to surrender; the appeal for
mercy—forming the horrid din of battle.

For a few brief moments the enemy stood and bravely
fought, and hand to hand, face to face, raged the contest; but,

quailing at length before the resistless force of our attack and
shrinking from the savage gleam and murderous stroke of our
swift descending sabers, they at length broke and fled in con-
fusion. We followed, and soon the whole plain for a mile in
extent was covered with flying columns engaged in a general
mêlée. This continued until the enemy came up with rein-
forcements, when we withdrew and reformed.

Trapped in a cross fire, a Lieutenant Robb, 10th New York,
spotted a Rebel horseman galloping down upon him. He spun
around to Sergeant Elias Evans and snapped, "Now 'Lias, what
will we do?"

"Follow me," Evans replied.

Jamming his spurs, Evans cleared a ditch and escaped. Robb's
horse stumbled and fell, pitching the lieutenant out of the saddle.
The horse scrambled to its feet, leaped out of the ditch, Robb clinging to him for 100 feet before he relaxed his grip.

Evans charged back to help his comrade. He turned and shot
at an oncoming Confederate. Charging in from the rear, a Rebel
officer lashed out at Evans with his saber. It whistled past the
sergeant's head. Instinctively, Evans ducked and his eyes caught
the gleam of bright steel as it hurtled through the sunlight, barely
missing. "I thought it best to get out of that place," remembered
Evans, and sped off down the road.

The battle at Brandy Station thundered to its climax. Rebel
lines began to waver. Batteries changed positions. Yankees charged.
Johnnies reformed. J. E. B. Stuart narrowly held the hill. At 5 P.M.
General Pleasonton withdrew his troops from the field since Con-
federate infantry from General Robert E. Lee's Army of Northern
Virginia was reported fast approaching.

Night fell on the Virginia countryside. It took a long time to
move the bone-weary horses back across the Rappahannock. The
Union dead and wounded—450 in all—had to be found. Pleasonton
insisted on counting the dead horses and was anxious to recover
the horse equipments. Roaming the woods and fields of Brandy
Station that night, soldiers failed to get an accurate count, but
streamed back to camp loaded down with saddles, bridles, nose
bags, halters, picket ropes, saddle blankets, carbine sockets, and link
straps—a respectable amount of salvageable equipment.

4th Pennsylvania Cavalry
by an unknown Civil War artist.

The battle of Brandy Station was not without effect. The Yankee cavalry had retreated from the field of action, but it had at last stood up to the Confederate horse soldiers in open combat. Man for man the Yankees felt themselves to be equal to the Confederates. Going into battle they had not known quite what to expect, but they had cleared the big hurdle in a credible way.

The Union cavalry had reason to be proud. It was now a different outfit from the clumsy conglomerate which had been wearing out good horses earlier in the war. Enlisted man and officer alike had learned their trade thoroughly—they were the survivors; the inept had fallen by the way.

Several months earlier General Hooker had consolidated all his army's forty cavalry regiments into one corps, three divisions. By concentrating the cavalry, its officers realized that they could outnumber the enemy at times and employ initiative as successfully as their opponents. With the assignment of young, aggressive leaders to the corps—John Buford, Hugh Judson Kilpatrick, Percy Wyndham, George Armstrong Custer—Hooker's cavalry became an effective fighting unit.

General Lee, commanding the Army of Northern Virginia, the decisive victor at Chancellorsville a month earlier, viewed the battle at Brandy Station in a conservative light, depressed that Stuart had been caught napping and saddened by the Confederate losses—523 men killed, wounded, or captured. Major H. B. McClellan, Stuart's assistant adjutant later recalled, "One result of incalculable importance certainly did follow this battle—it made the Federal Cavalry. Up to that time confessedly inferior to the Southern horsemen, they gained on this day that confidence in themselves and in their commanders which enabled them to contest so fiercely the subsequent battlefields."

The qualities of informality and extreme flexibility which for two years had given the Confederate cavalry a seeming advantage in numbers and initiative, by the spring of 1863, had brought about the beginning of a decline. The Rebels' defective system of supply and the excessive discretion exercised by Confederate horsemen became evident as twin evils. Had the South been able to supply its horse regiments with remounts, had Lee and General Braxton Bragg kept a tighter rein on cavalry generals Stuart and Morgan, events might have been altered.

Brandy Station signaled the beginning of the Gettysburg campaign. Captured Confederate papers convinced Hooker that Lee intended to invade Maryland and Pennsylvania. During the days that followed Brandy Station, the valleys echoed with the crack of rifles and the thud of field pieces as the two armies sparred cautiously. Yankee reconnaissance patrols fanned out. The cavalry skirmished at Aldie, Middleburg, Upperville. The Yankee march northward from Virginia was an arduous one. In one three-day stretch, troopers averaged twenty hours in the saddle without rest and with scarcely anything to eat. Horses by the score dropped from exhaustion along the road. Officers and men, begrimed past recognition, tramped along on foot, leading their worn-out mounts to save their strength, well knowing how much depended upon them. Dismounted cavalrymen, whose horses had fallen dead, struggled forward, some carrying their saddles and bridles, hoping to beg, buy, or steal fresh mounts.

General Lee's invasion of Pennsylvania culminated on the field of Gettysburg, "high-water mark of the Confederacy," forever a symbol of valor for Americans. Lee boldly sought the Federal army, now commanded by General George Gordon Meade, but he erred initially by permitting Stuart to separate himself from the army for a dashing but barren raid, depriving the Army of Northern Virginia of its eyes and ears. As a result the two armies met head on in a pitched battle on a terrain which neither adversary would have chosen.

As the guns thundered on July 1, the first day of battle, the little town of Gettysburg rang with the clang of military congestion. The Rebel cavalry under Stuart, cut off from all communication with Lee, was hastening to join him. On July 2, after encountering Colonel Judson Kilpatrick's 3rd Division at Hunterstown, Stuart arrived in the vicinity of Gettysburg and went into position on the left of the Confederate infantry.

On the 3rd was to come Lee's final effort—that fatal, gallant charge by General George E. Pickett up Cemetery Ridge. To divert the Yankees, Lee planned a simultaneous cavalry attack on the Federal's right flank. This cavalry diversion was to be no mere reconnaissance.

As morning dawned, Stuart's horsemen moved two and a half miles down the York and Harrisonburg highway and turned off to the right on a country road. There they occupied the elevated ground east of Gettysburg from which they could protect the flank of Lee's army while commanding a view of the routes leading to the rear of the Union foe. With woods screening them, Stuart's soldiers massed and maneuvered unobserved.

On the extreme right of the Union line, the Yankee cavalry had none of these advantages. Their position was lower, less commanding, more exposed. From early morning troopers heard the heavy firing on Culp's Hill. At 10 A.M. the bombardment ceased. The grim-faced horse soldiers looked at each other questioningly, uncertain. The entire battle line down Cemetery Ridge had become silent. Fields, ravines, and orchards, which for two days had shaken with constant bombardment, quieted in the July sun. The men, dismounted, moved into the shade of the trees.

As noon drew on the strain became intensified. The silence was appalling. The Federal cavalry learned that something big was brewing. General Pickett's attack was expected momentarily on the Union center. Reconnaissance reported Stuart's horse regiments were forming on the right, evidently planning an all-out assault on the Federal rear to cut communications and destroy ammunition dumps.

The Rebel barrage exploded at noon—convincingly. A maelstrom of sound thundered back and forth along the whole line as the big Confederate guns slammed steadily away. The sky brightened with the hot flash of cannon and along the slopes huge clouds of smoke began to bunch up on the air.

Near the Union center the dismounted 6th Pennsylvania Cavalry dove for cover. Union batteries opened up. At 3:00 P.M. the artillery fire slackened. The smoke lifted. Below, the 6th Pennsylvania saw the Rebel army advancing across the long, level plain, soldiers massed in close column by division. Pickett's charge had begun.

On came the gray coats with colors flying, bayonets glistening, keeping their lines as straight as if on parade. Yankees held their fire. The Confederates closed to within 100 yards.

A sergeant of the 6th Pennsylvania Cavalry put the rifle to his shoulder. He snuggled his cheek against its stock, and his eye glanced down the sights. So close were the Rebels now that the sergeant could see their scowling faces.

Someone yelled, "Fire!" The recoil jolted the sergeant's shoulder. For an instant white smoke blotted out everything.

Union artillery poured its storm upon the advancing lines. The 6th Pennsylvania fired and charged on foot. The Confederate van disintegrated momentarily, shrill cries of alarm and consternation filled the air. The Southerners rallied. Again they bulled their way toward the crest. Line after line surged forward to be mowed down like grass. Still they came, only to fall back, rally, reform, and recharge. Each time the ranks were smaller and thinner.

On the far Union right, Yankee cavalrymen stiffened. Sergeants growled orders. Officers spoke to their companies. They were old words, a thousand times delivered before a thousand previous engagements. It was a little after three o'clock.

Stuart's skirmishers, supported by mounted columns, emerged from the woods and pushed forward. A carbine spoke. Instantly there was a stutter of reports from a dismounted Pennsylvania regiment.

The 5th Michigan, dismounted, armed with Spencer repeating carbines, moved toward Stuart's skirmishers. The Johnnies opened up at almost point-blank range. The 1st North Carolina and the Jeff Davis brigade slowly and systematically repulsed the 5th.

Advancing boldly, the 7th Michigan met the 1st Virginia at a stone fence. The Yankees hesitated, then began firing their carbines. The Virginians pressed forward. A scorching fire hit their flanks. Southern reinforcements streamed up, firing rapidly until the 7th Michigan gave way.

In that whirlpool of men and horses, Captain Herman Moore, in whose company sixteen mounts had been killed, retired with the regiment, covering the retreat of his dismounted men. Amid fire, Moore's horse charged the wrong way and hesitated at a stone fence just as the enemy roared past. Glancing over his shoulder, Moore caught the gleam of a saber and ducked.

Suddenly Moore felt his horse buckle. All limp in the air the gelding went—from a thundering run to a long sliding fall. Stunned, his face scarred with gravel but still clutching his pistol, Moore struggled to his feet. The horse was dead, a bullet through its brain.

Moore heard a horse charging, swerved and fired the last shot in his revolver. A gray figure pitched forward sprawling so that his horse had to leap to avoid trampling him.

The strung-out 1st Virginia was exposed to fire from two Union batteries. A battalion of 5th Michigan, half mounted, galloped up and gradually crowded the Southerners back upon their supports.

The cavalry battle on the Union right waned momentarily. By this time Pickett's charge up the blood-soaked slope of Cemetery Ridge was falling apart before Yankee cannon.

On the Federal's left the horse brigades of General Elon Farnsworth and Wesley Merritt pushed near to the southern tip of Missionary Ridge. At his command post General Meade ordered them to hit and smash the exposed flank of General E. McIver Law's infantry division. But in the bombardment, Law pulled back and girded for the Yankee assault.

The Union brigades, Merritt's and half of Farnsworth's, dismounted, pressed against the Confederate infantry. Union General Judson Kilpatrick, division commander, spotting an opportunity for mounted action, sent in Farnsworth and his 1st West Virginia and the 1st Vermont. In a reckless, helter-skelter charge over fences and ditches, Farnsworth and his regiments plunged into a frightful fire from the 1st Texas and 4th Alabama. Followed by only a few men, Farnsworth fought his way forward until shot from his saddle. This assault, although viciously repulsed, diverted two southern infantry brigades, which might have strengthened Pickett at the Union center.

In the woods on the Federal right, General J.E.B. Stuart assembled the crack brigades of Wade Hampton and Fitzhugh Lee. If the enemy's right was to be swept from the field and the road to the rear of the Union army gained, now was the time. On this charge hung the fate of the Army of the Potomac at Gettysburg.

Off in the distance in the woods beyond the ravine, Yankee cavalry spotted Confederate horsemen, Stuart's last resource. A moment later every man in the blue line sucked in his breath as he saw them coming in close columns of squadrons, gathering speed, prancing as if in review. It was a gallant spectacle.

Union batteries hurled double charges of canister. The Rebel van wilted as though charging into an invisible wire. Men and horses flopped convulsively about the field, some turned back or fanned out, others lay still in mute clumps that those galloping in from behind had to hurdle.

The 1st Michigan advanced toward the Rebels. The colonel turned, ordered sabers drawn. General Custer rode up and placed himself at its head. Down upon the enemy the 1st Michigan roared—white horses, bay horses, black horses, piebald horses, necks outstretched, gaining momentum at every bound.

Blue and gray columns galloped nearer and nearer, the Confederates outnumbering their opponents three to one. General Wade Hampton's battle flag floated in the van of his Rebel brigade.

The Yankees could hear the orders of enemy officers. "Keep to your sabers, men, keep to your sabers!" *Charge* was ordered. The speed increased. Every man gathered his horse well under him and gripped his saber tighter.

Watching the enemy's front ranks, Custer straightened his legs in his stirrups, waved his saber, and shouted, "Come on, you Wolverines!" With a yell, the 1st Michigan plunged forward.

Moment after moment, in sheer fascination, Custer watched the enemy troopers hurtling down upon him. The Rebels' war cry grew in volume. They were a furlong away, a hundred yards. . . .

Captain William Miller, 3rd Pennsylvania, heard the two lines meet. The sound reminded him of the roaring crash when woodsmen felled a giant tree. Riders on each side pushed deep into their enemy's ranks. Men swore as they heard the sickening thud of bodies falling to the ground. Horses reared back, pawed the air, whinnied in fright. All formation dissolved. Scattered men of other Federal regiments charged the Southerners' flanks. Steel rang on steel. Small arms rattled.

Wade Hampton was helped from the field, bleeding, severely wounded by saber cuts about the neck. A Union general, joining the melee, had his jaw torn off by a Rebel color bearer who used his flagstaff as a lance.

The Confederate columns wore thin, the outside men drawing back. Suddenly, the Southern line broke, turned, and rushed pell-mell for the rear. As the Johnnies ran for safety, Pickett's survivors three miles away were limping down the slopes of Cemetery Ridge, also repulsed.

Hurrah! sheathe your swords! the carnage is done.
All red with our valor, we welcome the sun.
Up, up with the stars! we have won! we have won!

It had been a severe action for the Union cavalry— in three days it had lost 1,908. General Meade, who held the fate of the Confederacy in his hands that night, failed to reap the fruits of complete victory by swift, unrelenting pursuit. The next days saw Lee skillfully bring his battered Army of Northern Virginia through the Pennsylvania mountains to the Potomac.

The battle of Gettysburg was a Herculean effort which determined the war's final outcome. "We cavalrymen who fought . . . on the right flank at Gettysburg," recalled Lieutenant Colonel William Brooke Rawle, 3rd Pennsylvania, "have always maintained that we saved the day at the most critical moment of that, the greatest battle and the turning point of the War of the Rebellion. . . . So fierce was the main engagement, of which the infantry bore the brunt, that the fighting on the part of the cavalry passed almost unnoticed; yet this was one of the few battles of the war in which the three arms of the service fought in combination and at the same time, each within supporting distance and within sight of the other, and each in its proper sphere."

General Custer wrote in his report, "I challenge the annals of warfare to produce a more brilliant or successful charge of cavalry than the one just recounted."

chapter 12.

"We'll make coffee out of Cedar Creek tonight."

♞ ♞ ♞

GENERAL PHILIP SHERIDAN, AFFECTIONATELY CALLED "Little Phil" by his men, was a peppery, hard-fighting jockey of a man with a foul mouth. Bandy-legged, wiry, weighing a mere 115 pounds, Sheridan by custom wore a mud-splotched uniform with a flat black hat which always seemed two sizes too small for him. His square Irish face was cut across by a heavy cavalry mustache that accentuated his chin. He rode a black charger, *Rienzi*, at a thundering gallop when he made his rounds.

When General Grant was called East in early 1864 to assume command of the Union armies, he told President Lincoln that for chief of cavalry he "wanted the very best man in the army." Passing over every cavalry officer, Grant picked Philip Sheridan, erstwhile infantryman.

One of Sheridan's first acts was a complete reorganization of the Cavalry Corps. General George Armstrong Custer's Michigan Brigade—the 1st, 5th, 6th, 7th Michigan regiments—together with Colonel Thomas C. "Old War Horse" Devin's and General Wesley Merritt's brigades became the 1st Division. General Alfred T. A. Torbert, a slow but competent regular infantry officer, assumed command. General David McMurtrie Gregg headed the 2nd Division and Sheridan assigned General James Wilson who, like Custer had risen rapidly, to command the 3rd.

Despite the creation of the Cavalry Bureau with its six depots, Sheridan was appalled by the mounts. He discovered that a multiplicity of factors accounted for the rapid breakdown of the horses. Some were too young or in poor condition when purchased. Many were returned to duty before fully recuperated. Soldiers failed to give their mounts proper care, galloping them on trivial errands when a walk would have sufficed. Troopers let overheated horses drink their fill or permitted them to overeat. Improperly folded saddle blankets caused sores. Second only to lack of care as a killer was disease. Frequent and virulent epidemics of hoof-and-mouth disease, often described as "rotten hoof," cut down horses even before they reached the regiments. One brigade lost half its horses within one week.

Checking official reports, Sheridan was also astonished to find that General Meade, then commanding the Army of the Potomac under Grant, had rescinded the reorganizational policies of General Hooker. He wasted the cavalry's strength by a policy of disintegration, assigning regiments to protect trains and picket around infantry, subordinating horse operations to the movements of the main army.

At Willard's Hotel in Washington, Sheridan told a friend: "I'm going to take the cavalry away from the bobtailed brigadier generals. They must do without their escorts. I intend to make the cavalry an arm of the service." Immediately he cut picket details to a minimum.

Sheridan argued vehemently that cavalry should fight cavalry. Moving columns of infantry should take care of their own fronts. Little Phil strove to keep his troops together, concentrated in a compact, fighting force. He wanted to avoid another Brandy Station, the chaotic fight in which General Pleasanton had divided his divisions, diverting them in a three-pronged attack.

When General Meade reported to Grant that Sheridan had bragged that he would whip the Southern cavalry in open conflict if he could take his men and go off on his own, Grant smiled.

"Did Sheridan say that?" he asked. "Well, he generally knows what he is talking about. Let him start right out and do it."

In the spring of 1864 Union troops controlled the Mississippi River, held Tennessee, West Virginia, and Virginia north of the Rapidan River, and occupied most of the coastal forts from Virginia to Texas. Yet the core of the Confederacy was still unshaken. Rebels held the rich Shenandoah Valley, and two powerful armies,

Robert E. Lee's in Virginia and Joseph E. Johnston's in north-western Georgia stood ready.

The Army of the Potomac in early May pushed across the Rapidan River in Virginia and plunged into the Wilderness campaign. On May 9, Sheridan's cavalry moved south to stab deep into enemy territory toward Richmond with plans to ride behind Lee's army, severing communications, diverting Confederate cavalry.

Sheridan and his 10,000 troops pushed through the Virginia countryside at a walk, not at the trot usual for cavalry raids since the general wanted his soldiers and horses to be fresh when they caught up with Jeb Stuart. Sheridan had stripped his command of all impediments—unserviceable animals, wagons, tents. The necessary ammunition train, two ambulances to a division, several pack mules for baggage, and three days' rations comprised the outfit.

Blue columns rode into Beaver Dam Station during the night of May 9–10. They promptly seized the railroad station and squeezed from the telegraph operator the information that two trains—one from Richmond carrying ammunition and supplies for Lee's army, one from Lee's army with prisoners—would arrive in less than thirty minutes.

Off in the distance they heard the whistle "down brakes" and saw a train, hissing and puffing, lumber into the station and jerk to a halt. Quickly wrenching open the car doors, the troopers freed 378 Union prisoners. Minutes later they stopped the Richmond train several miles down the tracks and set fire to its cars and 1,500,000 rations and medical supplies for the Army of Northern Virginia. As the command moved out from Beaver Dam Station, they turned and watched enormous pillars of smoke and flame go tumbling upward. The roof of the depot crashed in, and yellow and black smoke poured out.

Early the next morning while preparing breakfast, Yankees were startled by the *whirr-boom, whirr-boom* of shells. Breakfast was left unfinished. The echo of the big guns had scarcely died away before Sheridan mounted his command.

The Confederate attack came from the rear. General Gregg thrust his 2nd Division against the oncoming Rebels and, after a short, sharp engagement, drove them off.

Sheridan's columns moved down the road. Scouts probing

the enemy picket lines came galloping back. Confederates, thousands of them, were up ahead.

"Cavalry or infantry?" snapped Sheridan.

"Cavalry!"

"Keep moving boys—we're going on through," shouted the general. "There isn't cavalry enough in all the Southern Confederacy to stop us."

Without encountering further action, Sheridan's command reached the South Anna River by nightfall and rested. The morning of May 11 dawned warm and sunny. At Ashland, fifteen miles from Richmond, the columns passed a smouldering wreck of railroad cars. Sheridan's advance patrols were doing their job.

At Yellow Tavern, Sheridan took the Brook Turnpike toward Richmond, six miles away. Artillery up ahead opened fire. Within an area of ten miles, 18,000 cavalrymen, Union and Confederate, began forming. Jeb Stuart's artillery kept up a steady barrage. Union lines were being shot to pieces. Islands of wounded and dying Yankees dotted the field.

General Custer surveyed the Rebel cannoneers swarming about their guns. Rammer staffs whirled as rounds were jammed down the black muzzles. Riding over to Wesley Merritt, commanding the 1st Division in Torbert's absence, Custer said sharply, "Merritt, I'm going to charge that battery."

"Go in, General, I will give you all the support in my power."

Custer galloped off. Pounding up to Merritt's position, Sheridan slid from his saddle. Merritt quickly explained the situation.

"Bully for Custer," Sheridan said. "I'll wait and see it."

With the 1st and 7th Michigan, 1,900 strong, Custer rode off to the right screened by trees on the hillside. The Johnnies, spotting the Union movement, changed positions. Artillery pieces fired, high. Fired again, high, the cannoneers unable to depress the guns enough.

Custer and his Michigan regiments, their musicians piping "Yankee Doodle," picked their way forward, around stone fences, over deep ditches. They reformed as squadrons when they came to the level field.

The trumpeter sounded *Trot*, then *Charge*. In a few seconds the squadrons were swallowed up in dust and smoke. It seemed that every weapon around them was firing.

Lieutenant Asa B. Isham, 1st Michigan, listened to the rising drum role of rifle fire. Beside him Major Henry W. Granger's pistols blazed. For a second Isham saw Jeb Stuart's Corps ensign. Amid the cannonade, the lieutenant swerved in his saddle to stare at Major Granger. He was firing at the horsemen off to the left, those gathered about Stuart's battle flag. Isham realized that Granger was aiming at General Stuart.

Sitting on his horse behind a line of dismounted troopers, Stuart was watching the Yankees sweeping down the field, firing wildly at his men. Just back of Stuart a man dragged a limp leg as he crawled over a rock, leaving a scarlet smear of blood.

Carefully with borrowed ammunition, Stuart began loading his pistol, calmly repeating, "Steady, men, steady. Give it to them."

He reeled in his saddle. In a stupor of agony, he turned and mumbled to a private, "Go and tell General [Fitzhugh] Lee and Dr. Fontaine to come here."

The courier sped off. When he returned after delivering the message, he saw soldiers lifting General Stuart into an ambulance. Mortally wounded, Stuart lay there without speaking, shaking his head.

Dismounted Union regiments crowded through the woods after Custer's charging horsemen. Sergeant L. E. Tripp, 5th Michigan, slogged forward as his colonel yelled, "Now, boys, keep a good line, for General Sheridan is watching us."

Caught in a crossfire on the left and from the rear, the 5th Michigan had no chance for cover. Right and left blue coated men spun, and fired in all directions.

Sergeant Tripp's tent-mate, Daniel F. Miller, dropped, shot through the skull. Custer stormed up on his horse and bellowed, "Lie down, men—lie down. We'll fix them! I have sent two regiments around on the flank!"

The Confederate line buckled and retreated. Sheridan's command rested two hours. It started to rain. It came straight down in bucketfuls. Everything not covered up was drenched in a matter of minutes. Soaked to the skin, still worn out from the battle, the force marched out for Richmond.

By daylight, May 12, the rain had stopped. Sheridan and his troopers were within the outer perimeter of Richmond's fortifications. "I could capture Richmond if I wanted," Sheridan boasted to his staff that morning, "but I can't hold it; and the prisoners tell me that every house in the suburbs is loopholed, and the streets barricaded. It isn't worth the men it would cost."

The Union columns turned, skirted the Confederate capital, and headed out to join General Benjamin F. Butler's army at Haxall's Landing on the James River. On that march General Custer wrote to his beloved, Libbie Bacon:

> We have passed through days of carnage and have lost heavily. . . . We have been successful. . . . The Michigan brigade has covered itself with undying glory. . . . We destroyed railroads, &c., in Lee's rear, mentioned in Sheridan's report to General Grant. . . . I also led a charge in which we mortally wounded Genl. Stuart and captured a battery of three cannon and a large number of prisoners. . . . Genl. Sheridan sent an aide in the battlefield with his congratulations. . . . We were inside the fortifications of Richmond. I enclose some honeysuckle I plucked there.

Again on the 16th Custer wrote her:

> . . . Suffice to say that our brigade has far surpassed all its previous exploits, and that your Boy has never before [been] the object of such attention, and has succeeded beyond his highest expectations. . . . I can tell my little one something that will please her: I have sworn less during the late battles than ever before on similar occasions—all owing to the influence of my beloved darling. During the battles, while I was in the thickest, with bullets whistling by me and shells bursting all around me I thought of you. You are in my thoughts always, day and night.

At Haxall's Landing Sheridan calculated his losses—715 men, 300 horses. The general had worried Lee's rear, partly relieved General Grant from molestation by Rebel cavalry, and had destroyed food, munitions, and railroad tracks. Reading the dispatches, Sheridan learned about the frightful losses in the early days of the Wilderness campaign—18,000 casualties, only 5,000 less than those sustained at Gettysburg. Resting but two days with Butler's Army on the James, Sheridan's bluecoats hastened northward across enemy country to meet Grant on his march for Cold Harbor.

After rejoining the Army of the Potomac, the cavalry suffered severely in the Wilderness. Grant, never retreating, kept pushing around Lee's wing deeper into Virginia. Crossing the James River, the Union army was halted by fortifications below Petersburg. Grant dug in and lay siege.

Days and months crept by. His army hopelessly mired in front of Petersburg, Grant's reputation as a general was seriously threatened and President Lincoln's reelection in November was in jeopardy. In many parts of the North violent opposition to the continuance of the war was becoming manifest.

The biggest stumbling block to victory was the Union's inability to drive Rebel armies out of the Shenandoah Valley, from where they could cross the Potomac into Maryland and Pennsylvania. Already the valley had consumed the reputations of Union Generals Nathaniel P. Banks, Franz Sigel, and David Hunter. Operating from the Shenandoah, General Jubal Early and his Confederate bands had forced several Union towns to pay exorbitant tribute under threat of total destruction. Early had even ridden into the suburbs of Washington. He had fallen back after this thrust, but there was always the chance that once again his butternut-clad troops might come pouring out of the Shenandoah.

Throughout the Civil War the Shenandoah Valley was known simply as "The Valley," a corridor shooting off to the southwest from Harper's Ferry, a broad land of rich farms sprawling between blue mountains with a river flowing gently among the fields and woodlands. Running from southwest to northeast, the Shenandoah was a screened way which led to Washington. The Blue Ridge gave concealment and protection.

The North could not win the war, reasoned General Grant, until Yankee might deprived the Confederacy of this fertile valley. Until the enemy was driven out and the Shenandoah laid waste, the Army of the Potomac before Petersburg would never be safe from assault from the rear.

Grant dispatched General Sheridan to Harper's Ferry and gave him command of the Middle Military Division. Under him was a scratch force composed of elements which had never worked together before, many of whom had come to accept defeat as a foregone conclusion. This Army of the Shenandoah included Sheridan's own cavalry, General George Crook's cavalry from the Department of West Virginia, the XI Corps, and part of the XIX Corps. It was Sheridan's task to fuse this mass of 35,000 men into a tough, efficient striking force to oppose General Early's army of 19,000.

Sheridan ordered General Torbert to "make the necessary arrangements and give the necessary orders for the destruction of the wheat and hay south of a line from Millwood to Winchester and Petticoat Gap . . . you will seize all mules, horses and cattle that may be useful to our army. Loyal citizens can bring in their claims against the government for this necessary destruction. No houses will be burned; and officers in charge of this delicate but necessary duty must inform the people that the object is to make this Valley untenable for raiding parties of the rebel army."

In mid-August, 1864, Sheridan's Army of the Shenandoah marched a third of the way up the valley with absurd ease. Already the general was making himself felt. Instead of asking for reports, Little Phil was forever roaring off at a gallop on *Rienzi* to see for himself. Soldiers grew accustomed to seeing his little flat black hat bobbing along the picket lines or weaving among the marching columns. He visited artillery lines, ambulances, supply wagons, and tents of isolated companies.

Learning that Lee had reinforced Early and still feeling cautious with his new command, Sheridan turned his army around and headed back for Halltown. As the columns began retracing their steps, horse soldiers fanned out in all directions and began to tear the valley apart, methodically, systematically. The plan was simple—burn the barns, destroy the crops. Anything that was of value to the Confederacy had to be eliminated.

Lieutenant Colonel Theodore W. Bean, 17th Pennsylvania Cavalry, recalled:

> . . . the torch was applied deliberately and intentionally. Stacks of hay and straw, and barns filled with crops harvested, mills, corn-cribs; in a word, all supplies of use to man or beast were promptly burned and all valuable cattle driven off. . . . The work of destruction seemed cruel and the distress it occasioned among the people of all ages and sexes was evident on every hand. The officers and soldiers who performed the details of this distressing work were met at every farm or home by old men, women and children in tears, begging and beseeching those in charge to save them from the appalling ruin.

These scenes of burning and destruction, which were only the prelude to those which followed at a later day further up the valley, were attended with sorrow to families and added horrors to the usual brutalities of war. . . .

The troops came into camp loaded down with supplies for man and beast, while droves of cattle, sheep, hogs and many good and serviceable horses and mules were turned over to the quartermaster's department.

While Sheridan's force wended its way down the Shenandoah leaving a swatch of desolation, the countryside swarmed with outlaws and with Rebels who were civilians six days a week and raiders on the seventh. Swooping down from the hills, ruffians picked off Yankee outposts, burned bridges, bushwhacked scouts, and destroyed supply wagons. One of Sheridan's aides was discovered in a barren field with his throat cut. Farther down the road Lieutenant Charles McMaster 17th Pennsylvania, lay wounded. Before he died he mumbled to friends that he'd been shot after he'd surrendered. Insanely furious, twenty-five volunteers from the regiment chased scattered bands of marauders, who went charging toward the hills. Before they could reach their hideouts, the Pennsylvanians overhauled six of them. They shot three dead on the highway and took the other three prisoners. A Michigan detail surrounded one of the guerrillas, a youth, and riddled his body with bullets. They hanged the other two in a small grove, their bodies dangling from a projecting limb of an oak tree.

Union patrols searched the valley for "Captain" Stump the infamous guerrilla chieftain. Late one afternoon Sergeant G. D. Mullihan, 17th Pennslyvania, was just mounting his horse in front of a barn when he saw a marvelous looking creature trot up to the gate. His saddle was equal to his mount—hand-tooled and glittering with silver ornaments. A carbine stock thrust up from the boot under the saddle leathers, and the man was triple-gunned with pistols. He carried bandoliers of ammunition strung over his shoulders and around his waist.

Failing to heed Mullihan's order to halt, the man kept riding up to the gate. Mullihan snapped out his pistol and fired. The figure in the saddle fell and sprawled on the ground, slightly wounded. The sergeant and his comrades, who by this time had converged on the scene, swarmed over the injured horseman and helped themselves to his pistols, carbines, and ammunition.

Mullihan asked if he were Captain Stump.

"No," the man drawled, "but I am Captain Stump's brother."

They remounted and with the Southerner in front they rode down the lane. Gaining the main road they galloped up to the rear columns of Sheridan's army.

"Whom have you there?" asked a major.

"Captain Stump, but he will not own up to it," replied Mullihan.

Looking at the Rebel, the major snarled, "You might as well own up to it, for there are plenty of people around here who know you and can identify you."

"I might as well own up to it: I am Captain Stump," retorted the Southerner.

"I suppose you know that we will kill you," said the major. "But we will not serve you as you have served our men, cut your throat or hang you. We will give you a chance for your life. We will give you ten rods start on your own horse, with your spurs on. If you get away, all right. But remember, my men are dead shots."

Stump wheeled about.

The major shouted: "Go!"

Shots thudded out almost together. Stump spun forward. He hit the ground, writhed, twisted his legs together, then lay still.

♘ ♘ ♘

During the month of September, General Grant rode in to the Shenandoah and prodded Sheridan to march along the valley pike to somewhere below Winchester, maneuver south of Early's army which was camped at Opequon Creek, and eliminate it.

The Army of the Shenandoah began the slow march through the valley, the infantry rolling in massive columns along the floor while artillery and transport clung to the pike and better side roads. Behind the infantry came the horse soldiers. By division, by regiment, by troop they rode slowly, trotting over upland fields, surging along the banks of creeks.

General Wilson's cavalry division sped across one of the fords of Opequon Creek early on September 19, and struck Rebel outposts. Galloping on, Wilson began probing Early's main defensive line. Unfortunately, Union orders were confused. The supporting columns closed slowly. During the battle, which narrowly missed resulting in a disastrous Federal defeat, Sheridan exhorted his men into line and saw them advance. The cavalry swept down on knots of resistance, broke them, scattered them, reformed at a trot, and galloped off in a fresh attack. The gray lines gave way in good order, eluding the Yankee force.

The Army of the Shenandoah pushed along the pike. Sheridan meant to whip General Early and to prevent his escape. Massing his foot soldiers for a frontal thrust, he dispatched mounted regiments to circle up the Luray Valley and cut back to the pike near New Market, obstructing the Rebels' escape route.

On September 22, the Union infantry attacked and beat back the Confederates. But General Torbert's cavalry failed to halt the Southerners' retreat and Early, outguessing Sheridan, had his cavalry regiments block the Federals at Milford and hold them off until his force had marched through.

Sheridan's army on October 6 moved back for the lower valley—a withdrawal, not a retreat, Sheridan was careful to say. Winter was coming on and his 190 mile supply line seemed dangerously long. As the army, trailed now by an ever-increasing stream of refugees—black and white—marched back, Sheridan reapplied the torch. Black rolls of smoke spread skyward. From a hillside Lieutenant Colonel Bean, 17th Pennsylvania, described the destruction:

> Looking southward from this eminence, the eye falls upon a broad valley, skirted by the Blue Ridge on the east and the Alleghenies on the west, traversed by highways in all directions; towns, villages and churches forming local centres among farms, the improvements upon which were the best in Virginia and possibly in the South. From all points of observation small bodies of cavalry could be seen, by the aid of field-glasses, on every public road, gradually spreading out like foragers at will, giving ample evidence of the thoroughness of their instructions and their methodical execution of the order. Slowly and deliberately our troops retired, applying the torch and driving off all manner of stock.
>
> . . . we do not think the annals of civilized warfare furnished a parallel to these destructive operations. It would be

an interesting chapter in the Annals of War to have the names
of the property owners and the estimated loss of property, real
and personal, suffered by fire within the lines of the Military
Divisions between August 1 and December 1, 1864. The work
of destruction was to be thoroughly done, and the blackened
face of the country. . . bore frightful testimony to fire and
sword.

First Lieutenant Luman Harris Tenney, 2nd Ohio Cavalry,
scrawled in his war diary:

Camped . . . on an old gentleman's farm. I had quite
a talk with him. He owned a farm, sterile and poor, of 200
acres in among the hills. He was 70 years of age. Moved there
34 years since when all was a wilderness. Had never owned a
slave. Had cleaned up the farm, built a long house and made
all the improvements with his own hands. It made him almost
crazy to see all going to destruction in one night—all his fences,
outbuildings, cattle, sheep and fowls. An only son at home,
an invalid. Had always been true to the government. Only
wished that God would now call him, that he might be with
his many friends in the church yard—pointing to it near by—
and this aspect of suffering and starvation be taken from him.

The Army of the Shenandoah continued to withdraw. Gen-
eral Early's advance force closed in behind and hotly engaged
Sheridan's rear columns. Upset over these rear-guard skirmishes,
Sheridan rode to see General Torbert.

At the house of a Mrs. Hendricks, Torbert and his staff sat
in the dining room demolishing a twenty-five-pound turkey. In
burst Sheridan, his face puckered with rage. His unsteady temper
exploded: "Well, I'll be d——d! if you ain't sitting there stuffing
yourselves, general, staff, and all, while the rebels are riding into
our camp! Having a party, while Rosser* is carrying off your guns!
Got on your nice clothes and clean shirts! Torbert, mount quicker
than h–l will scorch a feather!"

Sheridan strode from the room, jumped on *Rienzi*, and disappeared into the dark.

---

* General Thomas L. Rosser

General Sheridan's ride on **Rienzi**,
October 19, 1864.

On October 9, Yankee horse divisions engaged the Rebels in a vicious cavalry duel. It ended when the Johnnies turned and were pursued by Custer's troopers for ten miles. That evening General Early sat in his makeshift headquarters, writing: "This is very distressing to me, and God knows I have done all in my power to avert the disasters which have befallen this command; but the fact is the enemy's cavalry is so much superior to ours, both in numbers and equipment, and the country is so unfavorable to operations of cavalry, that it is impossible for ours to compete with it."

By mid-October Sheridan and his command were on a chain of low hills near a stream called Cedar Creek, twenty miles south of Winchester. With Early presumably whipped for good, Sheridan mounted *Rienzi* and rode off for Washington to plan his next move.

On the night of October 18–19, Private William F. McKay, 5th Cavalry, was sentry on Post No. 1. He had gone on duty at 2 A.M. and noted the air chilly and that a heavy fog had fallen. An hour later in the eerie darkness he was startled by picket firing up the line accompanied by muffled yells. Pinching himself to be sure he wasn't napping, McKay shook the bugler, ran to headquarters, looked inside and yelled, "General, there is something wrong on our front."

The general dashed out in his night shirt. The rattle of pistol fire was heavy. He spun around and exclaimed: "We're surprised; bugler blow 'boots and saddles.'" Turning to McKay, he said calmly, "Sentry, you are relieved. Report to your company."

All hell broke loose and mishap followed tragic mishap.

Captain Henry A. Dupont's first impression was that his pickets were chopping wood to make the morning fires. The gunfire increased. The flash of artillery fire added to the confusion. Dupont jumped out from his bedroll, pulled on his boots, and ordered the bugler to sound *Reveille*.

Corporal William Edward House, 7th Michigan, dreamed that he heard pickets firing. He awoke with a start to the reality. Three shots. Then another. Running from blanket to blanket, he roused his comrades. Most of them climbed out their bedrolls quickly; others complained, "Oh, it is only a false alarm."

Corporal House and his sidekick, William Kemp, stood with

their hands on their saddles, ready to mount. They heard someone shout, "Forward, charge!" and saw a streak of fire encircling the unit. *Fall in!* was confused with *Fall back!* Companies broke for the rear. The grey coats kept advancing. In the blood-pounding excitement House and Kemp turned and ran, stumbling, sprawling full length and rolling down the slope and picking themselves up and running faster than before.

Sergeant R. Marshall Bellinger, 7th Michigan, heard bullets whine. One of the men nearby swore and wrung his right hand, from the fingertips of which came a little spray of blood. Beyond another man sat down abruptly and leaned forward, his head resting on his arms, dead, shot through the head. Other troopers flattened themselves behind trees to escape the ricocheting bullets.

Down the line General Custer was worrying down some breakfast. The bombardment had grown alarmingly loud. Custer dispatched a messenger for information and with orders to put the division under arms.

The courier galloped back with distressing news. General Early had surprised the Union left and was at that moment punching his way toward the flank. Already he'd taken hundreds of prisoners. Thousands of Yankee soldiers were streaming down the road toward Winchester. All that stood in Early's way were the VI Corps, two brigades of the XIXth, and Custer's and Merritt's cavalry. Flushed with success, many Rebels halted to loot tents and wolf down abandoned Union breakfasts.

Waiting for onslaughts of the Rebels, Union soldiers heard a shrill roar of cheers welling up from the Winchester-Strasburg pike. It was Sheridan back from Washington, "Come on back, boys—Give-em Hell, G— D—— 'em. We'll make coffee out of Cedar Creek tonight." All along the line he was met by a storm of cries, "Sheridan! Sheridan!"

Without parleying with his officers, the general rode along the whole front of his army. He trotted up and down shouting, "Steady, lads, we'll give 'em hell yet."

Sheridan ordered an advance. The blue lines rushed forward. General Early shifted positions to strike the Union flank. Eagerly watching this movement, Sheridan spotted a weakness, a gap in the Rebel lines, and ordered Custer's whole cavalry division to hit it hard and chop Early's army in two.

Buglers sounded *Charge*. Troopers spurred their mounts toward the Confederates. Like a thunderbolt, Custer burst through and split the lines. The division kept on riding to Cedar Creek and, splattering across, waited for the Rebels to come storming back in full retreat before the onslaught of the Yankee infantry.

By early evening the Southerners started an orderly retreat. The pike was thick with batteries and wagons and red faced, cursing infantrymen. There was a horrible jam at Cedar Creek Bridge where a heavy cart had tried to turn.

A Confederate officer stood transfixed and watched Custer's troopers bear down. He recalled:

> There came from the north side of the plain, a dull, heavy swelling sound like a roaring of a distant cyclone, the omen of additional disaster. It was unmistakable. Sheridan's horsemen were riding furiously across the open fields of grass to intercept the Confederates before they crossed. . . . Many were cut off and captured. As the sullen roar from horses' hoofs beating the soft turf of the plain told of the near approach of the cavalry, all effort at orderly retreat was abandoned. The only possibility of saving the rear regiments was in unrestrained flight—every man for himself.

Rebels hightailed it for the woods, screaming, "We're flanked! We're flanked!" Soon the road south to Strasburg was littered with wagons full of heavy equipment and supplies, boxes of ammunition, forage carts, smashed ambulances, canteens, scores of weapons.

At Sheridan's headquarters that night officers rehashed the events of the day. Excitedly, General Custer came in, grabbed Sheridan in a bear hug, then lifted him into the air and whirled him around and around, shouting, "By Jesus, we've cleaned them out and got the guns."

The Battle of Cedar Creek was the last important action fought in the valley during 1864. Sheridan's army had inflicted a critical blow on the Confederate armies by destroying the fruitful fields which supplied them with food and forage. This was soon confirmed in the telegrams and letters from Lee's army at Petersburg, from North Carolina, and elsewhere.

ABOVE: Yankee Cavalry *seize* Confederate *battery near*
Cedar Creek, October, 1864. BELOW: Sheridan's *ride through* cheering
troops, Cedar Creek. From James E. Taylor's *illustrated diary.*

Three days after Cedar Creek, Lincoln penned a note to General Sheridan from the White House:

With great pleasure I tender to you and your brave army, the thanks of the Nation, and my own personal admiration and gratitude, for the months operations in the Shenandoah Valley; and especially for the splendid work of October 19, 1864.

In less than six months the Civil War would be over, a war which was the last general conflict in the Western world in which large bodies of mounted troops played a major role.

chapter 13.

"Most of 'em don't know what hardships are!"

🐴 🐴 🐴

THE NOTES OF THE BUGLE LINGERED IN THE HEAT ABOVE the Dakota plains. The thudding report of the swivel gun, fired during the interval between *Colors* and *Retreat*, had boomed, seeming to split the air above Fort Lincoln, Dakota Territory. It was a fine moment for the post, a time for relaxation after the day's routine of drill, parade, fatigue, and stable details were over. Troopers within sight of the flag released their salutes and resumed their activities. Across the parade the sound of feminine voices drifted along Officers' Row.

In one of the parlors Kate Garrett chatted excitedly with her sister, Mollie, wife of 2nd Lieutenant Donald McIntosh, 7th United States Cavalry. Kate had traveled by rail, boat, wagon, and cart from Pennsylvania to visit her sister. Although noticeably worn from the rough and tedious trip, she sat enchanted listening to Mollie's stories of the West and life at Fort Lincoln.

The post, explained Mollie, was regulated by the bugler, directly or indirectly, throughout the day. He sounded *Assembly* and *Recall* a dozen times in sixteen hours, and *Reveille*, *Mess*, *Tattoo*, *Taps*, and all the calls entailed in troop drill. Each day on the post, her husband's schedule was the same—*Reveille* sounded by trumpets and drums; first guard mount before breakfast; inspection of the soldier's mess at breakfast, dinner, and supper with samplings of the food prepared; dismounted drill and mounted drill according to the colonel's orders; inspection and supervision of the stables every afternoon; inspection of pasturage beyond the fort at suitable intervals; second guard mount in midafternoon; calls upon the men in the hospital; sanitary inspections; schooling of horses following afternoon stables; study of regulations, orders, and military court procedures when not otherwise occupied; retreat ceremonies; third guard mount before taps; *Taps.*

Women on the post fell into strict categories, the lines of which were never crossed—officers' wives, enlisted men's wives, and laundresses. The latter, the Spikes, the settlers of Suds Row were an institution of the service inherited from the British Army. Military regulations stipulated that each troop or company in the United States Army could hire four laundresses to wash the men's clothes, females who were to be paid fixed wages and given army rations, the money coming from deductions out of the troopers' pay. These rough, raucous women who lived together on the outskirts of the post amid squalor and children of dubious parentage were objects of incessant attention and rivalry among the troopers.

As with common law, the long established practices of the cavalry service were not set down in writing yet they became immutable. One custom prescribed that any cavalry officer who was publicly "policed" (thrown from his mount) must set up drinks for his brother officers. The cavalry toast of "How" was a shortened "Here's How." It was generally understood that the "HO" of *how* stood for H_2O, the "W" for whiskey, and, properly defined, "How" became half water, half whiskey.

Perhaps the most exasperating practice was "ranking out of quarters." Living accommodations on the posts were symbols of rank. A newly arrived officer would inspect the quarters of all those junior to him and make his selection. The officer "bumped" would then repeat the ritual and such maneuvers oftentimes resulted in a dozen shifts.

An officer's child was christened beneath the regiment's color; no officer or enlisted man in uniform could carry an umbrella, a collection of packages, or push a baby carriage; a junior officer walking or riding with a senior must take his position on the left; troopers addressed all officers by rank; officers addressed enlisted men by last names. Off duty, senior officers called their juniors by first or last name, but the junior never had the same privilege.

On the frontier the trooper's first allegiance was to his company—he bunked in company quarters, ate in company mess halls, played on company teams, danced at company balls. Units acquired individual characteristics. Known throughout the 7th regiment as a wild group, Troop A was dubbed "The Forty Thieves." Frequently a captain became so identified with his company that it was called by his name.

On an afternoon after Kate Garrett's introduction to the military mysteries at Fort Lincoln, the sisters were interrupted as Lieutenant McIntosh came bounding up the steps to dress for the parade. Hastily Mollie and Kate clambered into the buckboard and were trundled out to the wide, level plain where spectators had begun gathering in a huge semicircle—soldiers from the nearby infantry post, curious frontiersmen from neighboring ranches, Indian scouts and squaws mingled with the gaily clad men and women who had driven out from the town of Bismarck.

Kate, who had never previously witnessed the pomp and ceremony of a cavalry dress parade, stood up in the buckboard, entranced by the sight. She wrote later:

> As I recall my first impression of that mounted parade, I realize that it imparted a glamor to my army life that nothing ever quite equaled. I can see now those six troops of cavalry, the horses of which had been selected by experts and groomed to perfection, their glossy skins shining in the sun like cut velvet. Atop these superb creatures sat men like centaurs, their chins held in by the leather understraps of black helmets—or maybe they were of the deepest blue, which appeared black. Anyway, these helmets were decorated by gold spread eagles, and thick yellow plumes floated from gold spikes in the center of the crown. The cavalry uniforms were of blue and gold, and sabers swung at the sides. The officers' equipment was supplemented by kidney-shaped yellow and gold epaulets, bearing the insignia of rank, repeated on the collar. A gold thread saber belt, heavy gold cords and tassels worn across the breast, and broadcloth canary-yellow stripes which ran down the outside of the trousers, the latter encased in regimental high-topped boots, completed the outfit.

Officers and sergeants bawled out orders and advancing columns swept forward, flags and guidons whipping in the afternoon breeze. Lines formed and divided, undulating in trots and gallops, responding to the commands or bugle calls, all of which were understood by the horses.

The officers wheeled their mounts into line as the adjutant

galloping from the rear filled up the space left open for him. He yelled, "Officers, center, march!" The whole line advanced as one man and one horse toward the colonel and his staff while the band swung into a spirited march. Deftly the officers reined their horses to a halt. The band stopped playing. Officers saluted the colonel smartly, their hands at the visor until the salute was returned. Breaking the line, they turned, rejoined their troops, and awaited *Retreat.*

After the last notes died away, the band played, "The Star-Spangled Banner" and the parade ended. Dismissed, the officers sauntered back to the post. Riding in front of their men with sabers drawn, the first sergeants ordered "Post." With the band striking up a brisk march the columns left the wide plain.

Kate Garrett adapted quickly to life on the post-Civil War frontier. Released from the tensions and horrors of that struggle, Americans were pushing westward in tidal waves, moving along the major thoroughfares—the Santa Fe Trail to New Mexico and California; the Kansas Trail to Denver; the Oregon Trail to Nebraska and Utah and beyond; the Boseman Trail through Wyoming and Montana.

The Sioux, Apache, and other savages fought fanatically for survival, determined to war as long as hope remained. In that conflict the Indians gave no quarter as they saw themselves being relentlessly decimated and pushed off their ancient hunting grounds.

The United States Army represented the power of established order on the frontier and while defending the westward marching pioneer from the hostiles, it also protected Indian reservations and land grants from the encroachment of white settlers and enforced the law. Cavalry detachments drove cattle from one station to another, hunted down deserters, escorted paymasters, and guarded railroad construction.

Along the western frontier, cavalry and infantry posts stood at points near Indian territory or along the Mexican border. To the officers of the cavalry service and their wives, it was a source of wonder how the War Department selected the sites of the frontier garrisons. Wives were convinced it was the work of congenital idiots, men who either hated mankind or who had an astounding knowledge of western geography. They had a genius for locating posts in spots notable for dust, cyclones, impossible temperatures, and enough bugs and reptiles to delight the Smithsonian Institution.

The wives agreed that the men who had designed and constructed the temporary posts were a worse menace than those who had picked the sites. Cavalry women were horrified when they first inspected a miserable dugout with a dirt floor or a decaying log hut whose cracks and crevices let in the drifting dust and sand.

A miserable post was Camp Supply, Indian Territory. It stood in a barren and remote region. One lieutenant's wife complained: "This country itself is bad enough and the location of the post is most unfortunate, but to compel officers and men to live in these old huts of decaying, moldy wood, which are reeking with malaria and alive with bugs, and perhaps snakes, is wicked."

One of Elizabeth Bacon Custer's earliest memories of the plains was of a "forlorn little post—a few log houses bare of every comfort, and no trees to cast a shade on the low roofs. . . . The floor of uneven boards was almost ready for agricultural purposes, as the wind had sifted the prairie sand in between the roughly laid logs, and even the most careful housewife would have found herself outwitted if she tried to keep a tidy floor."

In the established regions of the West or, occasionally on the far western frontier, wives found well-constructed, permanent posts. The buildings were frame, brick, stone, log, or whitewashed adobe which at a distance looked like marble. A few of the frame buildings had shingled roofs and glass windows. Fort Stanton, New Mexico, located in magnificent country with a fine climate, was regarded as a desirable post, especially by those who enjoyed hunting and fishing. Fort Clark, Texas, had spacious quarters of limestone, finished with deep porches masked by screens of Madeira vines. "It is delightful to be in a nicely furnished, well-regulated house once more," Mrs. Fayette W. Roe said, describing Fort Shaw, Montana. "The buildings are all made of adobe, and the officers' quarters have low, broad porches in front. . . . There are nice front yards, and on either side of the officer's walk is a row of beautiful cottonwood trees that form a complete arch."

The ever-changing military situation determined the movements of military families. Some transferred stations twenty-one times within three years; others remained in one place for longer periods. If an entire regiment were shifted, it usually meant a cross-country move of a thousand miles or more with dependents traveling in ambulances across plains and deserts and over mountains.

When orders arrived for a transfer, women habitually cursed the War Department's edict which allowed a family to ship only a thousand pounds of personal gear at government expense. Everything else had to be paid for by the officer and the cost of freighting via civilian wagon was prohibitive in the West. As a result every officer owned three huge wooden chests, each stenciled with his name, into which he stuffed his most needed effects. For the women it was disheartening to sacrifice things they had cherished and to watch them being auctioned off to those that remained behind at half their cost.

"I have always thought army life would be delightful," said Mrs. Frances Boyd, "if there was the slightest certainty of remaining at any post for a given length of time; but this is so out of the question that many comforts which might have otherwise been procured are gradually tabooed."

Married only six months, Fran Boyd traveled by train, sled, and stagecoach from San Francisco to rejoin her husband at a military camp near Ruby, Nevada. Arriving tired and disheveled, looking forward to a well-earned rest, Fran, after the first warm embraces with her husband, learned that they must ride an additional 100 miles to their home at Fort Halleck. Climbing into a ramshackle ambulance, they started out across the plains. They jogged monotonously the first day, seeing not a sign of habitation, not a tree, nothing but the dreary flatlands outlined by the far mountains.

The ambulance was covered with canvas over bows and Fran sat under the cover, clutching her jewel box to her knees. That night was her first experience in camping out. At dawn they resumed the tedious journey and in late afternoon the ambulance rattled up before an eighteen-foot-square log hut which slept ten. As Fran opened the shack's door and entered, a crowd of rough, unkempt men ogled and stared. But they were extremely courteous and hospitable, insisting that she sleep in the only bed—a rough bunk of unplaned pine timber standing in one corner. Shrinking from the proximity of so many men, yet remembering camping out the night before, Fran was glad to get behind the improvised curtains which had been deftly arranged. Outside it began snowing.

On the last day of her journey, Fran arose feeling wondrously happy at the prospect of reaching Fort Halleck, only twenty miles beyond. Ten inches of snow clogged the road. After slogging two miles in the cold, the mules wandered off into a deep gully, plunging the ambulance into an enormous drift. Passing frontiersmen extricated them and Fran Boyd, seated in the center of that springless conveyance, huddled beneath five blankets during the remaining eighteen miles.

It was evening when they pulled into Fort Halleck. Any arrival at the garrison was an event, but one which brought a popular officer and his bride was spectacular. Fran saw all the officers and most of the troopers gathered at the main gate. She waved when they greeted her with cheers. Her husband vaulted from the wagon and she stepped down into his arms. They stood for a moment looking at their new home.

It was a dismal sight. Fran, bone-weary from the rugged trip, felt utterly dejected. Their quarters consisted of two windowless tents pitched together so one could be used as a sleeping room and the other as a parlor. A pathetic calico curtain divided them and a carpet of barley sacks covered the floor. Fran went to bed that night and cried and cried and cried.

Once cavalry wives settled into the routine of a post, they learned how to deal with the tame Indians, who continuously drifted into the garrison. Many a wife, bathing leisurely in her portable galvanized tub, discovered a grimacing redman peeping in the window or invading her quarters. If shouting and waving them away did no good, she reached for her robe, dashed to the door, and screamed for the Corporal of the Guard.

Mrs. Fred Klawitter, wife of an enlisted trooper, related her first brush with the Indians: "I have never seen an Indian before in my life, and here we were, ferried across the Missouri River right into the weirdest noises that human beings could ever make; but my husband told me it was nothing but an Indian war dance. . . . All night long the howling continued, and we just had a tent for protection! Believe me, that tent seemed pretty frail to me that first night. I could just feel the hands of an Indian reaching under the edge of the tent and dragging me out so quickly that my husband never even knew it. That's how scared I was of the Indians."

Life at Brenham, Texas, in the late 1860's was unbearable for Mrs. Ellen McGowan Biddle, doubly so since she lost all her baggage in Galveston while in transit. The Biddles made no friends or acquaintances in town as Texas, having sided with the Confederacy during the Civil War, stood aloof. Preferring a small house in Brenham rather than tent-living at the Army camp, Ellen had a wretched time. The outscourings of Texas roamed the streets fighting, shooting, gambling. "I was dreadfully afraid lest some of those terrible creatures would come in to rob and kill us. . . . My nerves got into a frightful condition. . . . One of our officers was brutally shot down, murdered, when he had gone out to make an arrest, and his body was not discovered for several months."

One afternoon when her carriage drove up in front of the house, Ellen noticed a strange driver. Upon inquiry she learned that her regular man was unwell. As the carriage wove its way through the streets and out into the country, Ellen noted the driver was drunk, so drunk that he was in danger of falling off his seat.

Suddenly the horses broke into a trot, then began to gallop faster and faster, the carriage careening behind. Scared, yet calm enough to react correctly, Mrs. Biddle ordered her children to lie flat on the bottom. Desperately she struggled through the window and clambered into the seat next to the driver. Grasping the reins, she guided the horses to a halt. She wheeled the rig around and headed back to Brenham. Signaling her husband, who stood talking with an officer on the street, Ellen managed to stop the horses before fainting dead away.

Most city-bred women who married officers had an inaccurate picture of military life out West. In the post-Civil War period, the Army faced difficulties supplying the isolated posts. Advertising in principal cities, the Commissary and Quartermaster depots awarded contracts to the lowest reputable bidder. The Army purchased clothing, blankets, and equipment on the Pacific Coast and in the East. Arms, ammunition, and other ordnance stores were sent from the various arsenals and depots. Fresh beef, grain, hay, lumber, and commissary supplies were bought from local markets if they could be secured economically.

Supplies did not always reach their destination without loss.

Meat hauled overland from Fort Yuma invariably spoiled. The utter absence of items considered indispensable in eastern homes created hardship. The government attempted to provide adequately, but the distances between the far-flung garrisons and the sources of supply, and the skyrocketing costs of transportation made the job almost impossible.

For months Marion Russell at Camp Nichols, built near today's New Mexico-Oklahoma border, cooked and ate Army rations—hardtack, bacon, coffee, beans, venison, and beef. This monotonous fare was supplemented by such delicacies as canned peaches for which her husband paid outrageous prices whenever a supply wagon rolled in. At Fort Halleck, Nevada, Fran Boyd's only luxury was dried apples and, tiring of these before a year was over, she tried to devise ways to disguise their taste.

Learning to survive without eggs, milk, or other common ingredients, cavalry wives traded recipes and information on food preparation. Stationed at a desolate post, Ellen Biddle was grateful that she had the recipes of a Mrs. Coolidge, who had lived and cooked on the western plains in the early 1850's.

MOCK CUSTARD

To make custard without eggs or milk: six tablespoonfuls of cornstarch; enough water to make it creamy thick when cooked; then add essence of lemon and sugar to taste; serve in custard-cups.

MOCK APPLE PIE

To make apple pie without apples: take soda crackers and soak them in water until soft—break not too fine; add essence of lemon and sugar and a great deal of nutmeg; bake in pastry with a top crust to the pie.

The wife of an enlisted man at Fort Lincoln, said Mrs. Klawitter, ate "Bacon, beans, hard tack with beef three times a week." "A fresh egg," she continued, "would have been a feast. But then after I learned how to use that hardtack we got along very nicely. Good Land, we had all our boxes full of it. Two cakes of it would fill a quart jar full if they were well soaked up. The company cook told me how to make pudding from hardtack and other dishes also; and then we lived much better."

To wives accustomed to luxury the lack of domestic help was a concern. If they imported maids from the East they saw them marry soldiers or settlers within weeks. Sometimes enlisted men would work after duty hours but they were rarely competent and proved unsatisfactory stopgaps.

When it could be secured, Chinese help was excellent. Chinese cooks were a colorful set and full of surprises. Frequently a cavalry wife, dining as a guest, ate from her own china or silverware as the Chinese hustled plates and utensils from house to house without consulting either owner or hostess. Impossible to stop, such practices became custom.

Childbirth on the frontier was often a frightening and hazardous experience. "Convent raised, my knowledge of childbirth was limited," confessed Marion Russell. "I had prepared no clothes for my baby. I scarcely knew I was going to have one. . . . The young army doctor was reduced to a hopeless wreck before my ordeal had hardly begun. . . . Hattie Eliza Russell was a large baby and she literally tore her way into my life. . . . I loathed and hated the thing that had caused me so much hideous suffering."

Tender and understanding, the midwife wrapped the newborn into castoff blankets and took it with her. "I fell asleep," remembered Mrs. Russell, and "when I awoke again. . . . I wanted my baby and I wanted her very much."

Whether on a dreary post in Texas or in the vastness of the Dakotas the wife discovered contagion almost nonexistent. Army brats rarely suffered from the childhood ailments of the cities and seemed to thrive in temperatures ranging from 122 degrees above in summer to 60 degrees below in winter.

Schools were scarce and most children were taught at home, although, occasionally, an educated soldier conducted classes on the post. When youngsters of officers reached high-school age, they were shipped East to complete their studies.

During the winter months when ice and snow blanketed the plains and cut off posts from the outside world, life grew increasingly monotonous and lonely. "The days for the women are all alike," confided Ellen Biddle at Fort Whipple, Arizona Territory, "had it not been for my children, my two boys in particular, who were hearty and thoroughly alive mentally and physically, I think I would have despaired. No one who has not lived an isolated life can appreciate what it is for a woman."

"Did you find army life a hardship?" asked a high-school teacher who interviewed Mrs. Klawitter in 1935.

"Oh, Lord yass, people talk about hardships nowadays! They should be ashamed of themselves; most of 'em don't know what hardships are! It was a big change from my usual independent life in Shreveport, I'm telling you."

To while away the hours, army wives sometimes found solace and escape in smoking Mexican cigarettes. Officers and men turned to liquor. Fanny McGillycuddy, wife of a surgeon at Camp Robinson, penned this cryptic entry in her diary for December 28–31, 1876: "Outfit all drunk." At Lower Brule Agency, enlisted men discovered a captain with his neck caught between the pickets of a fence, his body suspended. Investigation revealed that the captain had imbibed heavily the night before and, becoming nauseated, had leaned over the fence. Losing consciousness, he lurched forward, his head dropping between the pickets, and he strangled. At another fort, the surgeon complained that the soldiers, circumventing the colonel's prohibition order, were drinking extracts of lemon, vanilla, cinnamon, peppermint, ginger, Worcestershire and red pepper sauces, bay rum, cologne, and quack medicine.

At Fort Stevenson, Dakota Territory, one general griped: "Winter is a deplorable season in Dakota. Its excessive severity keeps us captives in our huts, and there the days go by in monotonous uniformity. . . . My military duties are reduced to almost nothing. . . . All this does not take me more than a few hours a week."

A feeling of utter hopelessness was expressed in a letter by the telegraph operator at Camp Brown, Wyoming: "I want to get out of the Army honorable but if I can't get out otherwise I will give the cursed outfit the 'Grand bounce.' I can not endure them much longer. None but a menial a Cur Could stand the usage of a soldier of the Army of today in America."

On the more settled posts, winter was the signal for increased gaiety. "Now that everyone is settled," wrote one wife, "the dining and wining has begun. Almost every day there is a dinner or a card party . . . and several very delicious luncheons. . . . The dinners are usually quite elegant, formal affairs, beautifully served with dainty china and handsome silver.

"Everyone is happy in the fall, after the return of the companies from their hard and often dangerous summer campaign, and settles down for the winter. It is then that we feel we can feast and dance, and it is then, too, that garrison life at a frontier post becomes so delightful."

During the winter months at Fort Lincoln, each company gave a ball and preparations were begun long in advance. Men pushed bunks from the barracks, festooned the room, stacked arms, and arranged the guidons in groups. They hung pictures of distinguished men, wreathed in imitation laurel leaves cut from green paper. Chandeliers and side brackets, carved out of cracker-box boards into fantastic shapes, were filled with candles. At either end of the long room, giant logs burned in the fireplaces throwing out a cheerful light.

When General and Libbie Custer stepped through the doors the music began, and the ball was opened by the first sergeant, who strode the whole length of the floor in an evolution of remarkable energy and invention. The cornet and drum faltered now and then as the players watched the general taking Libbie around the floor. He habitually nodded and waved to others inviting them to come on the floor and dance. Soon the laundresses with their partners and all the troopers who could find space danced in pairs following the general's furious example.

The first dance ended, and officers and their wives were escorted to the supper room in the company kitchen. General Custer delighted the ball managers by sitting down and consuming a huge dish of potato salad, well flavored with onions, a rarity on the Dakota plains.

Everyone at Fort Lincoln was fond of the general's wife. Libbie could not do enough for others. She interested herself in the problems and needs of the troopers' wives and children, and when there was anything of a party going on in officers' circles, she could be counted on to perform minor miracles. She had an eye and a hand for decorating and remodeling gowns until they looked like new.

When winter set in and the railroads in Dakota Territory stopped service, young mothers despaired about clothing for their

ABOVE: A social evening at the Custers. Fort Lincoln, 1875.
BELOW: The Custers tenting on the plains, 1868.

growing children. So the ladies at Fort Lincoln organized sewing bees. A roomful of busy women, cutting, basting, marking button-holes, and joining together the garments, soon had passable outfits for the youngsters and perhaps even a gown for the mother.

A rented piano from St. Paul, Minnesota, arrived at Fort Lincoln and troopers manhandled it into the Custers' quarters. From morning until late at night the post heard singing, old war songs, college choruses, Negro spirituals, songs that everybody knew. "The Girl I Left Behind Me" was particularly well liked.

> *Full many a name our banners bore*
> *Of former deeds of daring,*
> *But they were of the days of yore,*
> *In which we had no sharing;*
> *But now our laurels freshly won*
> *With the old ones shall entwin'd be,*
> *Still worthy of our sires each son,*
> *Sweet girl I left behind me.*
>
> *The hope of final victory*
> *Within my bosom burning,*
> *Is mingling with sweet thoughts of thee*
> *And of my fond returning.*
> *But should I ne'er return again,*
> *Still worth thy love thou'lt find me;*
> *Dishonor's breath shall never stain*
> *The name I'll leave behind me.*

Off in the barracks the troopers sang earthier songs.

THADDY O'BRIEN

> AIR: *Ta-ra-ra Boom de ay*
> *Thaddy O'Brien was a sergeant gay,*
> *In the U. S. Cavalry,*
> *The fresh recruit would often say*
> *"I earnestly long to see the day,*
> *When 'neath the sod he's put to stay,*
> *That son-of-a-bitch from Dublin Bay,*
> *That sergeant with the 'suparior' way,*
> *My life's burden every day"*

CHORUS: *Ta-ra-ra Boom de ay,*
                  Ta-ra-ra Boom de ay,
                  Ta-ra-ra Boom de ay,
                  Ta-ra-ra Boom de ay.

Too long were the trousers by a span,
The recruit received from Uncle Sam,
The sergeant bawls as loud as he can,
"Go and let out yer supinders man!"
The hat he drew was much too small,
And failed to stay on his head at all,
"Stretch it ye spalpeen!" Thaddy would call,
"Ye'll niver be a throoper at all!"

As the snows gave way to spring, visiting brass arrived on inspection tours. In 1878 Fort Whipple, Arizona Territory, girded itself for the coming of General William Tecumseh Sherman—with trumpet flourishes and drum ruffles, artillery salutes, and dress review. On the day of his arrival troopers were formed on the parade ground with all arms and equipment, each man standing by the head of his mount. At the gate the officers, mounted, awaited the general and his retinue. They came at a canter. Salutes were exchanged.

Sherman at once swung out of his saddle. He then set off at a brisk walk and soon had his companions puffing and sweating. It was a pace he kept up during the whole inspection.

Standing on the piazza, watching the ceremonies, Ellen Biddle and the other wives had already made up their minds that the general was going to be treated with excellence in all details. It was a matter of pride that on so distant a frontier, they should contrive a reception and dinner that would do credit to any army wife garrisoned in the East. The general would have ice cold soup and fileted brook trout. He would taste a salad of fresh cucumbers and long French lettuce, and discover that these were grown behind the barracks, as was the melon he would have for dessert, with his champagne.

In the evening just before "half after six" officers and their wives and bachelor officers stood in a receiving line. When Ellen Biddle was presented, Sherman beamed and said, "Why, my child,

I knew your father in California in eighteen hundred and fifty, in the stirring times, and if memory serves me right, your brother-in-law Harmony was there also, and I have known them ever since."

"I felt like a queen," Ellen confided later, "(for I was always a hero-worshipper), and never was prouder in my life."

The general was escorted into the dining room where the table was laid. The combined grandeurs of the officer families had yielded crystal, silver, linen, and lace, and the table looked heavy and rich. When the Chinese cook, called "Flang," served the trout, Ellen held her breath lest some nonthinking wife disclose to the general that enlisted men had dynamited the river to assure a sufficient supply. The conversation ran from politics to the military situation and from the general's travels to the latest Washington gossip.

To amuse themselves during the summer months, wives contrived ways to keep cool, played endless games of cards, or rode their horses out onto the plains, sometimes accompanying their husbands' patrols for the first day.

Every Fourth of July the inhabitants of Fort Rice were stung with excitement as they participated in a gigantic celebration. Typically, in late June, 1865, troopers began decorating the fort. Above the main entrance they painted "4th of July, 1776–1865. Peace, Founded, Sustained," and stars of red, white, and blue.

At sunrise on the Fourth the cannon fired a 13-gun salute and at 9:30 the band thundered and the colonel reviewed the troops. In sweltering heat the soldiers listened patiently to the colonel's overlong oration; then dismissed, they romped through the sports program. To the merriment of the onlookers—officers, wives, civilians, and Indians—troopers sweated through wheelbarrow and sack races, competed in shooting contests, demonstrated feats of skill, and raced horses around the fort. The day ended with a mock dress parade to the commissary where the thirsty tossed down glasses of rum punch and got uproariously drunk.

The prospect of a wedding always created a stir among the ladies of a post. Late one summer Fort Lincoln learned of Kate Garrett's betrothal to Lieutenant Francis Gibson, 7th Cavalry, who, with the rest of the regiment, was out on the plains campaigning. White material arrived from the East along with a dress pattern. With Libbie Custer supervising, Kate, her sister Mollie McIntosh, Annie Yates, and Charlotte Moylan started making the

ABOVE, left to right, first row: Lt. Bronson, Lt. Wallace, Gen. Geo. A. Custer, Lt. Benj. Hodgson, Mrs. Gen. Custer, Capt. Yates, Miss Annie Bates (Mrs. Maugham?), Gen. Carlin, Mrs. Lt. McIntosh, Capt. Myles Moylan, Lt. Donald McIntosh; second row: Mrs. Tom McDougall, Mrs. Capt. Yates, Mrs. Lt. Calhoun, Lt. Varnum, Mrs. Myles Moylan, Lt. Calhoun; third row: Capt. Tom McDougall, Capt. Badger, Chas. W. Thompson, son of Capt. Wm. Thompson, Col. Poland, Capt. Tom Custer; fourth row: Capt. Wm. Thompson. At Fort A. Lincoln, Dakota Territory. BELOW: Recruiting poster.

'HO! FOR THE PLAINS!'
RECRUITS WANTED!
50 MEN ARE WANTED

To complete the organization of the body of "Scouts" that are now operating upon the Kansas Frontier.

EVERY MAN TO FURNISH HIS OWN HORSE!

For further particulars enquire for five days at the

ADJUTANT GENERAL'S OFFICE, Topeka, Kan.

Topeka, Kan., June 23d, 1869.

COMMONWEALTH POWER PRESS PRINT, TOPEKA, KANSAS.

wedding gown, Libbie Custer doing the cutting and fitting, Kate the straight sewing, and Mrs. Moylan and Mollie the fancy hemming and ruffling. Once the gown was finished, Mollie made orange blossoms from little tufts of satin, using threads of yellow embroidery silk for centers.

Enlisted men swarmed over Mollie's house, hanging a cotton wedding bell in the window, and stretching white canvas over the floors of the parlor and dining room. A Mexican laundress strung bright-colored cheesecloth draperies. The maid, Iwilla, shuffled in and out of the kitchen complaining, "Miss McIntosh, dat onery army punch ain't got de right punch yet." Army punch known throughout cavalry service was a concoction of tea, whiskey, and citric acid.

On the last day of August the cavalry command pulled into Fort Lincoln, weary and begrimed. Bearded, their faces burned to a dull brown from the summer sun, their campaign hats ruined from the alkali dust, Frank Gibson and Donald McIntosh bounded up the steps of Officers' Row and into the arms of their waiting girls.

Frank proudly showed Kate the wedding gift from the bachelors of the regiment, a check for $50. The women of the post had already presented Kate with handmade lingerie. The faithful Iwilla gave the bride two small towels of unbleached linen embroidered with blue cornflowers. Libbie Custer ran over with a blue garter, "something new and blue," to complete the wedding costume, and Mollie loaned her sister their mother's brooch of moonstones surrounded by pearls and tiny diamonds.

Kate's wedding day dawned bright and clear. Thin high clouds filtered the sun's light until it made no shadows anywhere. No breeze moved.

By noon Mollie, Charlotte Moylan, and Maggie Calhoun were helping Kate into her gown. They could hear the clank of sabers hitting against the bannisters as young officers sprang up the stairs, two at a time, and clattered into the room where Frank was struggling into his regalia. The aroma of venison, prairie chicken, and ham drifted up from the kitchen.

The wedding march began. As Kate walked downstairs with Mollie, she glimpsed the living room, packed with gaily gowned women and officers in full dress uniform. At the foot of the stairs was Lieutenant Donald McIntosh, who gently gave Kate his arm and walked the length of the living room toward the wedding bell and the waiting chaplain. On the right was Lieutenant Francis Gibson, beside him Captain Myles Moylan, his best man.

When the last words were spoken, Custer and Captain Moylan, on each side of the newlyweds, crossed sabers over their heads. Instantly every officer sprang to the same position, while the Gibsons passed beneath the arch of metal. At that moment Kate gloried in the fact that she was "really one with the other army women, and our joys and sorrows would be mutual."

chapter 14.

"From Gary Owen in Glory."

♞ ♞ ♞

ROM THE CANADIAN BORDER TO MEXICO AND FROM THE
Missouri River to the Pacific, the plains, deserts, and mountains felt the fury of Indian attacks. Savages exacted a terrible
toll, swooping down on settlements, inflicting brutal ven-
geance. Scalps dangled from lodge poles. Pale-faced women slaved
in isolated Indian villages. Blackened heaps marked spots where
pioneer homes once stood.

The redman was an incredibly tough opponent, not only because
of his wiles, but because he could exist on the land. Lean, hardened,
needing only few supplies, mounted on the best horses in the world,
the Indian nimbly played hide-and-seek with cavalry detachments.
He possessed outstanding ability to camouflage his presence, to ride
extraordinary distances, to turn and fight at places of his own selec
tion. His hit-and-run attacks were so unpredictable they seemed to
materialize out of the ground. His audacious ambushes were master-
pieces. "The Indians of the plains," remarked a veteran officer,
"are the best skirmishers in the world . . . their ability to hide behind any obstruction in ravines along creeks and under creek and
river banks, and in fighting in the open plains or level ground, the
faculty to disappear is beyond one's belief." The savages, seldom
as well armed or disciplined as the trooper, could not hope to fight
the cavalry successfully in large-scale, prolonged attacks. The hostiles were raiders, skillful in ambush, surprise attack, and dispersal.

Aware of the urgent need for more men to defend the frontier,
Congress in July, 1866, authorized the Army to organize four more
cavalry regiments, the 7th through the 10th. The latter two, the
9th and 10th, were to be composed of Negro enlisted men with
white officers.

General Philip Sheridan was determined to bring peace to the frontier when he rode west in the spring of 1868 to assume command of the Department of Missouri. Poring over official correspondence at his headquarters at Fort Leavenworth, the general was appalled at the enormity of the problem. His command embraced 150,000 square miles of space in Kansas, Colorado, Indian Territory, and New Mexico. To police this area, he had but 2,600 men—1,200 troopers and 1,400 foot soldiers. Eighteen-hundred men were assigned to garrison duty at 26 forts. Against 4,000 Cheyenne, Arapaho, Comanche, Kiowa-Apache, and Wichita, each of whom had from two to ten extra horses, the general could throw a mobile force of only 800.

Drilled in the battle tactics of the Civil War, these soldiers were unprepared to cope with the type of fighting dictated by the enemy. Colonel Ranald S. Mackenzie, one of the greatest Indian fighters of the period, commented: "It differed so greatly from what we old Civil War veterans had seen, and so little was known of it that it proved to be an absolutely new kind of warfare . . . a kind we had never seen or encountered."

From a company point of view, the war in the West seemed to be nothing but a series of patrols, police actions, and campaigns. The majority of encounters with the Indians were hit-and-run brushes and skirmishes. Hundreds of routine, unknown, and forgotten raids took place and in many the casualties were heavy. Cavalry units usually fought dismounted, with every fourth man holding the horses. Few troopers could fire accurately from the back of a speeding horse and, while mounted, were easy targets.

Brooding over wrongs done them, the Cheyenne and Arapaho launched all-out war against settlers during the summer of 1868. Hordes of savages hurtled down upon Kansas and Colorado villages. The shriek of war cries and the thunder of galloping hooves grew in volume. Fierce young warriors, lashing their ponies, vied with each other to be the first to strike. In sixty days kill-crazy riders butchered 117 whites and took seven women prisoners.

"For God's sake," pleaded the acting governor of Colorado, "give me authority to take soldiers from Fort Reynolds. The people are arming and will not be restrained." The governor of Kansas wired that Indians had captured and destroyed a wagon train near Pawnee Fork, scalping and cremating sixteen men. Up and down

the plains the best cavalry in the army pursued in vain. They galloped to the calls for help, only to find that the warriors had murdered and raped and disappeared.

During the summer of 1868, General Sheridan shifted headquarters from Fort Leavenworth to Fort Hays, Kansas, where he
became the very soul and brains of the command. Sheridan was
convinced that the Indian must be taught that murder and rape
and theft did not pay. Punishment must be swift and sure. Moral
persuasion, Sheridan argued, could not always be used with the
redman.

Prior to the Civil War the frontier campaigns had been primarily defensive, the cavalry protecting settlements, keeping peace
among the tribes, and defending the redman against white intrud-
ers. But General Philip Sheridan, in 1868, switched to offensive
strategy—to crush the hostiles' power and force them to submit to
the supervision of the Indian Bureau. At Fort Hays, and on the
trail, he studied the opponent. One unalterable fact dwarfed all
others: the Indian was most vulnerable during the winter when
food and forage were scarce and his ponies were in no condition to
campaign. Discarding the well-worn stratagems of earlier periods,
Sheridan decided upon hitting the heart of Indian country in the
dead of winter when his powerful, well-fed horses could pursue and
overtake the hostiles. He agreed with General William T. Sherman's dictum: "The more we can kill this year, the less we'll have
to kill next year, for the more I see of these Indians the more I
am convinced that they all have to be killed or be maintained as a
species of paupers."

During the fall Little Phil carefully prepared a three-pronged
attack. From Fort Bascom, New Mexico, one column of 3rd Cavalry and two companies of infantry under the command of Colonel
A. W. Evans would march along the Canadian River. From Fort
Lyon, Colorado, seven troops of 5th Cavalry under General Eugene
Carr would move southward toward the Antelope Hills of north-
western Oklahoma. These two commands were to act as beaters,
driving the hostiles toward a third force riding out from Fort Hays
in the direction of the Washita River.

This third outfit, the spearhead of Sheridan's assault plans,
was composed of eleven troops of the 7th Cavalry, a battalion of
infantry, and the 19th Kansas Volunteer Cavalry Regiment. To

command this unit, the general picked a favorite of his from the Shenandoah Valley campaign, George Armstrong Custer.

Officers of the 7th knew Custer's record as they knew their own. Custer had graduated from West Point in 1861 at the foot of his class of thirty-four. During the Civil War, General Pleasonton jumped him to brigadier general and assigned him to a brigade of Michigan volunteers. Rescued from possible obscurity Custer served with distinction at Gettysburg and through the succeeding Virginia and Shenandoah Valley campaigns. But it was in pursuit of Lee's army in April, 1865, that he won his greatest glory.

After the war, the disbanding of the volunteer army stripped Custer of his temporary rank and left him a mere captain in the 5th Cavalry. When the 7th was organized, he was assigned to it with the rank of Lieutenant Colonel and took an active part in the muddled Indian campaign of 1867. That same year he was placed under a year's suspension as a result of a court-martial which convicted him of cruelty and illegal conduct. General Sheridan had now brought him west and placed him in command of the 7th.

At Fort Hays Colonel Custer and his officers drilled the men relentlessly. Troopers trained their horses until they moved with precision and practice-fired their carbines twice daily, working enthusiastically. Custer molded the 7th into a crack cavalry regiment with great *esprit de corps*. He loved martial music and his mounted band usually rode with the troopers into the field. "Garry Owen" became the regimental song.

> *Let Bacchus' sons be not dismayed*
> *But join with me each jovial blade;*
> *Come booze and sing, and lend your aid,*
> To help me with the chorus.

> CHORUS:　*Instead of spa we'll drink down ale,*
> *And pay the reck'ning on the nail;*
> *No man for debt shall go to gaol*
> From Garry Owen in glory.

One day during those months of training, 500 horses arrived from the East and passed in review before Custer's quarters. Among them the colonel spotted a spirited bay which he ordered detained.

Testing him all afternoon, Custer was convinced that the horse would prove equal to the rigors of the march and decided to exercise his option as an officer to buy the mount from the government.

He named the bay *Dandy*. It was well that the horse belonged to the commanding officer for on the trail *Dandy* would brook no horse running ahead of him. Custer found it difficult to keep him beside any other mount—he'd champ at his bit, toss his head, and pull furiously on the rein until the colonel let him stretch his neck in advance of the others.

Many obstructions marred smooth riding on the level-appearing plains. Buffalo wallows were one. Thundering up to these, *Dandy* learned to veer to one side and to leap in and out like a cat. He could clear buffalo trails with a bound, pick his way through prairie-dog villages unguided, and rarely did his hooves sink in subterraneous traps.

On October 4, at Fort Hays, Custer began a series of letters to his wife, Libbie.

> *I breakfasted with Genl. Sheridan and staff. He said "Custer, I rely on you in everything, and shall send you on this expedition without orders, leaving you to act entirely on your own judgment."*

Winter set in earlier than usual on the Kansas plains. Frosts reduced the grass to substanceless provender. No longer could Indian ponies feed. Warriors moved south and set up winter quarters on the banks of the Washita, Indian Territory, near present-day Cheyenne, Oklahoma. Here along the banks of the river, the Cheyenne, Arapaho, Comanche, Kiowa, and Apache encamped in winter quarters.

Sheridan's winter campaign commenced. From Fort Hays Custer and his 7th Cavalry moved to Fort Dodge and, on November 12, headed southward.

> *Yesterday my twelve Osage guides joined me, a splendid set of warriors, headed by a chief, Little Beaver. They are painted and dressed for the warpath, and well-armed with Springfield breech-loading guns. All are superb horsemen. A white woman has come into our camp, four days without food. I suppose her to have been captured by Indians, and rendered insane by their barbarous treatment. . . .*

On the first night out the command pitched camp near Mulberry Creek, where it was joined by 400 supply wagons and five companies of foot soldiers, detailed to establish a supply post further up the line. Before dawn the columns moved out, businesslike, efficient. Up ahead cantered the painted Osage and the buckskin-clad scouts trailed by Custer's advance. Behind them two equal columns of troopers flanked the wagons.

Horses and train rumbled southward, down the valley of the Beaver, to the spot Sheridan had picked for Camp Supply, in the angle formed by Wolf and Bear creeks. Custer calculated he was 105 miles from Fort Dodge, 25 miles from the eastern line of the Texas Panhandle, deep in Indian country. With saw and ax the soldiers attacked the countryside, chopping away the brush. The clearing spread.

General Sheridan rode into Camp Supply on November 22. After consulting with the general, Custer jotted to Libbie:

> . . . I move tomorrow morning with my eleven companies, taking thirty days' rations. I am to go south to the Canadian River, then down the river to Fort Cobb, thence south-east toward the Washita Mountains, then north-west back to this point, my whole march not exceeding 250 miles. The snow is five or six inches deep, and falling rapidly. . . .

At daybreak buglers sounded *Reveille*. Men crept from their tents into a raging blizzard. Twelve inches of snow blanketed the ground. Temperatures plummeted to below zero. *The General* was sounded. Tents tumbled down. Wagons were packed.

Encased in a military greatcoat, Custer trudged toward his orderly who held his horse, already saddled and nervously pawing the snow. For a moment the colonel surveyed the snowy field, then swinging into his saddle, he rode to Sheridan's headquarters.

Custer entered. Sheridan grumbled, "What do you think of this storm?"

"Just what we want. We can move and the Indians cannot. If this snow remains on the ground one week, I promise to bring you satisfactory evidence that we have met the enemy."

With quick, buoyant steps, Custer strode off into the storm where his command waited. He ordered *Mount*, then *Advance*. In that piercing cold the columns snaked out from Camp Supply,

the regimental band striking up "The Girl I Left Behind Me."
It was a march the like of which none of the troopers had ever
experienced before.

Plodding through the blizzard, they marched down the wooded
valley of Wolf Creek. It was slow going. At 2:30 P.M. they dismounted and camped in a protected ravine. Comforted by the
blazing fires, the men cleared away the snow and hoisted their
tents. Beyond, the earth spread away in frozen stillness.

Before dawn Custer's unit crunched forward. For three days
the columns, buffeted by the winds and snow, crept on across the
wasteland. Then, suddenly, the storm was gone. For the first time
in days there was no wind at all. The sun shone. They reached
the treacherous Canadian River, full of quicksand and holes. Here
the colonel detailed Major Joel H. Elliott with three troops to
ride upriver to search for an Indian trail.

Just as the last wagon forded the river, a courier from Elliott
dashed into camp and dismounted. The major had stumbled upon
the trail of a war party, 150 strong, leading due south. The rider
sped off on a fresh horse to tell Elliott to move up the path. The
main column would short cut and intercept him. The supply train,
guarded by eighty men, was to follow at its own pace.

Custer ordered *Advance*. At 9:30 P.M. his outfit joined Elliott's
and, after a brief halt, the horse soldiers in columns of four swung
into motion through the night.

> *. . . I rode, so as to be near as possible in the advance.
> The Cavalry followed, from a quarter to a mile distant, lest
> warning should be given by crunching of the crusted snow.*
>
> *Orders prohibited a word above a whisper, a match struck,
> pipe lighted, great deprivation to a soldier. Thus, silently, mile
> after mile, until it was discovered that the guides had halted,
> were awaiting my arrival. Word was passed back to halt, pend-
> ing enquiries. . . .*

Standing on a small hill, a scout pointed to the valley below.
Custer's eyes searched the darkness. He listened. In all the vastness of the country about him there was no sound. Suddenly,
Custer heard the faint tinkle of a bell. Then the cry of a child
split the night air. Stealthily, Custer and his scout retraced their

steps down the hill. Assembling his officers, the colonel informed them of the situation.

The Cheyenne slept. Double Wolf, the watchman, shivering in the cold, crept up to the lodge fire and fell asleep. Moving Behind, a girl of 14, was up and about, uncertain whether the camp would be shifted that night. The wife of Chief Black Kettle stood in the doorway of her lodge a long time, angry that the Cheyenne were not moving to safer quarters. "I don't like this delay," she said, "we could have moved long ago. The Agent sent word for us to leave at once. It seems we are crazy and deaf, and cannot hear."

It was 1:30 in the morning and bitter cold. A crust had formed on the snow. Osage scouts counseled caution, arguing that Custer did not know the size of the enemy's force. But Custer impetuously went ahead with his plans for an assault.

The soldiers lit no campfires. The guard changed every two hours. Every trooper knew that this was the night before *the day*. The dull cold wrapped and hugged them tight, seeping in under their woolens, slowing their bodies, stiffening but not quite numbing their fingers. Throughout the night little knots of men formed and stood or sat whispering earnestly.

Toward daylight soldiers prepared for the attack. They tightened cinches, buckled belts, checked weapons. Custer snapped out an order. The columns moved forward.

Moving Behind heard a woman whisper: "Wake up! Wake up! White men! White men are here! The soldiers are approaching our camp."

A Cheyenne woman, troubled with rheumatic pains, hobbled outside her hut for firewood. She saw something on the hillside, moving. Soldiers. She struggled back to her quarters, woke the children, and sent them scurrying off toward the river. Afraid to shout lest the enemy hear her and shoot, she followed without making a sound.

A barking dog roused Double Wolf, the sleeping sentry. Rubbing his eyes, he took his rifle and walked to the edge of the frozen river. A woman ran from the timber. "Soldiers!"

Double Wolf stiffened. He heard the unmistakable crunch of hooves puncturing the snow and ice. Behind a fallen tree, a blue-coated man lifted his gun and fired.

Bugles boomed *Charge*. Half-frozen musicians played a few bars of "Garry Owen." By the time the band had played one stanza, their instruments froze up.

The cavalry rushed the village from all sides. Guns exploded. Bedlam broke loose—the high soprano cries of women, the shrill screams of children, the curses of soldiers, the guttural exclamations of infuriated warriors.

In the excitement Black Kettle rushed from his lodge, firing. Troopers saw the great Cheyenne chieftain convulse and jump as bullets thudded through him. A horse ran riderless, tossing his head, turning in random lunges. Officers shouted commands and redeployed their men.

Moving Behind started for the door, but a friend grabbed her. "Don't go out, stay inside; the white men might see you outside, and shoot you."

Frightened but determined to escape, she fled the hut. Outside warriors were running helter-skelter. Moving Behind and her aunt, whom she found amid the chaos, dodged out of the village and hid in the snow-encrusted grass of a hillside. "It frightened us to listen to the noise and the cries of the wounded." When the racket subsided momentarily, Moving Behind raised her head to see what was going on. She shuddered as she saw the disemboweled body of a pregnant friend, dead, on a nearby hill.

From every vantage point Custer's men pumped lead. Several leaped from their horses and battled the savages hand-to-hand. Knives and hatchets slashed into bodies. A young captain, Louis McLane Hamilton, grandson of Alexander Hamilton, riding at the head of his column, turned and yelled, "Now, men, keep cool! Fire low, and not too rapidly."

Seeing Captain Albert Barnitz clasp his stomach in agony, Custer galloped to his side. Shot in the belly, Barnitz was barely

ABOVE: The Indian War—Sheridan on the Move.
BELOW: 7th Cavalry charging Black Kettle's village, November, 1868.

breathing. Thinking himself near death, he muttered a few last words for his family to be delivered by Custer. But Barnitz clung to life and, miraculously, recovered.

Heedless of danger, a teen-age savage saw Captain Frederick Benteen and his men emerge from the forest. He whipped his mount and charged the soldiers. It was weird and somehow insane. Benteen raised his arm in a sign of peace. But the lad spurned surrender, aimed and fired his rifle, once, twice. The third bullet grazed the neck of the captain's horse. Benteen fired. The youth bounced from the back of his galloping horse, and hit the ground with his legs jerking, dead before he struck.

A bugler dismounted and sat down, leaning his shoulders against the wall of a hut. The tufted shaft of an arrow protruded from just above his right eye. He tried to grab it with his two hands until he fainted.

Bloodstained and staggering, seventeen warriors were firing in desperation. Custer's sharpshooters moved forward and fired in unison. None of the seventeen remained on his feet, each had been shot through the forehead.

Two miles farther on, savages hastening to the scene of combat from below Black Kettle's camp, surrounded Major Elliott and his detachment of eighteen men, killed them, and mutilated their bodies.

After a time the roar of rifle fire degenerated into sharp cracks, then ceased altogether. The Cheyenne had turned and were hastening toward the ravines and forest along the banks of the Washita. Just before leaving they shot and killed Mrs. Clara Blinn, a captive from a wagon train, and crushed the skull of her two-year-old child against a tree trunk.

An aging squaw led a white boy toward the forest. Confronted by troopers, she hesitated a moment, her eyes rolling in panic, as she drew a knife and plunged it deep into the child. When he fell, she pounced upon him and ripped open his abdomen. The soldiers stood in frozen disbelief. Then with a kind of frenzied deliberation, they riddled her with bullets.

After the flight of the Cheyenne, Custer reported that the battle had been "real fighting, such as rarely, if ever . . . equalled in Indian warfare." In one ravine alone lay 38 dead savages. In his report the colonel listed 103 warriors slain, but those located later miles from the camp multiplied the number by a third. Osage scouts dragged in 53 women and children as prisoners.

In one part of the village surgeons worked swiftly. Among the wounded was the bugler boy, who had been struck above the eye. With difficulty a surgeon cut the shaft of the arrow and gently pulled out the steel head, leaving a gaping wound.

Visiting the wounded, Custer saw the boy just as the blood gushed out covering his face.

"Did you see the Indian who wounded you?" asked Custer.

Reaching down into his pocket, the lad jerked out an Indian scalp. "If anybody thinks I didn't see him, take a look at that."

Custer's losses, including those of Major Elliott's command, were twenty-two killed; and fourteen wounded.

The sight of the dead and dying and the unspeakable treatment suffered by the corpses had a profound effect on DeBenneville Randolph Keim, correspondent for the *New York Herald*. He accumulated all the details of each and every atrocity.

Major Joel H. Elliott, one bullet hole in left cheek, two bullets in head, throat cut, right foot cut off, left foot almost cut off, calves of legs very much cut, groin ripped open and otherwise mutilated.

Walter Kennedy, sergeant-major, bullet hole in right temple, head partly cut off, seven bullet holes in back, and two in legs.

Harry Mercer, corporal of Company E, bullet hole in right axilla, one in region of heart, three in back, eight arrow wounds in back, right ear cut off, head scalped, and skull fractured, deep gashes in both legs, and throat cut. . . .

William Milligan, company H, bullet hole in left side of head, deep gashes in right leg, left arm deeply gashed, head scalped, throat cut, and otherwise mutilated. . . .

Thomas Downey, company I, arrow hole in region of stomach, throat cut open, head cut off, and right shoulder cut by a tomahawk. . . .

Custer ordered K Troop to destroy all Indian property. Beginning at the upper end of the camp, soldiers ripped down tepees, piled them together on poles, and applied the torch. The fire mounted skyward in swirling towers of smoke and flame. Troopers tossed in all articles of personal property—buffalo robes, blankets, food, rifles, pistols, bows and arrows. One man found a bridal gown, adorned with bead work and elk's teeth. Starting to show it to his lieutenant, the soldier stopped as he passed the roaring fire, hesitated, then chucked it into the blaze.

As the flames consumed the last tepees, Custer ordered K Troop to kill all Indian ponies. The soldiers tried to rope them and cut their throats, but the mounts, panicking at their approach, fought viciously. Weary from battle and the work of destruction, the men called for reinforcements to complete the slaughter of 800 ponies.

On the rise near the village Custer peered through field glasses and saw clearly hundreds of Indian horsemen watching from a far hill. The colonel turned and stared at other occupied hilltops. He was surrounded. Interrogating Chief Black Kettle's sister, Custer learned that this village was only one of several along the banks of the Washita—below were the camps of Little Raven, Black Wolf, and Satanta.

To outwit the savages, Custer led his columns down the banks of the Washita toward the other camps. The watchers dashed off, intent upon protecting their homes. At last the sun slipped down over the western horizon and the afterglow faded into night's darkness. Abruptly the troopers wheeled, returned to the smoldering village of Black Kettle, and moved up the valley.

At 2:00 A.M. the next morning, they halted and ate their scanty rations before huge bonfires. They moved out at daylight, located the supply train by midmorning and, twenty-four hours later, Custer's advance trotted to the top of the hill southwest of Camp Supply. Then suddenly the whole command merged into full view of the garrison, parading diagonally down the slope.

Private James Albert Hadley, 19th Kansas Cavalry recalled:

Though it was thirty-nine years ago, and though most of those gallant fellows have lain in their bloody graves for three decades, I can yet see that striking and dramatic parade as if it were yesterday; men and horses in bold relief against the glittering snow. . . .

At the head of the column was a young man of medium height, slender, wearing buckskin hunting-shirt and leggings much befringed. . . . Across his saddle he carried a long rifle, with which he was expert. This was Custer at the age of twenty-nine. . . . There was nothing in either figure or bearing to indicate the great physical strength and iron nerve that made him one of the most expert shots and horsemen in the world.

First came the Osage scouts, headed by Hard Rope and Little Beaver, in gaudy and barbaric finery, prancing in circles, firing their guns in the air, chanting war songs. Then came the regimental scouts, marching in two platoons, and the band, following, piping "Garry Owen." Escorted by the entire regiment were the prisoners, the widows and orphans of Black Kettle's band. Closely trailing were platoons of sharpshooters and troop after troop, their lines perfectly dressed, intervals properly observed, were marching with precision. The supply train and guard brought up the rear.

General Philip Sheridan tarried in the area until late February, 1869, assuring himself that the Kiowa, Cheyenne, and Arapaho would bow to the government's edicts and remain on their reservations. He counted the Comanche as friendly. Confident that the Indian war was over, Sheridan moved north on February 23. From Fort Hays, correspondent DeBenneville Randolph Keim filed his last report for the New York Herald:

The Indian war has ended. . . . There is not a hostile Indian within the limits of the Missouri Department. The refractory tribes have been entirely subdued.

Despite Keim's optimism, the hostiles continued to plunder and raid, especially the Kiowa. Warfare flared up in the Southwest in the early 1870's and it was not until after the campaigns of Colonel Ranald S. Mackenzie and Colonel Nelson Miles in western Oklahoma and the Texas panhandle that the southwestern Indian menace was eliminated.

When the rough years on the southern plains ended and the Modoc uprising on the California-Oregon border had been quelled, trouble with the Sioux and Cheyenne on the northern plains assumed major proportions. From Fort Fetterman in south-central Wyoming, from Fort Lincoln in Dakota Territory, and from posts in western Montana, army patrols moved out and fought inconclusive actions.

On May 17, 1876 Colonel Custer and his columns of 7th Cavalry trotted out from Fort Lincoln toward their destiny, toward the 25th of June, toward the Little Big Horn.

chapter *15.*

"How many dead men did you find?"

♞ ♞ ♞

After repulsing the 3rd cavalry columns of colo-nel George Crook on the banks of the Rosebud in June, 1876, Chief Crazy Horse of the Oglala Sioux and his medicine man, Sitting Bull, led their people into the river valley of the Little Big Horn. Here with 12,000 people, including 2,500 warriors, they constructed a sprawling village. It was toward this camp that Colonel George Armstrong Custer and his regiment of 7th Cavalry were heading.

Custer was under orders from General Alfred B. Terry, commander of the Department of Dakota, who headed the expedition to which the 7th was attached. If the Sioux trail led to the Little Big Horn, Terry had counseled Custer, the 7th was to pass on and turn south to permit Colonel John Gibbon's infantry command with troops of the 2nd Cavalry to reach the mouth of that river. Terry envisioned the two columns uniting on June 26.

This order was modified by verbal instructions which allowed Custer more leeway. According to General Nelson A. Miles in his *Personal Recollections* these were: "Use your own judgment, and do what you think best if you strike the trail; and whatever you do, Custer, hold on to your wounded."

Stumbling upon the Indians' trail on June 24, Custer and the 7th Regiment followed it up the Rosebud River. After twenty-eight miles they halted and dismounted. Scouts reported more signs of the Sioux.

Testimony given at a Court of Inquiry, which was convened in Chicago, Illinois, several years after the battle of the Little Big Horn, reconstructed the actions which led to the tragedy of June 25, 1876. All the witnesses were attached to other columns of the 7th

Cavalry, which on the day Custer and his detachment fell, also participated in fights with the Sioux in the valley of the Little Big Horn.

The actions of the command on the night of June 24, were recalled by Fred F. Girard, a civilian interpreter:

About 11 o'clock on the evening of the 24, Gen. Custer* sent after me to report to his camp, and I reported; and he gave me my orders to take an Indian by the name of Half-Yellow Face, and an Indian by the name of Bloody Knife, and to ride at the head of the column with him. At half-past 11 or so we pulled out, and got to the head of the column and waited until Gen. Custer came up; and then he reported his orders to me to be sure to have the Indians follow the left-hand trail, no matter how small it might be—he didn't want any of the camps of the Sioux to escape him. He wanted to get them all together and drive them down to the Yellow-stone. I told the Indians what the orders were, and Bloody Knife remarked: "He needn't be so particular about the small camps; we'll get enough when we strike the big camps,"—and the Indians were halted, and I sat there with the General while the Indians were finding the trail. The next conversation came up about the number of Indians we would find the next day, between the General and myself, and he asked me what number of Indians I thought we would have to fight. And I told him I thought it wouldn't be less than twenty-five hundred [corrected later to read "1500–2000"]. . . .

While we were there, Gen. Custer asked those two Indians if he could cross the divide before daylight, and they replied "no." And he asked them if he could cross after daylight without being discovered by the Indians in the bottom, and they said "no."

In response to a question Captain Myles Moylan, 7th Cavalry, replied:

On the night of the 24th the command made a night march, leaving camp about 11 o'clock on the Rosebud river,

---

* Because Colonel Custer had held the temporary rank of brigadier general during the Civil War, his men still referred to him as "general."

or creek, and marched about two and a half hours; and they were bivouacked there without unsaddling, and orders were given for the men to lie down and sleep if possible, and guards posted, I suppose; and if possible to have coffee made for the men in the morning if water could be found. It was supposed we were on the dry fork. It was one of the streams tributary to the Rosebud. . . . It [the command] remained there until about 8 o'clock, and then it moved forward. . . .

The country was rolling. The country marched through was the valley of this dry fork that we had bivouacked on; and on either side, at a distance of half a mile in some places, to a mile and a half in others, were high, broken hills. . . .

Q. About that time, what indications were there of proximity to hostile Indians as far as brought to your knowledge?

A. There was a very fresh trail visible; a trail that had evidently been made but a day or two previous; and while at this second halt at the foot of the divide, between the Little Big Horn and the Rosebud, a sergeant of one of the companies returned on the trail some miles—I don't know exactly how far—for the purpose of recovering, if possible, some clothing of his that had been lost from a pack-mule the night before.

He had gone back several miles I presume, and on going over one of those knolls, over which the command had marched, he saw two or three Indians some four or five hundred yards in front of him, one of them sitting on a box of hard bread examining the contents of a bag, the contents of which I don't know. He thought that his duty was to return at once to the command and report it, and he did so. . . .

Realizing his trail was discovered and that he'd lost the advantage of surprise, Custer decided to go after the savages. The detachment climbed to the top of the divide.

Girard, the interpreter, testified concerning signs of Indians:

. . . I rode up a little knoll near where there was a lodge with some dead Indians in it; and from this knoll I could see the town, the Indian tepees, and ponies. I turned my horse sideways, and took off my hat and waved it, and then I hal-

looed to Gen. Custer: "Here are your Indians, running like
devils!" And I rode down from that knoll and joined Gen.
Custer, and he was still marching on.

Q. Describe this knoll or the place you rode up to Gen. Custer
and communicated that to him. . . .

A. It was where there were some lodges standing, with some dead
Indians in them. . . . I rode up to the right of this lodge where
the dead Indians were. It was not on the Little Big Horn, but on
one of the tributaries that empties into the Little Big Horn.

On the witness stand Captain Frederick W. Benteen recalled:

I think at the first halt, an orderly came to me with instructions for the officers to assemble at a point where he
[Custer] was, for an officer's call. No bugle was sounded for
officers' call: an orderly was sent to get them together. General Custer told us that he had just come down from the
mountain; that he had been told by the Scouts that they could
see a village, ponies, tepees and smoke. He gave it to us as
his belief that they were mistaken; that there were no Indians
there; that he had looked through his glass and could not see
any, and did not think there were any there.
Other instructions were given. . . . I had the advance.
We moved then probably 8 miles and halted in a kind of
valley surrounded by high hills. . . .

Custer divided his force into four detachments. Captain Benteen with three troops was to move far to the left to circle the
southern end of the valley; Captain Thomas M. McDougall with
one troop was to follow them with the pack train. Colonel Custer
and Major Marcus A. Reno would continue their march together
until they reached the valley of the Little Big Horn.

Captain Benteen declared:

My orders were to proceed out into a line of bluffs about
4 or 5 miles away, to pitch into anything I came across and
to send back word to General Custer at once if I came across
anything. I had gone about a mile when I received instructions

through the Chief Trumpeter of the regiment;—if I found nothing before reaching the first line of bluffs, to go on to the second line with the same instructions. I had gone, I suppose, a mile further, when I received orders through the Sergeant Maj. of the regiment, that if I saw nothing from the second line of bluffs, then to go into the valley; and if there was nothing in the valley to go on to the next valley. . . .

The ground was very rugged and we had to go through defiles and around high bluffs to get to the point to which I had been sent. I went to the second line of bluffs and saw no valley; and I knew the Indians had too much sense to go to any place over such a country; that if they had to go to any point in that direction, they had a much better way to go. . . .

As Benteen's troops and Captain McDougall's pack train moved out, the columns of Custer and Reno rode together until they reached the valley. Here they separated, Custer riding to the northwest with five troops; Reno marching straight down the valley with three troops and the scouts. Reno was to destroy the head of the Sioux camp near the mouth of the river, while Custer was to cross the high ground to the right to strike the lower end.

Girard responded to more questions:

Q. Did you hear any conversation between Maj. Reno and Gen. Custer, or any orders that were given by Gen. Custer, or through his adjutant [William W. Cooke]?

A. The General hallooed over to Maj. Reno, and beckoned to him with his finger, and the Major rode over, and he told Maj. Reno: "You will take your battalion and try to overtake and bring them to battle, and I will support you." And as the Major was going off he said: "And take the scouts along with you." He gave him orders to take the scouts along, and that is how I heard it.

Q. Then where did you go?

A. I joined Maj. Reno. . . .

Q. State how far this occurred from the place where you crossed the Little Big Horn river.

A. I should say a mile from the Little Big Horn to where the

215

orders were given to Maj. Reno. I didn't measure any of these distances, so I have to guess at it. . . .

Q. *State what directions the columns took . . . so far as you saw and know about the two, before Maj. Reno crossed the river with his command.*

A. My impression is that we were traveling due north from where we separated from Gen. Custer's command, following an old Indian trail; and we came to a little knoll, and the road went around it; and as we went around this little knoll we lost sight of Gen. Custer's command. I should say that was about a mile from where we separated. . . .

Q. *State whether or not you saw anyone before crossing the river, of Gen. Custer's column, after that; and state how it occurred.*

A. Yes, sir: I saw Col. Cooke [Custer's adjutant] and spoke to him, when we got to this knoll. The scouts were to my left, and called my attention to the fact that all the Indians were coming up the valley. I called Maj. Reno's attention to the fact that the Indians were all coming up the valley. I halted there a little time; I thought it was of importance enough that Gen. Custer should know it, and I rode back toward Custer's command. At this knoll I met Col. Cooke, and he asked me where I was going. I told him I had come back to report to him that the Indians were coming up the valley to meet us, and he says, "All right; I'll go back and report." And he wheeled around and went toward [Gen. Custer's command]. . . .

Reno's troops rode on into the valley, heading toward the Little Big Horn River and the Sioux and Cheyenne. Without warning the Indians struck. Reno's left flank crumpled before the mass of screeching, fast-firing savages. Quickly deciding to make a stand, the major ordered his men to dismount and form a solid line. The Indian attack gained momentum. With his soldiers falling all around him, Reno ordered *Mount* and retreated. The warriors closed in. The retreat became a rout. Those soldiers who were not cut down, struggled across the river and reached the bluffs on the other side. Casualties, killed, wounded, and missing, totaled 55 men out of 112—roughly 50 percent of Reno's command.

At the Court of Inquiry, Captain Myles Moylan, who rode with Reno and commanded A Troop, described the action:

After Maj. Reno's battalion had moved forward or separated from Gen. Custer's column, the command "Trot!" was given. His battalion took the trot and moved forward in column of fours down the valley of this tributary to the Little Big Horn, for some three or three and a half miles, reaching the Little Big Horn and crossing it. A slight pause was there made to allow the companies to close up after crossing the stream. When all were closed up, they moved forward again at a trot, the head of the column moving at a very fast trot, so that the two rear companies were galloping. They moved probably a third of a mile, when the companies were formed in line, before the . . . [advance] was made, on a little high ground on that side of the river.

An immense cloud of dust was seen down the valley, and a little opening in it occasionally, where we could see figures moving through it. After the line was formed, the command moved again in line, and the dust seemed to recede before the command until it passed over probably a mile futher, when it stopped. Then we could see Indians coming out of this dust mounted. They were so numerous that I suppose Maj. Reno thought it was more force than he could probably attack mounted; consequently he dismounted his command. At that time . . . the command was given to halt and dismount to fight on foot.

The companies were dismounted and the horse-holders ordered to take the horses into the timber for their better protection, and the dismounted portion of the companies deployed as skirmishers, company G on the right, my company to the centre, and M company on the left.

In about ten minutes after, I understood that Maj. Reno got information that the Indians were turning his right—that is, coming up the left bank of the river, and threatening his horses. The greater part of G company was withdrawn from the line and taken into the woods, so that it left an open space between the right of my company and the timber. I extended in on the right in order to cover that.

217

We remained there thirty minutes or longer—probably twenty-five or thirty minutes; and during this time there had been very heavy firing going on; in fact, the firing had commenced on the part of the Indians before we dismounted. We fired from our side, however, some; but after the skirmish line had been deployed, the firing was quite heavy on both sides; in fact, very heavy.

The Indians seemed to be withdrawing slightly from our front, and passing around the left flank of the line, some passing between the foot hills and some beyond the foot hills. Maj. Reno at that time was in the bottom superintending the movement of G company that he had taken down there. Fearing that these Indians were turning the left of his line and would close in from the left so as to necessarily cause a change of front on a portion of the front of the line, at least, I went to the edge of the hill and called to him to come up there and look at the situation of affairs himself, so that he might see how the thing was going.

He came in there and took in the situation, and ordered the line to be withdrawn. That movement was executed on the part of my company by a flank movement to the right, and the same movement on the part of M company. . . .

The order was then given to mount up the companies. The companies were mounted up, and, being unable to form in any order in the timber, I gave my men orders to mount up as rapidly as possible individually, and move up out of the timber in order that they might be formed out there. When about one-half of my company was mounted up, I went up out of the timber and formed the men in column of fours as they came up. M company came up very soon after and formed on my left at an interval of fifteen or twenty yards. G company, as I understood, did not mount quite so soon or did not get up quite so soon as the other two companies; but they were in the column before it reached the river.

During the time the companies were being formed, Maj. Reno was there on his horse overlooking the formation of the companies. He asked me as to my opinion as to the point we had better retreat to, as it became evident to him that our movement would be entirely on the defensive. It must necessarily be, owing to the force of Indians then in sight and coming down. I have almost forgotten what reply I made, but at any rate, he designated a point across the river at some high hills where we would go to and establish there, if possible, and await further developments.

I don't know what his intentions were. In a few moments he gave the order to move forward, and the command moved forward at a trot and then at a gallop. After the command was in motion at a gallop, the heads of the companies were almost on a line; the Indians closed in very close on the outer flank, and on the inner flank toward the timber—very close also, as there were a number of Indians in the timber; in fact, I know there were a great many Indians in there.

While the men were mounting up, one of my men was wounded just after mounting his horse, by a shot fired by an Indian who was between us and the river, in the woods. . . . A good many men had been wounded, and some killed, while the company was in motion. . . . When I reached the river myself, I found the river full of horses and men. There was no regular ford there, where they attempted to cross. They simply moved on the trail and into the river, and got onto the other side. . . .

While Major Reno's detachment fought in the valley, Custer's columns were searching in a different direction for the Sioux. John Martini*, H Company, who was Custer's trumpeter, gave testimony:

Q.   Tell how fast General Custer's column then went [after Major Reno had departed and after Custer had watered his horses at a little creek].

A.   General Custer left that water place and went about 300 yards in a straight line; then after that he turned to the right a little more and travelled that way for four or five hundred yards; then there was a kind of a big bend on the hill—he turned these hills and went on top of the ridge.

All at once we looked on the bottom and saw the Indian village; at the same time we could see only children and dogs and ponies around the village: no Indians at all. General Custer ap-

---

* Giovanni Martini (John Martin).

peared to be glad to see the village in that shape, and supposed the Indians were asleep in their tepees. . . .

After General Custer saw the village with no Indians in it, I suppose he was glad, and he pulled off his hat and gave a cheer and said, "Courage boys; we will get them, and as soon as we get through, we will go back to our station. . . ."

General Custer turned and called his Adjutant and gave him instructions to write a despatch to Capt. Benteen. I don't know what it was. Then the Adjutant called me. I was right at the rear of the General. He said, "Orderly, I want you to take this despatch to Capt. Benteen and go as fast as you can." He also told me if I had time and there was no danger in coming back to do so, but if there was danger or there were any Indians in the way, not to come back, but to remain with my company. My company was with Capt. Benteen, and report to him when I came down there.

Q. Tell what you did then—where you went and how fast.

A. My horse was kinder tired, but I went through as fast as he could go. The Adjutant told me to follow the same trail we came down. . . .

Q. Tell what you saw going back.

A. After I started from Gen. Custer to go back, I travelled 5 to 600 yards perhaps ¾ of a mile. I got on the same ridge where General Custer saw the village the first time. On going back over that ridge I looked down into the bottom, and I saw Major Reno's battalion was engaged. I paid no further attention to it, but went forward on my business. Then I went on to the edge of the stream and about 3 or 400 yards above the creek where we watered our horses, I met Capt. Benteen. . . .

I delivered my despatch and told him what . . . Cooke had told me—not to go back if there was any danger and to report to him when my company joined General Custer's command. Then Capt. Benteen took the despatch, read it and put it in his pocket, and gave me an order to take to Capt. McDougall to bring up the pack train and keep it well up.

Q. Did you say anything to Capt. Benteen about what you had seen in the bottom?

A. Capt. Benteen asked me where General Custer was. I said I supposed that by that time he had made a charge through the village, and that was all I said.

Captain Benteen's column rode over the rise from the east. They had seen no Sioux. The note delivered by Trumpeter Martini indicated that Custer was engaging the savages and needed ammunition. But where was Custer? Benteen was at a loss.

Under questioning at the Court of Inquiry, Captain Benteen declared:

. . . I met trumpeter Martini who brought a written order which I have.

Q. *What was that order?*

A. It has no date. It says: "Benteen, come on—big village—be quick, bring packs—P.S. Bring packs. W. W. Cooke." . . . After giving me that note I asked him about this village. He said the Indians were all skedaddling, therefore there was less necessity for me going back for the packs. . . .

At the time I received the order from Trumpeter Martini, I was riding 4 to 500 yards in advance of the battalion, accompanied by my orderly. Col. Weir [Capt. Thomas B.] was probably 200 yards in my rear. I waited till he came up and handed him the note. I asked him no questions nor did he volunteer any advice. When the command came up near enough to me, I ordered a trot. I went on ahead of it to the crossing of the Little Big Horn river at the ford; that was my first sight of the Little Big Horn. There I saw an engagement going on and I supposed it was the whole regiment.

There were twelve or thirteen men in skirmish line that appeared to have been beaten back. The line was then parallel with the river and the Indians were charging and re-charging through those men. I thought the whole command was thrashed and that was not a good place to cross.

To my right I noticed 3 or 4 Indians, probably 4 or 500 yards from me. I thought they were hostiles and rode with my orderly towards them and saw as I approached them, that they were Crows. They said there was a big "pooh poohing" going on, which I had already seen. Then I saw the men who were up on the bluff, and I immediately went there and was met by Maj. Reno [about 3 p.m.]. . . .

Q. State how long after you joined him on the hill was it that the pack train or any part of it arrived.

A. I should think it was an hour and a quarter. . . .

Q. State whether or not you stated to Maj. Reno the purport of the order you have received from Adjutant Cooke.

A. Yes, sir. I showed him the order. . . . I asked him if he knew where General Custer was. He said he did not; that he had been sent in to charge those Indians on the plain, and that General Custer's instructions to him, through Adjutant Cooke, were that he would support him with the whole outfit; and that was the last he had seen or heard of him, and did not know where he was. . . .

Q. From the order which you had received through Trumpeter Martini, or from any other information you had received, had you at that time any knowledge or impression where General Custer was, or on which side of the river?

A. No sir. My impressions from Trumpeter Martini were that the Indians were skedaddling. But my first sight of the fight showed that there was no skedaddling being done by the Indians and I, of course, thought that was the whole command; and, if it was the whole command, that it was whipped.

Q. Upon reaching Maj. Reno's position and finding that it was not the whole command, state what your impression was as to where General Custer must have gone.

A. I supposed he was down the river.

Q. Did you or not so state to Maj. Reno at the time of your conversation?

A. I don't remember having stated to him anything about it. He should have known more about General Custer than I could, as I had been started off some 12 or 15 miles back. It did not occur to me but that he knew more about it than I did. . . .

Q. *Did you at the time express anything of the kind [solicitude or uneasiness], asking him [Reno] for authority to proceed to make a divertion in that direction?*

A. Not at all; I supposed General Custer was able to take care of himself.

Lieutenant Charles A. Varnum, 7th Cavalry, who commanded a detachment of scouts, was on the bluff with Captain Benteen and Major Reno. He described his feelings about the fate of General Custer:

> I was thinking: "Has he got in the same fix we are in? What has become of him? Has he been thrown off?" But the idea of the command being cut up and wiped out as it was, I didn't think of such a thing. I don't know as there was any such feeling as that. It was: "What in the world has become of him? Has he been corraled as we are? Has he been thrown off toward the mouth of the river where Gen. Terry's command is?" I can't describe exactly what I felt. There was no feeling that he had been completely used up the way he was. I know I had no such feeling. . . . My impression was that he had been thrown off so he would connect with Gen. Terry's command, he being on the side of the village toward that command, I knowing that command was coming up. . . .

On that bluff near the Little Big Horn, Reno's force, more concerned with its own fate than Custer's, dug in. Suddenly, as if by signal, the Sioux turned and raced toward the northwest. From that direction the major's troopers heard gunfire. For Custer and his men, the end had come. It is a story no soldier lived to tell.

As suddenly as they had left the battle scene near Reno's command, the hard-riding Indians reappeared to renew the action. Savage and trooper fought that night and into the next day. Charge after charge was hurled back by the horse soldiers. In the late afternoon of June 26, the redmen withdrew, gathered up their women and children from the village, and rode off igniting the prairie grass behind them.

The next morning General Alfred B. Terry and Colonel John

Gibbons' columns arrived. Searching the terrain, their scouts fell upon Custer's battlefield.

Lieutenant George D. Wallace, G. Company, testified:

> In compliance with orders of Maj. Reno, I mounted my horse and rode down across the ford where we had retreated, and met Gen. Terry beyond the point where our skirmish line had fallen back. I reported to him that I had been sent out by Maj. Reno to show him the approaches to his position. He then asked me who were there. I told him Maj. Reno and seven companies, and he went on to ask me in detail what had occurred; how the fight had commenced, and the result. When I got time I then asked him where Gen. Custer was, and received a reply that gave me to understand that they had all been killed. . . .

Q. Did you go over the country between the position that Reno held, and where Custer and his men were found?

A. Yes, sir. I went over it on the 28th of June. . . .

Q. How many dead men did you find?

A. That I am unable to state. The way they were buried was the companies were formed in columns of fours and moved in parallel columns, and each company as it moved along would bring the dead it found, and after they had completed this duty the number that each company commander had buried was reported to me, and from that the sum total was made up.

Q. You could not tell from your own knowledge?

A. No, sir. . . .

Q. Where was the company under Capt. [James] Calhoun found?

A. That was found on top of the last ridge; not the one on which Gen. Custer was killed, but the one that ran at right angles to it. . . .

Q. Did Capt. Calhoun's men, from the position in which they were found lying, indicate that the line had been drawn up in order of battle?

A. There was some indications of a skirmish line.

Q. Had you seen before you reached that point any indications of a skirmish line?

A. None. I afterward saw in the ravine some men lying in skirmish order, but they were at the bottom of a deep ravine, and I don't know how it was.

Q. What company were they members of?

A. Of "E" Company—Lieut. Smith.

Q. After leaving Calhoun's then whose did you find?

A. Capt. [Myles] Keogh's.

Q. In what order were they?

A. They were lying half way down the northern side of the slope.

Q. Between Custer and Calhoun?

A. Between Custer and Calhoun, but half way down the slope, and they appeared to me to have been killed running in file.

Q. Was their position such that it indicated that they had been brought into skirmish line?

A. I don't know whether they were in skirmish line or not. They were killed at intervals, but, from their position, I don't think they could have been in skirmish line.

Q. How far from Calhoun's men were those men found?

A. Between Custer and Calhoun's men.

Q. At what distance?

A. The first was probably not more than twenty or thirty yards, and they were killed at intervals.

Q. They were scattered along?

A. Yes, sir; as they went toward Custer.

Q. After you passed Capt. Keogh's men where did you next find dead men?

A. His men occupied the most of the ground well on toward Custer. . . .

Q. Where was Custer?

A. He was near that point marked "E" on the map.

Q. In what position were those men found about Custer?

A. They were right around. Four or five of them were piled up in a heap beside a horse, and the body of Gen. Custer was lying rather across one of the men.

Q. Were there any indications of a prolonged struggle?

A. They had struggled, but I do not think for any great length of time. They had apparently tried to lead the horses in a circle on the point of the ridge, and had killed them there, and apparently made an effort for a final stand.

Q. How many men were gathered about Gen. Custer?

A. Well, there were about twenty or thirty, but not right around.

Q. Where did you find the men of the other companies?

A. They were scattered all over the hill, south and east of Gen. Custer. . . .

Q. With respect to cartridge shells, did you find any?

A. At one or two places I saw little piles of twenty-five or thirty.

Q. Where was this?

A. They were near where Capt. Calhoun was killed.

Q. Did you find any elsewhere?

A. A very few. You would find them scattered around, but whether they had been used by the men or the Indians we could not tell.

Q. Now judging by the number of cartridges at the position in which you found these men separated from each other, and at irregular intervals, did you think that the struggle with Gen. Custer and his command against the Indians lasted any considerable length of time?

A. No, sir. I think the Indians met him as he came down to this supposed crossing, and did not give him time to make a stand.

Q. What was the character of the country for the purposes of protection—was it such as would enable him to make a prolonged resistance?

A. No; his position was on a ridge. There was no way of his protecting himself. If he got behind the ridge to defend himself at one point he would expose himself at some other point. The land was a series of hills, and there were one or two points a little higher than the point he held. There were no possible means of sheltering himself on the ridge he occupied.

Q. Judging from the number of empty cartridges, and from the character of the ground on which these men fell, and from the position they occupied toward each other, what do you think was the duration of that fight?

A. Not much more than half an hour. . . .

Immediately following the Little Big Horn, the actions of Major Marcus Reno were severely criticized. The Court of Inquiry, held at the major's request, found that "while subordinates, in some instances, did more for the safety of the command than did Major Reno, there was nothing in his conduct that requires animadversion." Yet the shadow of the Little Big Horn continued to haunt Reno for the rest of his life. He was unequal to the burden and was twice court-martialed for conduct unbecoming an officer and was finally cashiered.

Custer's actions were censured. Even his friend and commander, General Philip Sheridan, remarked: "Had the 7th Cavalry been kept together, it is my belief it would have been able to handle the Indians at the Little Big Horn and under any circumstances it could have at least defended itself; but separated as it was into three detachments, the Indians had largely the advantage, in addition to their overwhelming numbers."

President Ulysses S. Grant wrote:

> I regard Custer's massacre as a sacrifice of troops, brought on by himself, that was wholly unnecessary. He was not to have made the attack but effect the juncture with Terry and Gibbon. He was notified to meet them on the 26th, but instead of marching slowly as his orders required in order to effect the junction on the 26th, he entered a forced march of

eighty-three miles in twenty-four hours, and thus had to meet the Indians alone on the 25th.

The victory in the valley of the Little Big Horn marked the beginning of the end for the Sioux and Cheyenne. A year after the battle soldiers defeated the hostiles in a series of sharp actions and pushed them back to the reservations.

In the same year, 1877, war raged in eastern Idaho. Fighting indecisive engagements with the Nez Percé, troops failed to stop their retreat until finally, 5th Infantrymen, mounted, and units of the 7th Cavalry besieged the hostiles' camp and, on October 5, received Chief Joseph's surrender.

In 1878 soldiers tracked the Bannock of Idaho through mountain passes and defeated them on the banks of Clark's Fort River in southwestern Montana.

In Colorado the cavalry intervened in a sporadic frontier war waged by the settlers and Ute Indians. This conflict was finally ended through the mediation of peaceful chiefs.

chapter 16.

"I could cry, Mame, if it would do any good."

🐴 🐴 🐴

ONFLICT FLARED ANEW IN THE SOUTHWEST WHEN THE
Apache hit the warpath in 1882. They fell upon ranches
and farms in Arizona and New Mexico. The federal government sent General George Crook to the Southwest. Crook
knew the Apache better than any officer in the Army's higher
echelons nor was his knowledge restricted to the Apache alone.
After the Civil War, Crook had served continuously in the West,
most of the time opposing those who thwarted the advance of
civilization. Sioux, Cheyenne, Blackfoot, Crow, Ute, and Apache
knew him, feared and respected him. In the 1870's he had beaten
the Apache and brought peace to the southwestern frontier before
being transferred north on the eve of the Sioux-Cheyenne outbreak
of 1876.

Returning to Arizona Territory in the summer of 1882, General Crook discovered that the prospect of permanent peace with
the Apache was unpromising. Detachments of 3rd and 5th Cavalry
already had encountered the hostiles. Saddling up his old mule,
Apache, Crook rode toward the mountains to investigate first hand.

Apacheland was a vast desert wilderness dominated by mountains. They were the cruelest, most inhospitable peaks in the nation.
Crook did not underestimate his adversary: "It is not to be denied
that the Apache is the fiercest and most formidable of all our Indians, when upon the warpath. Opinion may differ as to the place
in the scale of intelligence the Apache should occupy, but there
is no diversity of sentiment, at least not among army officers, as to
the skill and cunning with which this Indian conducts all warlike
operations."

Astride *Apache* Crook moved into the mountains. He found

Alchise and Pedro, old loyal friends. "What I want," explained the general, "is to get at all that has happened since I left here to bring about this trouble, this present condition of affairs. I want you to tell the truth without fear, and to tell it in as few words as possible."

Alchise replied: "When you left, there were no bad Indians out. We were all content; everything was peace. The officers you had here were all taken away, and new ones came in—a different kind. The good ones must all have been taken away and the bad ones sent in their places. We couldn't make out what they wanted; one day they seemed to want one thing, the next day something else. Perhaps we were to blame, perhaps they were; but, anyhow, we hadn't any confidence in them."

Old deaf Pedro told Crook: "When you were here, whenever you said a thing we knew it was true, and we kept it in our minds. . . . I used to be happy; now, I am all the time thinking and crying."

After listening to their complaints, Crook set off for Fort Whipple. Here in October, 1882, he outlined his policy. He banished squatters and unauthorized miners from the Indian lands. Coaxing and cajoling, he lured group after group of Apache back to the reservation.

But a menacing new leader had emerged, Geronimo. Cunning, bloodthirsty, cruel, this Apache was neither a chief nor a subchief. By sheer determination and brains, he had clawed his way to the leadership of about one-fifth of the braves. His raging hatred of all whites dated from an episode in the 1850's when the Mexican governor of Sonora and a band of cutthroats had slaughtered scores of Apache women and children, including Geronimo's mother, wife, and three children.

When Crook took command, Geronimo and his lieutenants were leading a nomadic existence south of the border in Mexico. Without provocation on March 24, 1883, Chato and twenty-five braves crossed the boundary to make a wild and gory raid. They shot white settlers, scalped Judge J. C. McComas and his wife, and kidnapped their little boy, Charlie. Quickly, Chato and his band slipped back into Mexico.

Crook moved swiftly. Patrols scoured the country in every direction, hoping by luck to intercept, retard, or even destroy the

ABOVE: General
W. T. Sherman's
Grimsley saddle, side view.
BELOW: U.S. Army Cavalry
boots 1880's.

raiders. To surprise the elusive Apache by direct pursuit was hopeless, although the trail that Chato had made crossing over from Mexico could be followed back by the troopers.

A new American-Mexican treaty allowed soldiers to cross the border. General Crook himself led a contingent of cavalry and a battalion of Apache scouts, commanded by Captain Emmett Crawford, 3rd Cavalry, into Mexico on May 1, 1883.

They moved through a desert dotted with the ruins of abandoned *rancherias*, burned to the ground by Apache. Every classic outrage was represented. After tours of these grisly exhibits, Crook and his men gave what little dignity and final order they could to the corpses. The bottomlands of the San Bernardino, once heavy with crops of wheat, were blanketed with a jungle of semitropical vegetation. Dense canebrakes choked the river banks.

On May 8, the expeditioners traveled into the Sierra Madre Mountains, which dominated that portion of Mexico. From the general altitude of 3,000 to 4,000 feet, the mountains swept upward to heights of 10,000 to 12,000 feet. Canyon walls towered. Pack mules slipped and fell over precipices. Temperatures varied in extremes—bake-oven by day, icebox by night. Signs of Apache depredations multiplied—butchered ponies and cattle in every stage of mutilation, and odds and ends plundered from Americans and Mexicans.

Up the face of the mountain the command toiled. High in the Sierra Madre, Crawford and his scouts surprised and destroyed an Apache village. Then suddenly—incredibly—Chato and 260 hostiles walked into camp and capitulated. Geronimo, Natchez, Loco, and others came in to surrender. Only Juh and a handful of warriors failed to give themselves up.

Around the campfire General Crook agreed to turn back for Arizona with the women and children. The braves promised to follow with their cattle and horses. On June 23, Crook's dusty columns loped into San Carlos reservation with 52 warriors and 273 women and children.

Fearful settlers refused to believe that Geronimo and Natchez would surrender peacefully. Anxious days followed until one afternoon Natchez and forty men trotted across the border. Six weeks later Geronimo himself, pushing a gigantic herd of cattle, moved into Arizona.

The Apache remained at peace for two years. They worked their ranches and raised thousands of pounds of corn, beans, and wheat to sell to the Quartermaster Department. But in Apacheland Indian agent and soldier fell to quarreling. Apache heard the bickerings and when their friend, Captain Crawford, lost an argument with an agent, they became suspicious.

Geronimo and the fighting chiefs bolted the reservation. Telegraphs hummed. "19 May 1885. About fifty Apaches under Geronimo left reservation about dark on Sunday and are thought to be making for Mexico."

Across the Southwest farmers and ranchers were filled with terror. Troops poured out from Camp Apache, Camp Bowie, Fort Grant, and other posts. Surprising a camp of horse soldiers, the renegades gunned down a sergeant and two privates, stole the horses, and set the tents aflame. The savages broke down the doors of a small ranchhouse and killed the wife. In the Hoya Mountains, American scouts retaliated by bushwhacking a band of redskins. Another patrol murdered a squaw and child. Apache killed seventy-three settlers and soldiers before reaching the border.

To General Crook and his men, it was painfully evident that the cavalry could not catch the swift-riding Apache.

As one officer said:

> Here is an enemy with a thousand miles of hilly and sandy country to run over, and each brave provided with from three to five ponies trained like dogs. They carry almost nothing but arms and ammunition; they can live on cactus; they can go more than forty-eight hours without water; they know every water-hole and every foot of ground in this vast extent of country; they have incredible powers of endurance; they run in small bands, scattering at the first indications of pursuit. . . .
>
> It is no exaggeration to say that these fiends can travel, week in and week out, at the rate of seventy miles a day, and this over the most barren and desolate country imaginable. One week of such work will kill the average soldier and his horse; the Apache thrives on it.

General Crook pursued the only possible course. He dispatched patrols to guard every mountain pass and every water hole, and organized two battalions of Indian scouts. One outfit—100 Apache and a cavalry troop accomplished little. The other detachment, consisting mostly of Indian warriors under Captain Emmett Crawford was successful.

Inside Fort Bowie those interested turned out to view the departure of Crawford and his scouts. Small groups of horse soldiers, most of them of the 3rd, stood at the edge of the parade. Curiosity had routed a number of infantry from their bunks. Officers including General Philip Sheridan fixed their eyes upon the mounted men in the center of the parade. Captain Crawford climbed into his saddle and gave the hand signal. The column headed out the main gate.

Deep into Mexico Crawford and his scouts rode. On December 22, they pulled into Huasabas in the valley of the Bavispe. Here word-of-mouth reports indicated that the Apache were murdering Mexicans far to the south. The command, winding through the mountains, finally arrived at a point sixteen miles south of Nacori, where Crawford sent two pack trains back to New Mexico for supplies.

With the toughest part of the journey ahead, Crawford decided to leave the weaker members of the expedition behind. Seventy-nine men with twelve days' rations trudged out on foot and labored up the high hills. The trail was only six days old.

Dusk was settling in the canyons on January 9, 1886, as Noche, the Indian sergeant, dispatched a courier back to Crawford with the message that the Apache camp was twelve miles ahead. Halting his men for a brief respite, the captain called his officers together. They decided to march all night and attack at daylight.

"I cannot easily forget that night's march," recalled an officer, "All night we toiled on, feeling our way. It was dark and moonless. For much of the distance the way led over solid rock, over mountains, down cañons so dark they seemed bottomless. It was a wonder the scouts could find the trail. Sometimes the descent became so steep that they could not go forward, but would have to wearily climb back and find another way."

Daylight. Crawford carefully adjusted his field glasses on the hostiles' camp. Noiselessly, the men nudged forward. A burro brayed in the distance. Apache hurried to investigate. Suddenly alerted, their rifles flamed. Reports echoed and reechoed. Americans watched them descending the mountain side, disappearing below. Although Crawford's scouts stormed the village, their quarry had melted away.

A squaw made her way back to camp, bringing a message from Geronimo. The hostiles wanted to talk. Surprised and delighted, Captain Crawford sent back word that he'd meet the chief the next day.

Early on January 11, a patrol of Mexican soldiers, hunting the Apache, rode through Crawford's outposts. Suspecting the Indian scouts to be hostiles, they opened fire and wounded three. Crawford and Lieutenant Marion Maus raced up. Maus, who spoke Spanish, explained the situation. Major Corredor, commanding the Mexicans, glanced at the troopers and scouts in the rocks above. He could hear the snap of breechlocks as cartridges were inserted.

Crawford yelled: "For God's sake, don't let them fire!"

Corredor pleaded: "No tiras!" (Don't fire)

Somewhere a rifle cracked. Captain Crawford stumbled forward a few steps, then collapsed in the dirt. Instantly, there was a deafening stutter of reports from the American line. Maus saw a Mexican in midstep topple forward. Mexican lieutenant Juan de la Cruz fell as he ran, pierced by thirteen bullets. Two others trying to reach cover never made it.

Maus sprang forward. Bullets squealed in every direction. He flopped on the ground, prostrate. A spray of dirt stung his face. He crawled toward Crawford and found him behind a boulder, stretched out on the ground, coughing, clutching a blood-smeared handkerchief.

Outnumbered by the Mexicans, Lieutenant Maus chose to retreat. With the unconscious Crawford on a litter, the Americans marched northward. That night Maus met with Geronimo outside of camp. Listening patiently to his grievances, Maus promised the Apache that General Crook would talk with him and hear his complaints. The conference ended. Old Nana and eight braves walked into Maus' camp and surrendered. During the march homeward, Captain Crawford succumbed.

On March 25, 1886, at Canyon des Embudos, twenty miles southeast of San Bernardino Springs near the border in Sonora, General Crook and his retinue of officers and interpreters rode up to Geronimo, Natchez, and the subchiefs. Geronimo began to speak. Crook listened. At sundown Crook and the Indians parted and trotted back to their respective camps.

Two days later they met again. This time Chihuahua spoke: "I surrender myself to you because I believe in you and you do not deceive us. You must be our God. I am satisfied with all that you do."

Then in solemn tones Geronimo said: "Two or three words are enough. I have little to say. I surrender to you."

General Crook rode out immediately for Fort Bowie, leaving the Apache to come in under cavalry escort. That night a bootlegger sold enough rotgut whiskey to the Apache to make the outfit rip-roaring drunk. Crazed with liquor, Geronimo and Natchez with part of the band lit out for the hills. True to their word about surrendering, eighty braves including Chihuahua marched into Fort Bowie.

Crook wired General Sheridan, general-in-chief of the Army. He was convinced that the only way to subjugate Geronimo was by relentless pursuit. In Washington General Sheridan censured Crook's campaign and prescribed a policy of defense and the abandonment of offensive operations. Deeply hurt, Crook asked to be relieved of command.

On April 2, 1886, one of the most successful Indian fighters in the United States Army, General Nelson A. Miles, was assigned to command the Department of Arizona. Already Miles had subdued the Kiowa, Comanche, Sioux, Nez Percé, and other Plains' Indians and now, leaving Fort Leavenworth, he went south and west to face the Apache.

At Bowie Station on the Southern Pacific Railroad, General Miles stepped off the train. Here a battalion of 2nd Cavalry had their tents strung out along the tracks. The heat was stifling. Flies swarmed everywhere. Fresh from the field, the troopers were disheartened. Riding into Fort Bowie, the general halted momentarily to inspect the cemetery. He read the wooden headboards: "Killed by Apaches," "Tortured and Killed by Apaches."

That night Miles penned a letter to his wife, Mary:

I arrived today after a long, hot and very dusty trip. I think this is the most barren region I have ever seen. From

what I can see and hear of the troops, they are very much discouraged by being kept in the field so long and by the prospect
that the campaign must be continued for some time to
come. . . .

In many respects this is the most difficult task I have ever
undertaken, on account of the extensive country, the natural
difficulties and the fact that the hostiles are so few in number
and so active. Still I can only make the best effort possible.

Sizing up the situation in the days that followed, Miles cut the
territory into districts, each with a troop commander; dispatched
infantry to hunt the redskins through the mountains; sent cavalry
units on longer pursuits. In General Field Orders No. 7, dated
April 20, 1886, Miles emphasized:

To avoid any advantage the Indians may have by a relay
of horses, where a troop or squadron commander is near the
hostile Indians he will be justified in dismounting one-half of
his command and selecting the lightest and best riders to make
pursuit by the most vigorous forced marches, until the strength
of all the animals of his command shall have been exhausted.

Miles organized a flying column of hardened, desert-tested
soldiers and Indian scouts. He picked Captain Henry W. Lawton,
4th Cavalry, to head the outfit. This tough officer, who had an
enviable Civil War and frontier record, believed that the Apache
could be hunted down and tamed.

To help track the enemy, the general used the heliograph, a
contrivance consisting of a mirror which reflected the sun, and
established twenty-seven signal stations atop mountains from
twenty-five to thirty miles apart. Experts began transmitting messages in Morse Code 800 miles or more over inaccessible terrain.

The Apache swept northward again across the Mexican border
on April 27, 1886, and raced up the Santa Cruz valley. Geronimo,
Natchez, and eighteen warriors massacred several cowhands, forced
a rancher to witness the torture of his wife, and kidnapped a thir-
teen-year-old girl.

Five thousand American soldiers, 500 Indian scouts, and hundreds of Mexicans searched the wastelands. Weeks dragged on endlessly. From all visible evidence it looked as though the hunt might

go on indefinitely. Captain Henry W. Lawton's hand-picked command in Mexico marched up one mountain and down another. Heliographs winked reports and several times a day the captain huddled with his staff to evaluate intelligence. The pursuit assumed the proportions of an epic.

Push on. Eat dust. Eat sand. Sweat. Keep moving. Before them the Apache trail danced mockingly. The landscape faded in the heat. From time to time the men buried their faces in their arms and gasped for breath. Water was scarce. In some troops there were soldiers who had served with the British in India and they confessed that the campaign against the Apache was the hardest, most exacting duty they'd ever endured.

Bearded and hollow-eyed, Lawton and his men bore little resemblance to a military outfit. They were in various stages of dress and undress, sleeveless shirts, legless pants, no shirts at all. Shoes, made at Leavenworth Prison and issued by the Quartermaster, crumbled to pieces and had to be replaced by moccasins.

By July 5 Lawton had driven Geronimo south of Oposura. Eight days later scouts, far ahead of the main body of troops, fell upon the Apache camp and attacked. The charge miscarried and the Indians fled.

Chagrined at letting Geronimo slip through his fingers, Lawton wrote a long letter to his wife that night:

> I saw two scouts running towards me. . . . They were wet with perspiration, and handed me a note, saying the scouts had come on the hostiles' camp and would attack it at once, and for me to bring up the Infantry at once; that the camp was about eight miles from us.
>
> I started at once with the Infantry and was guided by the scouts to the top of a high mountain, from which we could see the horses in the Indian camp, and in a few minutes I heard several volleys fired and the Indians shouting. I started the Infantry down towards them, but when we got there our scouts were in the camp and found no hostiles. They had taken alarm in time to make their escape. . . .
>
> I could cry, Mame, if it would do any good and I know Gen'l Miles will be terribly disappointed and will probably think I have been careless or negligent, and we have worked so

Captain Lawton's
pursuit of Geronimo.

hard and under such trying circumstances, it seems too bad to fail and now it is all to do over again, only a hundred times more difficult, as the hostiles know we are after them and will watch all our movements, and I had so hoped I could finish the war and come home.

Back at Fort Bowie General Miles was confronted with the pioneers' clamor for the extermination of the Apache or for their removal from the territory. To secure permanent peace, Miles decided that the hostiles must be resettled at a distant location, preferably Florida.

In mid-July the Apache were reported near Fronteras, where a woman confided to authorities that Geronimo wanted to surrender. Miles picked his emissaries and briefed them for their mission. Lieutenant Charles B. Gatewood, 6th Cavalry; loyal Apaches Kaeta and Martine; and the chief of scouts, Tom Horn, headed for Fronteras. The four of them, riding toward the enemy's camp, were not unconscious of the peril. They rode more or less together, drifting apart to make observations, halting briefly, then moving on again.

After a short layover at Fronteras, Gatewood and his men wheeled south, carrying high a flour sack knotted to a stick as a flag of truce. On August 23, Martine and Kaeta came across Geronimo's band on the banks of the Bavispe River. Swiftly, Geronimo took Kaeta hostage while sending Martine back to Gatewood with the Apache demands. The Indians would talk only with Gatewood, and he must come alone.

The cavalry lieutenant and the warriors met in the river valley. Geronimo was the last to arrive. Dismounting, he laid down his rifle and shook hands with Gatewood. Pipes were lit. The Apache wanted to know General Miles' terms.

Gatewood replied: "Surrender, and you will be sent with your families to Florida, there to await the decision of the President as to your final disposition. Accept these terms or fight it out to the bitter end."

Never moving, the Apache looked at Gatewood and waited. Finally Geronimo passed a hand across his eyes and then, holding both hands before him, asked the cavalryman for a drink. Gatewood shook his head, explaining he'd left Fort Bowie too quickly to pack whiskey. Satisfied with this excuse, Geronimo began talking of trivia. The lieutenant, picking his words carefully, guided the conversation back. The Apache, countered Geronimo, would surrender only if Miles let them return to their reservation in Arizona, reoccupy their farms, and be guaranteed exemption from punishment.

After much smoking and more conversation, Geronimo observed that he did not know General Miles. The Apache listened to Gatewood's description. After a pause, Geronimo said, "He must be a good man, since the Great Father sent him from Washington, and he has sent you to us."

As dusk crept up the river the lieutenant started his return to camp, where Lawton and his outfit awaited him. Geronimo urged Gatewood to wait. "We want your advice," explained the chief. "Consider yourself not a White Man but one of us; remember all that has been said today and tell us what we should do."

Gatewood snapped, "Trust General Miles and surrender to him."

Geronimo said he'd hold a council that night and let the American know the result first thing in the morning. Shaking hands with the Indians, Gatewood slipped into the saddle and rode off.

Early next morning Apache sentries passed a call for "Bay-chen-day-sen," Gatewood's name among the hostiles, meaning "Long Nose." With his interpreters, the lieutenant met Geronimo, Natchez, and the subchiefs. The Apache wanted Gatewood to repeat his description of Miles. When the facts were repeated, Geronimo agreed to talk with the general.

Under Captain Lawton's escort, twenty-four warriors, fourteen women and children started northward for the United States on August 25, 1886. On September 3, the sole remaining fighting leader of the Apache faced General Miles in Skeleton Canyon. They conversed in low tones for over an hour. At sunset the Apache turned back for his camp. The next morning he and his band capitulated. The Apache war had ended.

Troops met Geronimo and his people at Fort Bowie and loaded them on a train. Within hours the Apache began their long trek to Florida. A day later General Miles sent off a letter to Mary:

We have at least been most successful. I am making a clean sweep of the hostile Apaches out of this country and it has been a feeling of relief and security to thousands of homes that they have never felt before. If you had been here you would have seen me riding in over the mountains with Geronimo and Natchez. . . . It is a brilliant ending of a difficult problem.

While horse soldiers were playing a decisive role in bringing peace to the plains and deserts, other cavalrymen were exploring new frontiers. Lieutenant Fred Schwatka, 3rd Cavalry, and seven men pushed to the headwaters of the Yukon River in Canada and then by raft and boat swept down its entire length through Alaska. Scouring the upper reaches of the Copper River in Alaska, Lieutenant Henry T. Allen, 2nd Cavalry, slogged northward to the Arctic Circle.

In 1881 Lieutenant Adolphus Washington Greely, 5th Cavalry, leading an Arctic expedition, erected a camp on Ellsmere Island across the strait from the northwestern tip of Greenland. Two of his men reached latitude 83°-24', the farthest north civilized man had yet penetrated. Heading southward in the summer of 1883, the unit arrived safely at Cape Sabine.

Relief efforts to reach the explorers failed and the contingent, its supplies exhausted, was compelled to spend another winter in the Arctic wastes. Buffeted by wind and plagued by cold, seven starving survivors from the original expedition of twenty-five were finally rescued in June, 1884, by a Navy relief ship. Lieutenant Greely, who was eventually elevated to the rank of general, became a legend in Arctic exploration.

chapter 17

"Where's Cuba at?"

♞ ♞ ♞

AT WOUNDED KNEE CREEK, DECEMBER 29, 1890, THE United States Cavalry fought its last big Indian battle. After this bloody skirmish, troopers continued to patrol the plains and deserts and track down renegades, but never again did they engage hostile redskins in a major encounter.

For the first time in fifty years peace came to the American West. Yet from all parts of America young men continued to enlist in the mounted arm of the United States Army. Ragtag assortments of greenhorns arrived periodically at cavalry posts. They were counted off into "awkward squads" and handed over to sergeants who drilled them in setting up exercises and the manual at arms. At night rookies pored over *The Soldier's Handbook*, which included Army Regulations, the Articles of War, and chapters on guard mounting, discipline, physical fitness, saluting, and care of animals.

When the new cavalryman had settled into a routine and had progressed sufficiently in training, he attended "stables." Trumpeters blew *Stable Call* twice daily—after breakfast and in late afternoon. Falling in, dressed in white overalls, troopers hupped-two-three-four to the stables where noncoms taught them how to tie, groom, feed, and water the mounts.

In fair weather they groomed the horses in the open air with the animals tied at intervals along a high picket line stretched between two posts. Equipped with brush and currycomb, men rubbed and scraped the mounts until their coats glistened. Gently and carefully, the animals' nostrils, eyes, and ears were wiped with damp cloths; manes and tails were washed.

A regular detail of troopers, supervised by stable sergeants, fed the mounts and, after dumping forage into each stall, they shook down the horses' beds for the evening. Each mount had a window venting his stall, which was fitted with a manger and straw bedding on the floor. Saddles and bridles hung on pins and, customarily, the horse's name and the name of his rider appeared over each stall.

Cavalry horses came from all parts of the United States. The mounts ranged in size from 15½ to 16 hands high, weighed between 950 to 1,150 pounds and, although selection boards paid little attention to color, they rejected white horses as being too conspicuous. The prescribed age was from four to eight years. No limit in price was fixed by regulation but the Army paid no more than $150, generally considerably less.

Lieutenant S. C. Robertson, 1st Cavalry, judged the ideal horse as sound and well-bred, gentle under the saddle, devoid of vicious habits, and with free and prompt action at the walk, trot, and gallop. He was a horse with a plain but well-shaped head set upon a good, strong muscular neck, with shoulders oblique, broad and well-placed and covered with suitable muscle. The chest, Robertson went on, should be well-shaped and full with great depth of girth; the body full and round with a short, straight powerful back—the saddle place should be as nearly as possible in the middle of the back with plenty of room beneath the belly.

Before accepting animals into service, military purchasing boards, experts in horseflesh, explored the shoulders, withers, loins, and hindquarters of each horse. After mounts passed this first examination, officers subjected them to further tests under the saddle, appraising speed, durability and stamina, all prime requisites for the cavalry.

After the new cavalrymen had mastered the art of grooming, noncoms drilled them in bareback riding. They learned how to sit, hold the reins, how to walk and trot the mounts. Issued blankets and surcingles for the horses, the men repeated the drill. The rookies, gaining confidence, were handed McClellan saddles and instructed how to place and cinch them, and how to sit on them properly. They trained in riding halls, where tan bark lay so thick on the floors that when recruits fell from their mounts, they experienced little discomfort.

When he was completely at home in the saddle, the private learned saber drills, cutting, jabbing, and slashing at dummy heads.

Announcement.

Extraordinary!!
≋
By Special Request, a

Grand Indian Club Exhibition

will be given at the

POST AMUSEMENT HALL, *Fort Robinson, Neb.,*
Saturday, July 15th, at 8 o'clock in the evening,

By Mr.

James J. Dougher,

Company C, 8th Infantry, in his Unique, Scientific and Skillful manipulation of Indian Clubs, performing the most Difficult, and Original Executions and Graceful Movements ever accomplished by any Athlete, or Gymnast, using Clubs of many descriptions and handling them with the Utmost Dexterity, which baffles all observers.

In addition to the Club Swinging there will be a Grand

⟩⟩⟩ Concert ⟨⟨⟨

by PROF. GUNGL'S ORCHESTRA, 9th Cavalry Band. Their choice musical selections with airs from the latest operas and popular songs, will be both interesting and entertaining.

This entertainment is sure to please all. Door will be open at 7,30.

General Admission 25c.   Reserved Seats 35c.

TICKETS FOR SALE AT POST EXCHANGE.

1893

PROGRAMME
—FOR—
JULY 4TH, 1893,
Fort Robinson, Nebraska.

FORE-NOON, 10 O'CLOCK.

Blindfold Wheelbarrow Race. *First Prize: $3.00. Second Prize: $.200.*	**"TUG-OF-WAR."** 12 men on each side.
Three-legged Race. *First Prize: $3.00. Second Prize: $2.00.*	1. Between C and D Co's. *Prize: 1 keg of Beer.*
Sack-race. *First Prize: $3.00. Second Prize: $2.00.*	2. Between 1st and 2d Squadrons. *Prize: 3 kegs of Beer.*

AFTER-NOON, 1,30 O'CLOCK.

Horse-Races.

QUARTER MILE DASH. *1st Prize: $8.00. 2d Prize: $4.00.*	ONE HALF MILE RACE. *1st Prize: $20.00. 2d Prize: $10.00.*
SIX HUNDRED YARDS. *1st Prize: $12.00. 2d Prize: $ 6.00.*	PONY RACE. Free to all Post-Ponies. *1st Prize: $5.00. 2d Prize: $3.00.*

FOOT-RACE, 600 yards. *1st Prize:* $4.00. *2d Prize:* $3.00.

Contestants must be on hand promptly at the hours named.
Entries of horses close at 8 o'clock p. m., July 2d, to Capt. *Corliss at the Officers' Club.*

COMMITTEE:	JUDGES:
Lieut.-Colonel *R. F Bernard.* Captain *A. W. Corliss.* 1st Lieut. *E. F. Ladd.* Benj. *S. Paddock.*	Lieut.-Colonel *R. F. Bernard.* Captain *A. W. Corliss.* 1st Lieut. *E. F. Ladd.*

Announcements of social events at Fort Robinson, Nebraska, 1893.

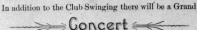

Fort Robinson Club Punch · · ·
ⱲⱲⱲ

Juice of 12 Lemons (¼ pint of juice); ½ doz. Lemons—sliced; ¼ pint Curacoa; 1 pint Port Wine; 1 quart St. Cruz or Jamaica Rum; 1 quart Brandy; 1 can Pineapple; 1 pint strong tea; 1 stick Cinnamon; little nutmeg; ¼ pint sugar. Make day in advance. Add 4 quarts Champagne and Apollinaris water to weaken.
Enough for hop for 30 people.

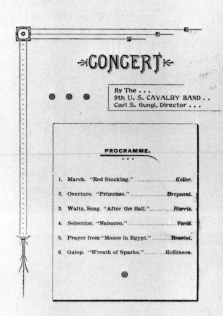

⟩CONCERT⟨

By The . . .
9th U. S. CAVALRY BAND . .
Carl S. Gungl, Director . . .

PROGRAMME.
. . .

1.	March. "Red Stocking."	*Keller.*
2.	Overture. "Primrose."	*Brepsant.*
3.	Waltz, Song. "After the Ball."	*Harris.*
4.	Selection. "Nabucco."	*Verdi.*
5.	Prayer from "Moses in Egypt."	*Rossini.*
6.	Galop. "Wreath of Sparks."	*Rollinson.*

FORT ROBINSON, NEBRASKA,
June 10th, 1893.

Noncoms, repeating over and over, "Fire is everything, the rest is nothing," explained the intricacies of the carbine and pistol. A popular small-arms practice was mounted revolver shooting. Work details set up empty hardtack boxes approximating the height of a man. Troopers began firing, first at a walk, then at a trot, finally at a gallop. They also underwent intensive instruction in dismounted firing, a cardinal principle with the American cavalry. Training at point-blank, middle distance, and long range, the men were taught how to fire standing, kneeling, and lying down, both by volley and singly at simulated battle targets.

In combined maneuvers at the Cavalry and Light Artillery School, Fort Riley, Kansas, regiment was pitted against regiment in sham battles. Actual collision was avoided; firing ended at sixty yards; cavalry charges at eighty. The regiment failing to meet charge with charge was defeated. When equal bodies of cavalry met head on, victory belonged to the side bringing up the last-formed reinforcements. Full written reports with topographical sketches were turned in after each day's work along with the decisions of the umpires and the comments of the Commandant.

The United States Cavalry was the glamour organization of the United States Army, a top choice of many high-ranking cadets at West Point. The cavalry had an unequaled tradition of which its officers and men were fiercely proud. But technological progress was making the horse obsolete. Critics charged that the range, accuracy, and rapidity of modern arms placed the mounted regiments in an inferior position to infantry and artillery. Advancing to the attack, horse units could be subjected to a withering fire from artillery at a range of 3,500 yards, from machine guns at 2,000.

Cavalrymen hotly retorted that the mounted arm was essential. Although infantrymen might be the most important on the field of battle, it was cavalry which veiled their movements while on the march. It was cavalry that guarded their ammunition supply. It was cavalry that scouted, reconnoitered, screened, and foraged.

As modern conditions discouraged frontal assaults, the cavalry relied upon wide-turning movements and surprise. The combination of mounted and dismounted action offered scope for the cavalry in its tactical role. A dismounted force on the defensive could draw the enemy's fire, while the mounted detachments charged his flanks and rear. By combining dismounted fire and mounted charge the regiments preserved their mobility and fortified it with the solidity of infantry. The duty of observation gained importance during the 1890's and was performed by patrols, which sought to penetrate opposing cavalry screens, to see without being seen, and to report back the location, strength, and direction of the enemy's march.

♞ ♞ ♞

As the Civil War is identified with Grant and Lee, the Indian Wars with Custer, so does the Spanish-American War conjure up the picture of Roosevelt and his Rough Riders charging up San Juan Hill. In April, 1898, shortly after the outbreak of hostilities with Spain, Theodore Roosevelt, erstwhile rancher, police commissioner, and Assistant Secretary of the Navy was given a lieutenant colonelcy in the 1st United States Volunteer Cavalry. Speedily the Army mustered units composed of cowpokes, hunters, and prospectors from the western territories. Overall command rested with Colonel Leonard Wood and his friend, Theodore Roosevelt.

Recruiters galloped across Oklahoma, Indian Territory, New Mexico, and Arizona filling their quotas. With a telegram from the governor of New Mexico stuffed in his pocket, Albert W. Thompson cantered into Clayton, slipped from his saddle, and strode into the "Favorite Saloon," headquarters for the cowhands of the area. A dozen roughly garbed men hung about the bar or lounged awkwardly on the saloon's pool table.

Thompson drew out the governor's telegram and handed it to "Red," the barkeeper. "Read it aloud," said Thompson.

"Enlist immediately thirty able-bodied men, your quota from Union County for the First United States Cavalry, Rough Riders, now being formed. Cowboys and men trained in the use of arms to be given preference."

Thompson filled in the details.

"Who's General Wood and this feller Roosevelt?" asked a cowboy.

Wood had fought the Apache with Lawton in Arizona, explained Thompson. Roosevelt was once a rancher in Dakota, rode the range and worked on the roundup.

"Them Cubans ought not to be hard to lick," volunteered the barkeeper. "Greasers mostly. Greasers fight like sheepherders. Reckon it'll be a mounted outfit that's goin' after 'em, won't it?"

"Where's Cuba at?" somebody asked.

"Cuba is an island in the Atlantic Ocean south of Texas."

"Toler'ble fur I reckon."

Next morning Thompson along with John L. Robinson, roundup boss of the Bar T Cross Ranch, entered the "Favorite Saloon."

"Come up, fellers," shouted Robinson, "what yer goin' ter drink? They're on me. I'm goin'."

Presently Thompson and Robinson were in the street. Mounting his bay Robinson said, "Adios," and started down the avenue. "Reckon I'm the first to enlist, ain't I,—sorter number one like?"

"You certainly are, Jack," said Thompson, smiling.

When it became know that the Bar T Cross roundup boss had volunteered, cowpokes from all over the county hurried to town. Men living as far south as lower Ute Creek, seventy-five miles from Clayton, rode all night to join up.

In Washington the Army upped the Rough Rider quota to 1,000. This gave Colonels Wood and Roosevelt a chance to sign up Easterners, college boys from Harvard, Yale, and Princeton; socialites from clubs like the Somerset of Boston and the Knickerbocker of New York—"The Swells," "The Millionaire's Sons," "The New York 400"—and men who belonged neither to university nor club but who spoiled for a fight. "The Rough Riders," said an observer, "were the most composite lot that ever gathered under a regimental standard. . . . The cowboy, the Indian trailer, the Indian himself, the packer . . . touched elbows with the New York policeman . . . the college athlete, the football player and oarsman, the dare-devil mountaineer of Georgia with the society man, the child of luxury and wealth."

It was at training camp in San Antonio, Texas, that hard-bitten Westerners first glimpsed the sons of Harvard and Yale. They were dumbstruck at a chap attired in morning coat, pinstripe trousers and spats, picking his way through horse droppings in the street.

Cowboys were even more astonished by their lieutenant colonel, Theodore Roosevelt. He was short, wide, bandy-legged, wore

ABOVE: Parade at Fort Riley, Kansas, 1897.
BELOW: Teddy Roosevelt and the Rough Riders, Cuba, 1898.

steel-rimmed glasses, and seemed to be eternally flashing his toothy grin. His uniform didn't fit. He looked the most unsoldierly soldier in the outfit.

On the drill field Roosevelt strove to weld the Rough Riders into a regiment. He drove the unit hard, first on foot, then on horse-back, by squad, by troop, by squadron, by battalion. In their slouch hats, blue flannel shirts, brown trousers, leggings, and boots, with handkerchiefs loosely around their necks, the Rough Riders trotted out through the adjoining countryside to drill wherever they found open ground.

The already furious pace became frantic. Roosevelt's enthusiasm was catching. Cowboys and college athletes fought for work. Captains and looeys volunteered for lowly chores, anything that might speed their departure overseas. "They were the finest fellows," Roosevelt said later, "and they were dead game. It was the privilege of a life time to have commanded such a regiment."

In exactly thirteen days the officers accomplished what a regular cavalry outfit did in thirteen weeks—they organized, equipped, and trained a full regiment of horse soldiers. On Sunday, May 29, 1898, the command moved out of their dusty, mosquito-ridden camp and crammed themselves and 1,100 horses and mules into ancient railroad cars. The trains jolted eastward across Texas, Louisiana, Mississippi, Alabama, and into Florida. After four night-marish days and nights the Rough Riders arrived at the pine-covered sand flats outside of Tampa. Tents shot up. Drills began promptly.

To his children—his "Blessed Bunnies"—Roosevelt wrote from Tampa on June 6:

> It has been a real holiday to have darling mother here. Yesterday I brought her out to the camp, and she saw it all— the men drilling, the tents in long company streets, the horses being taken to water, my little horse Texas, the colonel and the majors, and finally the mountain lion and the jolly little dog Cuba, who had several fights while she looked on. . . .
>
> Mother stays at the big hotel about a mile from camp. There are nearly thirty thousand troops here now, besides the sailors from the war-ships in the bay. . . . Our camp is on a great flat, on sandy soil without a tree, though round about

are pines and palmettos. It is very hot, indeed, but there are no mosquitoes. . . . A general was out to inspect us when we were drilling to-day.

The 1st United States Volunteer Cavalry did not linger in Tampa. An expedition, including the Rough Riders, was ordered on transports for an unnamed destination. Horses were left behind. Only eight troops of Rough Riders were to board the ships. Colonel Wood's contingent was brigaded with the 1st and 10th regular cavalry under Brigadier General S.B.M. Young. The Rough Riders were part of the 2nd Brigade, the 1st consisting of the 3rd, 6th, and 9th regular cavalry.

A former Confederate, Major General Joseph Wheeler, commanded the two brigades of cavalry.

Tramping up to the Tampa docks, Rough Riders elbowed their way through a swarm of humanity and struggled up the gangway of the transport, *Yucatan*. Thirty-two black-painted troopships, bloated with men and equipment, cast off lines, reversed engines, and finally anchored in the bay.

Dawn brought no sailing orders. One day, two, three, the ships rode at their hooks in the man-killing heat. Suddenly on the evening of June 13, the troopships seethed with activity. Engines throbbed. Windlasses whirred. Anchor chains rattled. The transports steamed slowly ahead. Bands crashed, "There'll Be a Hot Time in the Old Town Tonight." Riggings were cluttered with soldiers, cheering and yelling at those left behind.

For six days the ships bore down upon Cuba, ships of every description—rust-scarred freighter, small ocean liner, slim torpedo boat, hulking cruiser, converted yacht. Army officers enjoyed every minute of their passage and called the cavalcade of ships "impressive, unforgettable."

Theodore Roosevelt wrote to his family:

Last evening we stood up on the bridge and watched the red sun sink and the lights blaze up on the ships, for miles ahead and astern, while the band played piece after piece, from the "Star-Spangled Banner" at which we all rose and stood uncovered, to "The Girl I Left Behind Me."—But it is a great historical expedition, and I thrill to feel that I am part of it.

The troops below decks were glad to be under way despite the discomforts. "From the very start," said Private John G. Winter, Jr., "we had a tough time of it. The grub was horrible; 'Salt horse,' hard tack, one-eighth can of tomatoes, and watery coffee constituted a ration. The lack of variety at first made the food disagreeable, then nauseating."

Early on June 20, the armada closed to the coast of Cuba. The convoy steamed past Guantánamo Bay and, in early evening, sighted Spanish-held Santiago Harbor. For two days the ships wallowed in the seaway, waiting for the decision to land. On June 22, troopships steered for shore near the village of Daiquiri.

Guns on warships swung into action to dislodge the enemy from the beaches. The entire area erupted in a storm of fire. Great clouds of black smoke darkened the air. The maelstrom of sound thundered back and forth as the big ships slammed steadily away.

Soldiers—cavalry, infantry, and artillery—jammed the rails of transports waiting their turn to scramble into the landing boats. Bobbing lines of craft, packed with men and equipment, headed for shore.

The surf pounded. Boats capsized or were tossed about like Yo-Yos. Green water sloshed over everyone. Mules drowned. A sergeant thrashed by one boat, arms and legs flying through the water, yelling that he couldn't swim.

Sodden, seasick soldiers struggled through the combers. All along the shore the flotsam and jetsam of the invasion piled up—equipment and supplies, canteens, life preservers, and tools were strewn everywhere. Reels of wire, ration boxes, scores of weapons littered the sand. The Rough Riders pushed through the noise and congestion on the beach and into the rugged hills. They camped that night on a dusty, brush-covered flat surrounded by jungle.

The next afternoon the cavalry brigades reformed and slogged forward in the heat. That night they shuffled into Siboney, a squalid coastal village, and pitched tents. Around the flickering fires, clusters of men sat and conversed in low tones. The waiting, the gnawing uncertainty all lay ahead. Private Winter was uneasy: "I calculated the percentage of lost of every battle of the Civil War." There was little sleep. Restless men talked constantly of the coming battle.

Sunrise. The dismounted cavalrymen moved out for Santiago.

General Young and four troops of the 10th and four of the 1st were to head down the road which snaked through a valley. Colonel Leonard Wood, leading the Rough Riders, was to march along a hill trail to the left. Battle plans called for the two units to rejoin at a point where the road went over a mountain spur.

Probing the jungle, an advance from Young's outfit fell upon the enemy. The Spaniards' guns opened up. Young's regulars clawed their way forward. After a hot exchange, the enemy broke and made for the rear.

Simultaneously, the Rough Riders, footsore and weary from the previous day's march, were moving along the trail. Wood set a furious pace, double-timing up the steep hill. Private Winter marched—exhaustedly, gasping for breath as everybody did. After reaching the hilltop, the trail became easier leading through a luxuriant tropical forest.

Abruptly the columns halted. Lieutenants clipped orders: "Load magazines."

Yard by yard, cautiously, the Rough Riders sneaked forward. Scouts fanned out.

Enemy guns crashed and then crashed again as though they were firing in unison. Private Winter heard commands come in rapid succession: "L Troop deploy as skirmishers," "F Troop . . . double time, deploy as skirmishers." Winter and F Troop sprinted for the brow of the hill, the extreme left of the firing line.

The air was full of steel. "Mauser bullets began to whistle around my ears," recalled Winter, "but with some difference of effect upon my nerves. Represented as well as I can, those high above my head sounded like zir-ah-ah (long drawn out); those that came close, zip."

Creeping forward, sometimes on their knees, sometimes on their bellies, the Rough Riders sought the concealed enemy. Colonel Roosevelt hustled to the front to mark out the enemy's position. War correspondent Richard Harding Davis hailed him, "There they are, colonel; look over there; I can see their hats near the glade."

Everyone stared. Officers focused their glasses. The ravine swarmed with Spaniards, hidden behind dense foliage.

Yankee bullets ripped into the jungle. The enemy fell back. Stubbornly, the Rough Riders pursued until, across the ravine, they recognized General Young's regulars furiously waving their guidons. In the flame and clamor and smoke, Rough Riders worked toward a group of ranch buildings. As they ran some seemed to pause and bow their heads; they sank carefully to their knees and rolled over without a murmur to lie quiet in the grass. A few yelled when they were hit, grabbing frantically at limbs or torso before they tumbled forward.

Slugs tore into Harry Heffner, G Troop. In a stupor of agony he fell, wounded through the hips. Two buddies dragged him behind a tree. Here he propped himself up and began firing fiercely. He continued loading, firing, reloading, until his companions surged past and left Harry Heffner to die in the shade.

Panting and worn-out Rough Riders gained the ranch buildings. The firing died out. The enemy had vanished.

On June 30, the narrow, muddy track along which the Rough Riders were encamped was choked with marching columns. At noon the cowboys struck camp and lined up to the rear of the 1st and 10th Cavalry. The wait stretched out. Toward midafternoon the units trudged ahead. At 8:00 P.M. they veered left, crawled atop El Poso Hill and rested.

The first of July was the day of Theodore Roosevelt's "crowded hour." At dawn Rough Riders fell in. A battery of field guns was manhandled up the hill.

Word was passed—the main fighting was to be done by the infantry, which was to capture El Caney several miles to the right. The cavalry brigades were to make a diversion.

The first reports of cannon from El Caney boomed across the jungle. An explosion almost pitched Wood and Roosevelt on their faces. Then another, and still another.

The stunning noise went on. In columns of four, cavalrymen moved ahead on foot. Up Kettle Hill Sergeant George Berry, 10th Cavalry, bore not only his own regimental standard, but that of the 3rd, whose color-sergeant had been cut down. Above the noise Berry yelled: "Dress on the colors, boys, dress on the colors."

The Rough Riders ran straight into the left wing of the 9th Cavalry. After a brief consultation with the captain in charge of the rear guard, Roosevelt seized the initiative. Glancing around for the 9th's absent colonel, he barked: "Then I am the ranking officer here and I give the order to charge."

ABOVE: 6th U.S. Cavalry National Standard, Spanish-American War.
BELOW: Crayon drawing of the Battle of San Pascual.
(Not authentic as it shows charge in full uniform on horseback.)

As the captain hesitated to take orders from a stranger, Roosevelt needled: "Then let my men through, sir." Watching the cowboys rally and push ahead the regulars sprang forward and bounded up the hill.

In the excitement men performed astonishing feats. His left arm riddled with bullets, Sergeant Charles Karsten continued running and firing, refusing to go to the rear. Trooper Hugo Brittain was hit, but hurried the regimental colors forward, waving them to and fro, cheering the men onward.

The battle surged around Private Winter. "The full significance of the phrase, 'the art of war,'" he related, "burst upon me when I saw my friend's head shot to pieces by an explosive bullet. He fell with a thud, and I ran past his body."

Atop Kettle Hill Rough Riders and Regulars got a real reception. The enemy opened fire from trenches. Americans scampered for safety, a few ducking behind a huge iron kettle used for sugar refining. Here they had a splendid view of the infantry's charge upon the San Juan blockhouses to the left.

Rough Riders volley-fired against the Spaniards on San Juan Hill. The enemy spilled from the rifle pits and ran. Roosevelt ordered *Charge*. The cowboys came with a rush, shooting, cheering, yelling. Before the onslaught, the Spaniards retreated. When the Rough Riders reached the trenches, they found dead men, scattered shell casings, and rows of ammunition.

There was great confusion on San Juan Hill. Regiments were intermingled—white regulars, Negro regulars, Rough Riders. Officers merged them together and they drove ahead shoving the retreating Spaniards past a line of palm trees and over the crest. When they reached it, Americans discovered themselves overlooking the city of Santiago.

The wounded were quickly found and cared for. The burial detail wrapped the dead in blankets and laid them side by side in one grave. The chaplain read the Episcopal burial service. Grouped around the solitary grave, the Rough Riders sang, "Nearer My God to Thee." The bugler sounded *Taps*. The burial detail filled the grave and the cowboys and college men slowly moved back toward their camp. The charge of the Rough Riders was history.

chapter 18.

"What we want is Villa."

A HUGE BOLL OF DUST FLOATED HIGH ABOVE THE MEX-
ican desert, isolated, like a solitary brown cloud. Three
black Dodge touring cars swayed and lurched and banged
in low gear, spouting steam from their radiators, grind-
ing their way through the sand.

On the right fender of the lead car flew a small American flag;
on the left waved the single star of a brigadier general. The driver
glanced backward, his face white where the sand and dust had
crusted over. He spoke a few words to the clean-shaven, grey-haired,
six-foot brigadier general, who sat munching a saltless cracker. John
J. "Black Jack" Pershing gazed about the harsh and ugly Chihuahua
countryside. It hadn't changed much since 1886 when, as a shavetail
in the 6th Cavalry, he had ridden over these same wastes in search
of Geronimo. Now, in March, 1916, his quarry was the social
revolutionary, Francisco "Pancho" Villa. Commanding the
United States Punitive Expedition, Pershing was motoring over
the desert on a flying trip of inspection. In the two cars that followed were a military escort of five enlisted men and three newspaper correspondents.

Periodically since 1910, virtual anarchy had swept Mexico. In
the confused struggles and counterstruggles, many lives had been
lost. In the recent upheaval among the warring candidates for leadership of the country, the one most favored by President Woodrow
Wilson was Don Venustiano Carranza. His major rival for power
was Pancho Villa, the bandit-turned-general.

Pancho Villa was 37 years old, two inches under six feet,
chubby, with a handlebar mustache. The masses of northern Mexico loved him and regarded him as a Robin Hood. On the trail the

chieftain usually wore a brown turtleneck sweater under a dirt-smeared sombrero. Often he wore an unpressed dark suit, a vest, and a white shirt open at the neck.

Pancho Villa seethed with anger when, in October, 1915, the United States recognized Carranza as the de facto head of the Mexican government. On November 1 at Agua Prieta (south of Douglas, Arizona) in Sonora, Villa's bands were severely repulsed by those of Carranza—a victory attributable to American assistance. Villa's revenge came on January 10, 1916. His horsemen dragged seventeen Americans of the La Cusi Mining Company from a railroad train near Santa Ysabel in Chihuahua and murdered them.

Two months later on March 9, 1916, Mexicans armed with rifles, pistols, and belts of ammunition swept across the border into Columbus, New Mexico. The American sentry died gasping noiselessly. Shouting, "Viva Villa! Viva Mexico! Muerte a los americanos!" Villistas raced up and down Broadway, smashing, looting, burning. The Commercial Hotel was buried in pillars of smoke and Mexicans paused on their mounts to gun down guests as they came out running. Cavalrymen of the 13th tumbled from their cots, half asleep, to fire at the raiders. Villa's bugles blew Retreat. Troopers formed up and pursued the bandits across the border, crashing through guard blocks, killing 120. American losses at Columbus, civilian and military, numbered 17.

Newspapers across America carried the details, blotting out news from Europe where French and Germans were locked in mortal combat at Verdun. The celebrated entertainer, George M. Cohan, expressed popular feeling as he sang:

> Let's quit talking of Kaisers and Kings,
> Get Villa!
> Let's quit talking of all foreign things,
> Get Villa!
> Let's quit talking political views,
> Let's quit wasting our words to abuse,
> Come Americans—Christians and Jews,
> Get Villa!

The town of Humboldt, Iowa, put up a $10,000 reward for Villa, dead or alive. Colonel Herbert Slocum, commanding the 13th Cavalry, offered $50,000 of his own money for Villa's capture.

President Wilson, uncertain whether Carranza's troops were strong enough to punish Pancho Villa, decided to send a "punitive expedition" into Mexico. The War Department chose a cavalryman, Brigadier John J. Pershing, to command. Pershing had served with distinction with the 10th Cavalry in the 1890's. During the Spanish-American War he fought at Santiago—"the coolest man under fire I ever saw," observed his commanding officer—and next performed brilliantly in the Philippines at the turn of the century. President Theodore Roosevelt had promoted him to brigadier general from the rank of captain, jumping him over 862 senior officers.

The core of the Punitive Expedition was cavalry, a force ideally suited to tracking down marauders in the rugged Mexican countryside. Pershing picked the 7th, 10th, 11th, and 13th Regiments, the last two units having been created in 1901 to maintain order in the new territories won in the Spanish-American War. The general also selected infantry regiments to protect supply lines, field artillery detachments to strengthen the expedition's positions, and used airplanes of the 1st Aero Squadron to reconnoiter the deserts and canyons. All along the border in March, 1916, 4,800 men and 192 officers waited Pershing's signal to advance.

It came at 11:30, March 15, 1916. The 13th Cavalry Regiment trotted out of Columbus amid cheers. At the railroad station the engineer of the Golden State Limited tooted his whistle enthusiastically. To a chorus of chiming equipment and knocking hooves Major Frank Tompkins' advance crossed into Mexico. Mexican border guards drowsed in the sunshine or waved at the passing columns. Twelve hours later General Pershing astride a horse in traditional cavalry style rode across the boundary line. He soon dismounted and climbed into a Dodge touring car, from which he was to conduct the remainder of the campaign. Already motor vehicles and modern weaponry were beginning to doom the importance of the horse soldier. The United States Punitive Expedition was the last major expedition of horse cavalry in the world.

Toiling southward American soldiers, horses, mules, wagons, and trucks churned up the dust. Sand was underfoot. Sand was everywhere. Grit enveloped them as the wind, more powerful and as hot as an open oven, hit the columns and swirled about them.

While on that march, a young cavalry officer found time to write home to his family:

We have had a terrible 24 hours. Our last camp was a
terror. Dust 3 inches deep, and the wind blowing like the devil.
It quieted for a time as we went to bed. It looked like rain, but
no one thought it would rain here, where the rain comes but a
few times a year, so few of us bothered to put up shelter tents.
About 11, I was awakened by a gentle downpour. It was cold
as the deuce and I hesitated to get out of bed for half an hour,
hoping that the rain would stop. Finally gave up hope and got
up. Was fully dressed except for footgear, as one dresses up to
go to bed here.

Spent half an hour in the dark trying to put up my tent.
The dust refused to hold pins. By digging a hole in each place
I finally got in three pins at the front of the tent and had to be
content with that. With the tent and slicker I kept fairly dry
and slept intermittently the rest of the night.

We broke camp in the rain and started on. Marched
about 18 miles and came to what would have been a good
camp, excellent, in dry weather. . . . To cap the climax, the
mare got kicked and will be lame for some days. We have had
supper and I have changed into my hunting boots. . . .

The trail of the troops is marked by empty ration cans
and an occasional dead mule. . . . Passed the place this morning where Villa hanged three Palomas company men. . . . We
are all anxious to go on. The truck trains and wagon trains
pass daily going both ways. . . . I am feeling fine.

Pershing's cavalcade continued to push southward. Westward
were the towering peaks of the Sierra Madres, which work southward in a broadening mass. To the East a plain, 6,500 feet above
sea level, merges with the desert. This was Pancho Villa's habitat,
his lair. Like Geronimo, Villa knew every inch of terrain, every
mountain pass, every waterhole.

By late March Pershing's various commands converged on
Colonia Dublan near the Casas Grandes River, where they established a major encampment, 125 miles from Columbus. Here the
1st Aero Squadron joined the expedition—ten officers, eighty-two
enlisted men and eight airplanes, all Curtis JN–2s or "Jennies."

Each day that General Pershing and his columns stayed in
Chihuahua increased the danger they might be assaulted by groups

of Mexicans other than Villistas. The camp was full of rumors. Spies reported suspicious movements of Carranza's forces. Mexicans brought in a pair of bloody boots and a bullet-riddled vest— Pancho Villa, they proclaimed triumphantly, was dead. A few days later Villa was reported murdered at Santa Ana.

"Do you believe it?" correspondents asked Pershing.

The general hesitated, then hedged: "I don't know any more than you do. We get a lot of reports that he is dead, but when they are sifted, they all seem to come from the same source. Frankly, I can't say. If he is dead, well and good; the job's done. Anticlimax, possibly, but what we want is Villa."

Pershing and his aides devoted their energies plotting the pursuit, consulting maps, checking the probable routes. Up until now the trail had been easy to follow. The raiders had marched close to the Casas Grandes River, a fine source of water for men and mounts. Along the way the Americans saw carcasses of horses, which the Mexicans had ridden hard. These served as excellent markers for the pursuers as did the buzzards which circled above the trail. But at Colonia Dublan, the quarry wheeled and veered off and his tracks were no longer discernible. To confuse the Americans further, the wily Villa split up his army into several bands.

Detachments of the 7th, 10th, 11th, and 13th Cavalry searched the desert and mountain vastness. Trails became twisting nightmares. Exhaustion became chronic. Their horses were near their limits. Sometimes the men dismounted and led them. The hope that by some miracle they might come up with Pancho Villa kept them going.

At Colonia Dublan, Pershing issued his first communique to the correspondents. Standing near his tent, his campaign hat pulled well down on his head, the general summarized troop movements to date and traced Villa's line of retreat southward.

"Our troops seem to be pressing him," he said, militarily, "but I won't hazard any predictions. Villa is no fool. It may be that the campaign has just started."

A scout in a red shirt glanced up from where he squatted. "As I figure it, General," he drawled, "we've got Villa entirely surrounded—on one side."

Pershing laughed. Everybody did. The news conference ended. That was the situation on March 27, 1916, twelve days after the command had ridden across the border. Out of touch with the advanced cavalry units, marooned near Casas Grandes, Pershing decided to move south by motorcade to direct personally the forces pursuing Villa. Leaving the main body of the command behind, Pershing and his aide, Lieutenant George S. Patton, stepped into their touring car and drove southward trailed by two other automobiles full of troopers and correspondents. The general sat silent, erect, thin-lipped. The road was good and Pershing's chauffeur met the turns like the veteran he was. Sixty miles below Colonia Dublan they rattled into the town of El Valle and bedded down that night in a haystack.

Pershing was up at dawn. He shaved and washed his face from a canvas bucket, a collapsible affair that looked like a horse's nose bag. At breakfast he told reporters: "I think we've got Villa."

Twenty minutes later the cars were speeding southward. All that day, March 29, Pershing's caravan bumped over the Mexican countryside, bearing south and west. Evening twilight. Pershing pushed on. Reaching Namiquipa, where he learned that bands of Villistas were swarming the neighborhood, the general turned back and drove into San Geronimo Ranch, 270 miles from the American border. He discovered that Villa had routed and butchered Carranzista troops the previous day, only twenty miles to the north. In the fracas Villa had been severely wounded.

Associated Press correspondent H. W. Blakeslee and Frank Elser of the New York Times were a day behind the general. Their car had broken down and they were unable to keep the pace. At nightfall, March 30, they arrived at Namiquipa and were directed to the tent of Major Frank Tompkins, 13th Cavalry. He was holding a lantern, reading, as they entered. It was a dispatch from the general. He handed it over to Elser.

San Geronimo Ranch, March 30, 1916. Sir—Col. [G. A.] Dodd's force [of 7th Cavalry] yesterday at 7 A.M. struck Villa's force at Guerrero, scattering it and driving it northeast toward Providencia and Santa Ana. You will take two troops of your command at once and move via Santa Ana, arriving at Providencia at day light and working through the mountains, cooperating with Major [Robert L.] Howze, who is working west through the mountains from Bachiniva.

ABOVE: Colonel Leonard Wood. BELOW: General Pershing and Expeditionary Forces in Mexico crossing Santa Maria River, in their hunt for Pancho Villa.

It was near midnight when Blakeslee and Elser drove into San Geronimo Ranch. At daylight they found Pershing sitting on his bedroll, pulling on his boots. The general got into the touring car to write dispatches. Correspondents filed their copy regarding the fight at Guerrero.

The Villistas had fired first. The 7th Cavalry had answered. The horse soldiers came up and closed in. Both sides charged and countercharged, but finally the Mexicans broke through a trap, split into small groups and fled to the hills. Colonel Dodd listed enemy losses at sixty killed and a large number wounded. But he was disgruntled and frustrated. Had his columns reached the enemy camp a few hours earlier, the colonel was convinced that his men could have sealed off all avenues of escape and captured Villa.

On April 1 Dodd's tired and hungry troopers marched into Providencia and reported to General Pershing. Reporters began speculating upon the capture of Pancho Villa within the next few days. In Washington news of the victory was especially welcome in the inner circles of the Wilson Administration. Each day that Villa evaded capture and punishment increased the criticism of the President's policies.

At his camp Pershing asked Major Frank Tompkins, who had rejoined the command, "Where is Villa?"

"General, I don't know, but I would like mighty well to go find out where he is. . . . I would head for Parral and would expect to cut his trail before reaching there."

"Why?"

"The history of Villa's bandit days shows that when hard pressed he invariably holes up in the mountains in the vicinity of Parral."

"How many mules do you want?"

"Twelve."

The two men shook hands and Tompkins, saluting, departed.

The next morning Pershing told the major: "Go find Villa wherever you think he is."

On April 2, with five days rations, 500 silver pesos and Troops K and M of the 13th, the major astride his Arabian stallion, *Kingfisher*, moved out.

Pershing ordered Colonel C. W. Brown and the second squadron of 10th Cavalry, then operating in the area of San Diego Del

Monte, to head southward, a day's march to the east and to the rear of Tompkins. To the major's right, Pershing sent Major Robert Howze and a column of 11th Cavalry. To support these elements, a squadron of 11th Cavalry under Lieutenant Colonel Henry T. Allen was ordered into the field.

On April 10, a little more than a week after Tompkins' detachment left camp, it was heading for Parral over a rock trace which wormed through rolling country. In late afternoon, the men forded the Concha River and entered Valle de Zaragoza on the south bank, singing:

> We left the border for Parral
> In search of Villa and Lopez, his old pal.
> Our horses, they were hungry,
> And we ate parched corn
> It was damn hard living
> In the state of Chihuahua
> Where Pancho Villa was born.

When it was light the next morning the major led his soldiers out of the village and, by nightfall, trotted into Santa Cruz de Villegas. A Mexican officer from the Carranza garrison rode into town and promised Tompkins a royal welcome at Parral, where they would find pasturage, food, supplies, clothes, and even railroad transportation for the march south.

The troops broke camp at 7:10 A.M., April 12, and headed down the road. As the detachment neared Parral, the town looked white, cool, and attractive. But Tompkins and his men knew it to be a foul hole. Step off the main street and you found yourself in a maze of narrow, evil-smelling alleys. Towns like this one dotted the state of Chihuahua.

No Mexican officials came out to greet the Americans. Tompkins thought this odd. He and his soldiers went forward with care. Down the main street they rode. People came out to watch them. Ruffianly men and dark, sullen women scowled at the cavalcade.

At military headquarters, a shambling, two story structure, Tompkins halted his command, dismounted, and pushed open the door. Inside General Ismael Lozano, the Carranzista commander, shook hands with him and showed him upstairs to an office. The general blandly tried to mislead Tompkins into believing that Villa was in the north, operating near Satevo. The major knew this to be a lie. When he saw that the American was not deceived, Lozano flared and told him to get out of town. Tompkins retorted that he'd leave as soon as he was shown where to camp.

Outside a surly mob had gathered, chanting, "Viva Mexico! Mexico por los mexicanos." Shopkeepers locked their doors and bolted their shutters. The crowd pressed forward as General Lozano and his staff followed by Tompkins walked out of headquarters. Stiffly, the Mexican officers mounted horses and rode to the head of the American column. As the outfit got into motion, the mob surged close behind, hooting and shouting, "Viva Villa! Viva Mexico!" Troopers noticed fifty mounted Mexicans cantering into a cross street.

A rifle report exploded. Another. Then no more shots. Nobody was hit. Tompkins jerked his horse around and rode back to the tail of the column, spending a few minutes in a swift survey of the ground. The detachment continued out of town, across the railroad tracks, and into a ravine between two hills.

Tompkins galloped up to Lieutenant Lininger and eight troopers and snapped orders. They dismounted and ran behind a railroad embankment. To cover them, Captain Frederick Turner and his men occupied the easternmost of the two hills.

Tompkins, seething with anger, rode back to the head of the column. He glowered at Lozano and pointed to the mob. Lozano threw up his hands as if to ignore the business, turned, and rode off up a hill, 600 yards to the south from where Lininger's troopers waited.

Defiantly, Mexicans hoisted a Carranzista flag. The hill sprouted increasing numbers of armed Mexicans. Tompkins spotted a force beginning to move toward his left flank, but he was reluctant to fight. His orders called for avoiding hostilities with the forces of the de facto government.

To disperse the Mexicans, Tompkins clambered up the railroad embankment, waved his hands, and yelled for them to go back. They kept coming. The major spun around and asked Sergeant Jay Richley for his rifle, intending to cut down the approaching flag bearer. Before the major could fire, Carranzistas' rifles erupted. Turning to give Richley his rifle back, Tompkins saw the sergeant lying motionless behind the embankment. A bullet had struck him in the left eye. He had died instantly.

About the Americans sounded the *phit-phit* of bullets. Here and there leaden slugs kicked up little clouds of dust. The Americans returned the fire. But with his meager force, Tompkins could not hope to extend his lines to meet the enemy's flanking movements.

Two others besides Richley lay mortally wounded: Corporal Benjamin McGee, shot in the mouth; Private Hobart Ledford, a bullet in one lung. Tompkins decided to fall back for Santa Cruz de Villegas, where he could gain a good defensive posture. Quickly, the khaki-clad troopers retreated up the road.

Discarding attempts to outflank the Americans, Carranzistas charged. Tompkins, Lininger, and the rear guard dismounted behind a stone wall and opened fire.

Two troopers struggled with their horses, who madly tossed their heads and bucked at each report. One of the men, spying Tompkins empty-handed, shouted: "Hold my horse, Major." The other called: "Mine, too." Although this negated military etiquette, Tompkins smiled and grabbed the reins.

The Mexican attack slackened momentarily. Lininger and the rear guard raced back to the main column. The retreat continued.

Convinced that the enemy was preparing another head-on charge, Tompkins ordered Captain Turner and twenty men to dismount and deploy across the road.

Spurring their mounts, the Mexicans raced forward in an unruly mob without order, yelling and firing. Turner's troopers flattened themselves to escape the ricocheting bullets, refusing to reply to the Mexican fire at long range.

The horde closed in. "Now!" barked Turner. With a single clap like an explosion, the volley of twenty-one rifles burst out. It was difficult to believe the execution Turner's men had done. One hundred paces from the firing line was a welter of struggling horses. Mexicans flopped or lay motionless on the ground. One volley had taken out the first line of oncharging attackers.

The second line stumbled over the fallen and swirled about them. Mexicans pulled their horses to jolting stops. The charge disintegrated. Carranzistas wheeled and galloped off.

Tompkins and his soldiers entered Santa Cruz de Villegas and

deployed in defensive lines. Three men rode out of the ranch com-
pound, heading northward in search of Colonel Brown and his
column of 10th Cavalry.

The Mexicans reformed and moved toward Santa Cruz, ban-
ners snapping in the wind. Atop one of the ranch buildings, Captain Aubrey Lippincott watched them come. A crack shot, he
estimated the range, figured the wind direction and speed of the
enemy, raised his rifle, aimed, and squeezed the trigger. A half mile
away a rider tumbled silently from his saddle. Lippincott leaned
out over the roof and called down to Tompkins: "I got one at eight
hundred yards, Major!"

Troopers saw the Mexicans rein up, turn and trot out of rifle
range. A Carranzista messenger, holding high a white flag, rode
forward toward Santa Cruz. He entered the gates, dismounted, and
handed Tompkins a note. General Lozano threatened to renew the
attack.

There was no moon that night. Grimly, Tompkins and his
men waited. Around 7:30 they heard horses coming. It was Colonel
Brown.

Tompkins swung open the gates and greeted the detachment
warmly. He yelled out: "By God! They were glad to see the Tenth
Cavalry at Santiago in '98, but I'm a damn sight gladder to see you
now. I could kiss every one of you."

Major Charles Young, one of the six Negro officers in the
United States Army, grinned and answered: "Hello, Tompkins.
You can start on me right now."

With the arrival of Brown's contingent, the Mexicans' numerical superiority shrank to insignificance. The Carranzistas withdrew
from the area, ending the threat of an assault. On April 15, Lieutenant Colonel Allen and his troops arrived at Santa Cruz followed
two hours later by Major Howze's unit.

Back at headquarters, Pershing shot off a telegram to General
Frederick Funston, commanding the Army's Southern Department
at San Antonio, Texas. He requested that all units of the expedition
be increased to maximum strength and that another cavalry regiment be ordered to Mexico. Pershing then sat down and wrote
Funston a lengthy letter:

It is probable that the real object of our mission to Mex-

ico can only be attained after an arduous campaign of considerable length. Its possible that the truth of this statement may not be fully appreciated. But it should be realized that the country through which our cavalry is now operating is unfamiliar to every member of the command; very few white men of any class know it in the interior; it is sparsely settled by ignorant people usually unreliable, and almost wholly terrorized by roving bands of robbers and bandits. . . .

Under these conditions, our various forces have had to rely for their guidance upon the inaccurate knowledge of untried American employees, or else upon the uncertain information of frightened or unwilling natives. Thus have well laid plans often miscarried and the goal has moved further and further into the future. . . .

As long as Villa remains at the head of an organized band and moves about there is a possibility of overtaking him or of cutting him off, but when his forces divide into small detachments that scatter to different areas to become part and parcel of the people then the problem becomes more difficult.

Awaiting word from General Funston, Pershing moved northward to the American base at Namiquipa and wrestled with the problem of supplying his units. Brown's command at Santa Cruz de Villegas totaled 34 officers, 606 men, 702 horses, and 149 mules. Each day this force needed 9,000 pounds of grain for the animals and 2,000 pounds of food for the men. Extending the supply lines southward was difficult. The terrain was tortuous; the number of motor trucks, inadequate. Finding no satisfactory solution to the problem, Pershing ordered Brown's troops at Santa Cruz de Villegas withdrawn northward eighty-three miles to Satevo. The active pursuit of Pancho Villa had ended.

Intelligence information indicated that the Carranzista government was determined to force Pershing's expedition out of Mexico. Mexican troops were reported moving toward the Parral area. As a result of the rising hostility of the Carranzistas toward Americans, Washington ordered Pershing to consolidate his command. Hope of catching Villa was abandoned.

Pershing wrote:

The work of the Cavalry has been splendid. It has naturally borne the brunt of the campaign. I do not believe the Cavalry in all its experience has done as hard work on this campaign. This Expedition has been a great thing for the Cavalry, as it has demonstrated beyond question the necessity for this arm for the future service of this kind.

By the end of May, 1916, Pershing's command was centered at Colonia Dublan. The soldier's life became increasingly monotonous. To relieve the boredom, Pershing ordered daily drills. The cavalry trained in the wide-open country and developed a system which enabled whole troops to charge and fire pistols directly over the horses' heads at an enemy.

Regularly, Pershing dispatched mounted patrols here and there, scouting, watching for bands of Villistas and Carranzistas. On the trail a cavalry captain wrote home:

> The sun is very bright and I have to use my own shadow to write in. The last real letter I wrote you was along the irrigation ditch four days ago. The next day we had 34 miles to go. It was all in the mountains, over them, and through deep canyons. We started at 6:15, marched 6 miles, watered, and then grazed an hour, with 28 miles of h——l ahead of us. During that day we had 25 minutes' trotting. The rest was walk, lead, walk ad infinitum.
>
> No water on the way, down and up rocky roads, terrible roads, filled with loose stones in some places and large bedded stones in others, dusty, and fearfully hot, ye gods! We got to camp at 5:10 that evening, and then the horses went out to graze. . . . The next day's march was 24 miles, but over nice roads, comparatively speaking. Our water was little alkali pools. The next day, yesterday, we did but 12 miles, walking and leading. At base camp . . . men got new shoes and socks and I got some cigars and socks and shirts. My socks were going fast and shirts get soiled quickly.
>
> We left there this morning. . . . Got a good bath to-day and have on clean clothes. Have a small can of peaches with me. Got one letter from you, 10 days coming. We still are in mountains and little valleys. . . . Have had no papers or packages for a week or 10 days. Must be accumulating in Columbus. . . .

The cavalry is certainly doing the work down here and the necessity for a strong force of it, if only for border duty, must be evident. To-morrow we have 26 miles to the lake, where we stop, for how long we do not know. We are well and get plenty to eat.

There was a fight at Ojos Azules when troopers of the 11th engaged a vicious band of Villistas. In June, Carranza's commander in the north advised Pershing to go home, that Mexico would not permit him to move soldiers south, west, or east. This ultimatum was followed by the imbroglio at Carrizal where a cavalry force, because of the ineptitude of its captain, lost ten men killed, ten wounded, and twenty-three captured.

Autumn came and went. Natives reported Villa organizing a new army equipped with German small arms. Most of the Punitive Expedition (the "perishing expedition" it was being called) sat in Colonia Dublan, fighting off flies, enduring dust storms and rattlesnakes.

The campaign was being overshadowed by the struggle in Europe.

By January, 1917, President Wilson was certain that war with Germany was inevitable. A simultaneous war with Mexico would be disastrous. To keep the Punitive Expedition in the field courted such a conflict. Pershing's command was serving no purpose in its present situation, yet its presence was a standing invitation for the Mexicans to attack.

On January 28, Pershing received orders to withdraw. The men were jubilant, happy to leave Chihuahua to the Mexicans. The withdrawal included 10,690 soldiers, 9,305 animals, plus 2,700 American, Mexican, and Chinese refugees with more than 300 wagons and hundreds of privately owned beasts. From beginning to end the caravan stretched out five miles in length.

On Monday, February 5, 1917, the cavalcade crossed the border and headed for Columbus. Arriving in town ahead of the columns, Pershing mounted a reviewing stand festooned with red, white, and blue bunting. From here he watched his troops march past. Bands blared "When Johnny Comes Marching Home." The last unit crossed the border at 3:00 P.M.

The Punitive Expedition was the last time the horse cavalry played a significant role in any American military undertaking. On April 6, 1917, two months and a day after Pershing and his command returned to Columbus, President Wilson signed a joint resolution of Congress which plunged the United States into war with Germany. Along the Western Front, where the world's manhood perished in trench warfare, cavalry proved of little value. But in Eastern Europe the Russians and Austro-Germans employed huge numbers of horsemen, and British victories against the Turks in the Near East were gained largely by cavalry.

Only the 2nd United States Cavalry Regiment went to France, where troopers were assigned the unchivalrous task of operating various remount stations for mules and horses. The bulk of the American cavalry continued to police the Mexican border. German agents swarmed across Mexico and encouraged resentment fathered by the Punitive Expedition. Many patriotic Mexicans were eager to retaliate by marching into New Mexico and Texas.

The automobile and truck, barbed wire, and the new weapons wrought in World War I revolutionized land warfare. The cavalry's functions could be performed more efficiently by the tank and airplane. The development of the modern rifle with its flat trajectory and long range, and the advent of the rapid fire field guns of tremendous power made frontal assaults, even by infantry, things of the past.

The American army was slow to accept the inevitable. Cavalryman John J. Pershing doggedly maintained: "There is not in the world today, an officer of distinction . . . who does not declare with emphasis that cavalry is as important today as it ever has been." But theorists argued that the day of the horse soldier was over and that cavalry units should be relegated to reconnaissance and orderly duty.

In the years following the Armistice in 1918, Congress slashed military budgets and the number of horse regiments shrank from seventeen to fourteen. Congress made further cutbacks during the 1920's, reducing the cavalry to half-strength by assigning certain squadrons to inactive status.

Finally the War Department ordered the 1st and 13th dismounted and mechanized and, later, merged these outfits with infantry tank battalions to establish the Provisional Armored Corps.

The 4th and 6th Regiments were converted into Horse-Mechanized Reconnaissance regiments.

The success of the German panzer divisions early in World War II demonstrated the superiority of mechanized units. Three months after Pearl Harbor, in March, 1942, the War Department abolished the horse cavalry. Dismounted, the 1st Cavalry Division was sent to the Pacific Theater and trained in jungle fighting. Regiments kept their names and traditions, but became vehicular reconnaissance units. Fighting over all kinds of terrain and in extremes of climate which rendered motor vehicles ineffective, an occasional field commander pleaded for horse cavalry. The War Department was unresponsive.

After the war the Army sold the cavalry horses, equipment, and posts. Except for a few ceremonial mounts, the horses were gone. But cavalrymen of today's modern regiments, fiercely proud of their tradition, do honor to Dodge, Kearny, Sheridan, and Custer, by again serving on freedom's frontiers.

Near An Khe, South Vietnam, the First Cavalry Division (Airmobile) welcomed the new year, January 1, 1966, with a message to the Viet Cong. The division artillery fired sixty-six rounds, and a psychological warfare plane equipped with a loud speaker flew over the Viet Cong area blaring out to the Communist insurgents: "This is the Year of the Horse [Oriental calendar]. We are the horse. The horse will seek you out and destroy you."

Bibliography

I am indebted to the following individuals who helped make this bibliography possible: JOHN TAYLOR, ELMER PARKER, and SARA JACKSON, National Archives; ROGER PRESTON, Manuscript Division, Library of Congress; MARGARET ROSE, State Historical Society of North Dakota; ROBERT BRUBAKER, Illinois State Historical Library; Colonel RAYMOND C. BALL and MARY LEE STUBBS, Office of the Chief of Military History; JAMES S. HUTCHINS, Smithsonian Institution; JANET K. WHITE and CATHERIN RAFTER, Minnesota Historical Society; ANDREW M. LOVELESS and JOHN GARCON, Custer Battlefield National Monument; ROBERT W. HILL and PAUL RUGEN, Manuscript Division, New York Public Library; GERALD C. STOWE, West Point Museum; the entire staff, Henry E. Huntington Library.

Abbreviations: New Mexico Historical Review, NMHR; Kansas State Historical Society Transactions, KSHT; Harper's New Monthly Magazine will be cited as Harper's.

MANUSCRIPTS: New York Public Library: William Struckman Letters; A. H. Sydenham Diary. Library of Congress, Manuscript Division: Papers of Edward Steele Godfrey, Henry Ware Lawton, Frank McCoy, John J. Pershing, Philip H. Sheridan, and miscellaneous letters and diaries. National Archives: Adjutant General Files, Record Group 94; World War I Organization Records—Punitive Expedition to Mexico, Record Group 120. Illinois State Historical Library: Papers of Benjamin Grierson. Minnesota Historical Society: Miscellaneous letters and diaries. State Historical Society of North Dakota: Miscellaneous letters and diaries. Rutherford B. Hayes Library: Papers of George Crook. Henry E. Huntington Library: Miscellaneous letters.

UNITED STATES GOVERNMENT DOCUMENTS: "Affairs in Utah." *Senate Exec. Doc., No. 1,* 35 Cong., 2 sess., vol. II (1859); "Affairs in the Department of Texas." *Ibid.;* "Cavalry Horses in America." U. S. Commissioner of Agriculture, *Report* (1863), 159–175; *Cavalry Tactics* (1841, 1862); "Journal of Captain A. R. Johnston, First Dragoons." *House Exec. Doc., No. 41,* 30 Cong., 1 sess. (1848); [Lt. T. B. Wheelock's] "Journal of Colonel Dodge's Expedition from Fort Gibson to the Pawnee Pict Village." *American State Papers, Military Affairs,* V (1860), 373–382; [Lt. W. H. Emory's] "Notes of a Military Reconnaissance, from Fort Leavenworth, in Missouri, to San Diego, in California." *House Exec. Doc., No. 41,* 30 Cong., 1 sess. (1848); [A. Wislizenus'] "Memoir of a Tour to Northern Mexico, Connected with Col. Doniphan's Expedition in 1846 and 1847." *Senate Misc. Doc., No. 26,* 30 Cong., 1 sess. (1848); "Message from the President of the United States." *Senate Exec. Doc., No. 5,* 34 Cong., 3 sess. (1856); *Official Record of a Court of Inquiry Convened at Chicago, Illinois, January 13, 1879, by the President of the United States upon the Request of Major Marcus A. Reno, 7th U. S. Cavalry, to Investigate His Conduct at the Battle of the Little Big Horn* (1951); *Record of Engagements with Hostile Indians within the Military Division of the Missouri, from 1868 to 1882* (1882); *Regulations for the Uniform and Dress of the Army of the United States* (1851, 1872); "Report of a Summer Campaign to the Rocky Mountains, &c., in 1845." *House Exec. Doc., No. 2,* 29 Cong., 1 sess. (1845); "Report of Lieut. J. W. Abert, of his Examination of New Mexico in the Years 1846–'47." *House Exec. Doc., No. 41,* 30 Cong., 1 sess. (1848); *Soldier's Hand-Book; for the Use of the Enlisted Men of the Army.* By N. Hershler (1893); *War of the Rebellion: a Compilation of the Official Records of the Union and Confederate Armies.* 128 v. (1880–1901).

CORRESPONDENCE AND COLLECTED WORKS: *Battles and Leaders of the Civil War.* 4 v. (1887–88); Bieber, Ralph P., ed. *Marching with the Army of the West, 1846–1848.* (In Southwest Historical Series, IV, 1936); Id. & Averam B. Bender, eds. *Exploring Southwestern Trails* (In Southwest Historical Series, VII, 1938); "Correspondence of Governor Geary." *KSHT,* IV (1886–88), 403–519; "Correspondence of Governor Wilson Shannon." *Ibid.,* 385–403; Correspondence of John Sedgwick, Major-General. 2 v. (1902–03); Hafen, LeRoy & Ann W. Hafen, eds. *The Utah Expedition* (1958); Hamlin, Percy G., ed. *The Making of a Soldier. Letters of General R. S. Ewell* (1935); Hammond, George P., ed. *Campaigns in the West, 1856–1861. The Journal and Letters of Colonel John Van Deusen DuBois* (1949);

Hammond, Otis G., ed. "The Utah Expedition, 1857–1858. Letters of Capt. Jesse A. Gove." New Hampshire Historical Society, *Collections*, XII (1928); Jones, J. William. *Life and Letters of Robert Edward Lee* (1906); King, W. C. & W. P. Derby. *Camp-Fire Sketches and Battle-Field Echoes of '61–5* (1886); "Letters of Catharine Wever Collins." *Colorado Magazine*, XXXI (1954), 241–273; McLarty, Vivian K., ed. "Letters of William H. H. Gist." *Missouri Historical Review*, XLVIII (1954), 237–248; Merington, Marguerite, ed. *The Custer Story. The Life and Intimate Letters of General George A. Custer and His Wife Elizabeth* (1950); Morison, Elting E., et al., eds. *The Letters of Theodore Roosevelt.* 8 v. (1951–54); Pratt, Henry E., ed. "Civil War Letters of Winthrop S. G. Allen." *Journal of the Illinois State Historical Society*, XXIV (1931), 553–577; Roe, Frances M. A. *Army Letters from an Officer's Wife* (1909); Salter, William, ed. "Letters of Henry Dodge to Gen. George W. Jones." *Annals of Iowa*, 3d ser., III (1897–98), 220–223, 290–296, 384–399; Sanborn, F. B., ed. *The Life and Letters of John Brown* (1885).

DIARIES, JOURNALS, REPORTS: Alter, J. Cecil & Robert J. Dwyer, eds. "Journal of Captain Albert Tracy." *Utah Historical Quarterly*, XIII (1945), 1–128; Ames, George W., Jr., ed. "A Doctor Comes to California. The Diary of John S. Griffin, Assistant Surgeon with Kearny's Dragoons." *California Historical Society Quarterly*, XII (1942), 193–224, 333–357; Athearn, Robert G., ed. "The Civil War Diary of John Wilson Phillips." *Virginia Magazine of History and Biography*, LXII (1954), 95–123; "A Trooper's Diary. From Amherst to the Presidio." *Outlook*, LIX–LXI (1898–99), 775–779, 15–19, 521–527, 724–727, 908–913, 356–358; Bieber, Ralph P., ed. *Journal of a Soldier under Kearny and Doniphan* (In Southwest Historical Series, III, 1935); Brininstool, E. A., ed. *Campaigning with Custer and the Nineteenth Kansas Volunteer on the Washita Campaign* (1928); Brooks, Clinton E. & Frank D. Reeve, eds. "James A. Bennett: A Dragoon in New Mexico." *NMHR*, XXII (1947), 51–97, 140–176; Cannon, Carl L., ed. *A Journal of the Santa Fe Expedition under Colonel Doniphan. By Jacob S. Robinson* (1932); Cowan, Robert, ed. "Journal of John McHenry Hollingsworth." *California Historical Society Quarterly*, I (1923), 207–270; "Diary of John Taylor Hughes," in William E. Connelley. *War with Mexico, 1846–1847. Doniphans Expedition and the Conquest of New Mexico and California* (1907); "Diary of an Officer of the 'Army of the West.'" *Niles' National Register*, LXXI (10 Oct. 1846), 90–92; Drumm, Stella M., ed. *Down the Santa Fé Trail and into Mexico. The Diary of Susan Shelby Magoffin* (1926);

Emory, W. H. "Unofficial Journal." *Niles' National Register*, LXXI (31 Oct., 7, 14 Nov. 1846), 138–140, 157–159, 174–175; Ezell, John S., ed. "Excerpts from the Civil War Diary of Lieutenant Charles Alley, Company 'C', Fifth Iowa Cavalry," *Iowa Journal of History and Politics*, XLIX (1951), 241–256; Gardner, Hamilton, ed. "March of the 2d Dragoons. Report of Lieutenant Colonel Philip St. George Cooke on the March of the 2d Dragoons from Fort Leavenworth to Fort Bridger in 1857." *Annals of Wyoming*, XXVII (1955), 43–60; *Id.*, ed. "Report of Lieut. Col. P. St. George Cooke in his March from Santa Fe, New Mexico, to San Diego, Upper California." *Utah Historical Quarterly*, XXII (1954), 15–40; Hull, Myra E., ed. "Soldiering on the High Plains: The Diary of Lewis Byram Hull." *Kansas Historical Quarterly*, VII (1938), 3–53; Jones, Harold W., ed. "The Diary of Assistant-Surgeon Leonard McPhail on his Journey to the Southwest in 1835." *Chronicles of Oklahoma*, XVIII (1940), 281–292; "Mark Kellogg's Diary." *North Dakota History*, XVII (1950), 165–176; "Messages from Mexico. Letters of a United States Cavalry Officer." *World's Work*, XXXII (1916), 430–436; Mumey, Nolie, ed. *March of the First Dragoons to the Rocky Mountains in 1835. The Diaries and Maps of Lemuel Ford* (1957); Pelzer, Louis, ed. "A Journal of Marches by the First United States Dragoons, 1834–1835." *Iowa Journal of History and Politics*, VII (1909), 331–378; *Id.*, ed. *The Prairie Logbooks* [of Lt. J. Henry Carleton] (1943); *Id.*, ed. "Captain Ford's Journal of an Expedition to the Rocky Mountains." *Mississippi Valley Historical Review*, XII (1926), 550–579; Perrine, Fred S., ed. "Hugh Evans' Journal of Colonel Henry Dodge's Expedition to the Rocky Mountains in 1835." *Ibid.*, XIV (1927), 192–214; *Id.* & Grant Foreman, ed. "The Journal of Hugh Evans, Covering the First and Second Campaigns of the United States Dragoon Regiment in 1834 and 1835." *Chronicles of Oklahoma*, III (1925), 175–215; Rister, Carl C., ed. "Colonel A. W. Evans' Christmas Day Indian Fight." *Ibid.*, XVI (1938), 275–301; Stewart, Edgar I. & Jane R. Stewart, eds. *The Field Diary of Lt. Edward Settle Godfrey* (1957); *War Diary of Luman Harris Tenney* (1914).

AUTOBIOGRAPHIES, MEMOIRS AND REMINISCENCES: Armes, G. A. *Ups and Downs of an Army Officer* (1900); Barrett, S. M., ed. *Geronimo's Story of His Life* (1906); Batchelder, Roger. *Watching and Waiting on the Border* (1917); Betzinez, Jason with Wilbur S. Nye. *I Fought Geronimo* (1959); Bigelow, John, Jr. *On the Bloody Trail of Geronimo* (1958); Bloom, Lansing B., ed. "Bourke on the Southwest." *NMHR*, VIII-X (1933–35), 1–30, 33–77, 159–183, 273–289, 375–435, 1–35, 271–322; Bourke,

John G. *An Apache Campaign in the Sierra Madre* (1886); Id. *On the Border with Crook* (1891); Boyd, Orsemus B. *Cavalry Life in Tent and Field* (1894); Biddle, Ellen McG. *Reminiscences of a Soldier's Wife* (1907); Carr, E. T. "Reminiscences Concerning Fort Leavenworth in 1855-'56." *KSHT*, XII (1911–12), 375–383; Carter, R. G. *On the Border with Mackenzie* (1961); Id. *The Old Sergeant's Story* (1926); Cooke, Philip St. G. *Scenes and Adventures in the Army* (1857); Id. *The Conquest of New Mexico and California* (1878); Custer, Elizabeth B. *"Boots and Saddles"* (1885); Id. *Following the Guidon* (1890); Id. *Tenting on the Plains* (1887); Custer, George A. *My Life on the Plains* (1874); Daly, H. W. "The Geronimo Campaign." *Arizona Historical Review*, III (1930), 26–44; Davis, Britton. *The Truth about Geronimo* (1951); Drips, J. H. *Three Years among the Indians in Dakota* (1894); Ediger, Theodore & Vinnie Hoffman, "Some Reminiscences of the Battle of the Washita." *Chronicles of Oklahoma*, XXXIII (1955), 137–141; Elliott, Richard S. *Notes Taken in Sixty Years* (1883); Edwards, Frank S. *A Campaign in New Mexico with Colonel Doniphan* (1847); Emmett, Christopher. "The Rough Riders." *NMHR*, XXX (1955), 177–189; Ferguson, Samuel W. "With Albert Sidney Johnston's Expedition to Utah." *KSHT*, XII (1911–12), 303–312; Finerty, John F. *Warpath and Bivouac. The Big Horn and Yellowstone Expedition* (1955); Forsyth, George A. *The Story of a Soldier* (1902); Id. *Thrilling Days in Army Life* (1900); Fougera, Katherine G. *With Custer's Cavalry. From the Memoirs of the Late Katherine Gibson* (1942); Gatewood, Charles B. "Lieut. Charles B. Gatewood, 6th U. S. Cavalry, and the Surrender of Geronimo." *Arizona Historical Review*, IV (1931), 29–44; Glazier, Willard. *Three Years in the Federal Cavalry* (1870); Grant, Blanche, ed. *Kit Carson's Own Story* (1926); Hadley, James A. "The Nineteenth Kansas Cavalry and the Conquest of the Plains Indians." *KSHT*, X (1907–08), 428–456; Hood, John B. *Advance and Retreat* (1880); Johnson, Richard W. *A Soldier's Reminiscences in Peace and War* (1886); Keim, DeB. Randolph. *Sheridan's Troopers on the Borders* (1870); Kidd, James H. *Personal Recollections of a Cavalryman with Custer's Michigan Cavalry Brigade in the Civil War* (1908); King, Charles. *Campaigning with Crook* (1890); Kirwan, John S. "Patrolling the Santa Fe Trail." *Kansas Historical Quarterly*, XXI (1955), 569–587; Lane, Lydia S. *I Married a Soldier* (1964); Larson, James. *Sergeant Larson, 4th Cav.* (1935); Lowe, Percival G. *Five Years a Dragoon* (1906); McConnell, H. H. *Five Years a Cavalryman* (1889); Maury, Dabney H. *Recollections of a Virginian* (1894); Mazzanovich, Anton. *Trailing Geronimo* (1926); Miles, Nelson A. *Personal Recollections* (1896); Id. *Serving the Republic* (1911);

Mulford, Ami Frank. *Fighting Indians in the 7th United States Cavalry* (1878); Opler, Morris E. "A Chiricahua Apache's Account of the Geronimo Campaign of 1886." *NMHR*, XIII (1938), 360–386; Peck, Robert M. "Recollections of Early Times in Kansas Territory." *KSHT*, VIII (1903–04), 484–507; Pershing, John J. *My Experiences in the World War*. 2 v. (1931); Price, George F. *Across the Continent with the Fifth Cavalry* (1883); Rodney, George B. *As a Cavalryman Remembers* (1944); Roosevelt, Theodore. *Theodore Roosevelt. An Autobiography* (1920); Sheridan, Philip H. *Personal Memoirs*. 2 v. (1888); Shields, Alice. "Army Life on the Wyoming Frontier." *Annals of Wyoming*, XIII (1941), 331–343; Steele, James W. *Frontier Army Sketches* (1883); Summerhayes, Martha. *Vanished Arizona* (1908); Surby, Richard. *Grierson Raids and Hatch's Sixty-Four Days March* (1865); Thoburn, Joseph B. "Indians Fight in Ford County in 1859." *KSHT*, XII (1912), 312–329; Thompson, Albert W. "I Helped Raise the Rough Riders." *NMHR*, XIV (1939), 287–299; Tompkins, Frank. *Chasing Villa* (1935); Toulmin, Harry. *With Pershing in Mexico* (1935); Whitcomb, Mary R., ed. "Reminiscences of Gen. James C. Parrott." *Annals of Iowa*, 3d ser., III (1898), 364–383; Wilson, James H. *Under the Old Flag*. 2 v. (1912); Zogbaum, Rufus F. *Horse, Foot, and Dragoons* (1888).

SIGNED CONTEMPORARY ARTICLES: Baird, G. W. "General Miles's Indian Campaigns." *Century*, XLII (1891), 351–370; Bourke, John G. "General Crook in Indian Country." *Ibid.*, XLI (1891), 643–660; [Brown, A. C.] "The Utah Expedition." *Atlantic*, XXX (1859), 361–375, 474–491, 571–584; Dodge, Theodore A. "Some American Riders." *Harper's*, LXXXIII (1891), 2–8; Dunn, Robert. "With Pershing's Cavalry." *Collier's*, LVIII (Sept. 23, 1916), 8–9, 25–27; Ellis, Wilmot. "The American Cavalry Horse." *Munsey's*, XXXIII (1905), 53–57; Elser, Frank B. "General Pershing's Mexican Campaign." *Century*, XCIX (1920), 433–450; Forsyth, George A. "A Frontier Fight." *Harper's*, XCI (1895), 42–62; *Id*. "Sheridan's Ride." *Ibid.*, XCV (1897), 165–181; Godfrey, Edward S. "Custer's Last Battle." *Century*, XLII (1892), 358–384; Huidekoper, Frederic L. "Boots and Saddles." *Munsey's*, XXVI (1901), 416–421; King, Charles. "Custer's Last Battle." *Harper's*, LXXXI (1890), 378–387; Merritt, Wesley. "Three Indian Campaigns." *Ibid.*, LXXX (1890), 720–737; Remington, Frederic. "The Essentials at Fort Adobe." *Ibid.*, XCVI (1898), 727–734; *Id*. "A Sergeant of the Orphan Troop." *Ibid.*, XCV (1897), 327–336; *Id*. "A Scout with the Buffalo Soldiers." *Century*, XXXVII (1889), 899–912; *Id*. "Our Soldiers in the Southwest." *Harper's*

Weekly, XXX (Aug. 21, 1886); Rhodes, Charles D. "Uncle Sam's Four-Footed Friends." Lippincott's, LX (1897), 837–843; Riis, Jacob A. "Roosevelt and His Men." Outlook, LX (1898), 287–293; Roosevelt, Theodore. "The Rough Riders." Scribner's, XXV (1899), 3–20, 131–151, 259–277, 420–440; Stowell, Fred W. "On the Trail of Geronimo." Overland, 2d ser., VII (1886), 348–356; Wilson, James G. "Famous American War Horses." Outlook, LV (1897), 51–59; Winter, John G., Jr. "The Fight of the Rough Riders." Ibid., LX (1898), 19–20.

UNPUBLISHED DOCTORAL DISSERTATIONS AND MASTERS' THESES: Hartje, Robert. "Major General Earl Van Dorn." Ph.D., Vanderbilt University, 1955; Hughes, Willis B. "The Army and Stephen Watts Kearny in the West, 1819–1846." Ph.D., University of Minnesota, 1955; Johnson, Robert B. "The Punitive Expedition: A Military, Diplomatic, and Political History of Pershing's Chase after Pancho Villa, 1916–1917." Ph.D., University of Southern California, 1964; Mitten, Hamilton F. "Army Life on the Plains During the Indian Wars." M.A., University of Nebraska, 1930; Nohl, Lessing H., Jr. "Bad Hand: The Military Career of Ranald Slidell Mackenzie, 1871–1889." Ph.D., University of New Mexico, 1962; Thiele, Thomas F. "The Evolution of Cavalry in the American Civil War: 1861–1863." Ph.D., University of Michigan, 1951.

MAGAZINES AND NEWSPAPERS: Army and Naval Journal; Frank Leslie's Illustrated Newspaper; Journal of the Military Service Institution of the United States; Journal of the U. S. Cavalry Association; Military Collector & Historian; United Service Magazine; Winners of the West.

HISTORIES OF CAVALRY UNITS: Anon. History of the Third Pennsylvania Cavalry (1905); Beach, William H. The First New York (Lincoln) Cavalry (1902); Boudrye, Louis N. Historic Records of the Fifth New York Cavalry (1868); Brackett, Albert G. History of the United States Cavalry (1865); Id. "The Story of a Regiment [2d U. S. Cavalry]." American Historical Record (1872), 488–494, 538–543; Carter, W. H. From Yorktown to Santiago with the Sixth Cavalry (1900); Chandler, Melbourne C. Of Garry Owen in Glory: The History of the Seventh Cavalry Regiment (1960); Crowninshield, Benjamin W. A History of the First Regiment of Massachusetts Cavalry Volunteers (1891); Davenport, Edward A., ed. History of the Ninth Regiment Illinois Cavalry Volunteers (1888); Deibert, Ralph C. A History of the Third United States Cavalry (1933); Denison, Frederic. Sabres and

Spurs: The First Regiment Rhode Island Cavalry in the Civil War (1876); Denison, George T. *A History of Cavalry from the Earliest Times* (1877); Id. *Modern Cavalry* (1868); Ewer, James K. *The Third Massachusetts Cavalry in the War for the Union* (1903); Glass, Edward L. N. *The History of the Tenth Cavalry* (1921); Gracey, S. L. *Annals of the Sixth Cavalry* (1883); Hall, Hillman A. *History of the Sixth New York Cavalry* (1908); Herr, John K. & E. S. Wallace. *The Story of the U. S. Cavalry* (1953); Hildreth, James. *Dragoon Campaigns to the Rocky Mountains, being a History of the Enlistment, Organization, and First Campaigns of the Regiment of United States Dragoons* (1836); Isham, Asa B. *An Historical Sketch of the Seventh Regiment Michigan Volunteer Cavalry* (n.d.); Kirk, Charles H., ed. *History of the Fifteenth Pennsylvania Volunteer Cavalry* (1906); Lambert, Joseph I. *One Hundred Years with the Second Cavalry* (1939); Lee, William O., comp. *Personal and Historical Sketches and Facial History of and by Members of the Seventh Regiment Michigan Volunteer Cavalry* (1902); Lothrop, Charles H. *A History of the First Regiment Iowa Cavalry Veteran Volunteers* (1890); Norton, Chauncey S., ed. "The Red Neck Ties," *History of the Fifteenth New York Volunteer Cavalry* (1891); Norton, Henry, ed. *Deeds of Daring, or History of the Eighth N.Y. Volunteer Cavalry* (1889); Preston, N. D. *History of the Tenth Regiment of Cavalry, New York State Volunteers* (1892); Pyne, Henry R. *The History of the First New Jersey Cavalry* (1871); Rhodes, Charles D. *History of the Cavalry of the Army of the Potomac* (1900); Rodenbough, Theo. F. *From Everglade to Canon with the Second Dragoons* (1875); Id., ed. *History of the Eighteenth Regiment of Cavalry* (1909); Scott, William F. *The Story of a Cavalry Regiment. The Career of the Fourth Iowa Veteran Volunteers* (1893); Tobie, Edward P. *History of the First Maine Cavalry* (1887).

MISCELLANEOUS ARTICLES: Adams, Charles Francis. "Cavalry in the War of Independence." *Massachusetts Historical Society, Proceedings,* XLIII (1910), 547–593; Beers, Henry P. "Military Protection of the Santa Fe Trail to 1843." *NMHR,* XII (1937), 113–133; Bender, A. B. "Frontier Defense in the Territory of New Mexico, 1846–1861." *Ibid.,* IX (1934), 249–272, 345–373; Id. "The Soldier in the Far West, 1848–1860." *Pacific Historical Review,* VIII (1939), 159–178; Byrne, P. E. "The Custer Myth." *North Dakota Historical Quarterly,* VI (1932), 187–200; Camp, Charles L. "Kit Carson in California." *California Historical Society Quarterly,* I (1922), 111–151; Clendenen, Clarence C. "General James Henry Carleton." *NMHR,* XXX (1955), 23–43; Id. "The Punitive Expedition of 1916: A Re-evaluation." *Arizona and the West*, III (1961), 311–320; Deland, Charles E. "The Sioux Wars." *South Dakota Historical Collections*, XV (1930), 1–730, XVII (1934), 177–551; Dorris, Jonathan T. "Michael Kelly Lawler: Mexican and Civil War Officer." *Illinois State Historical Society Journal*, XLVIII (1955), 366–401; Forbes, Stephen A. "Grierson's Cavalry Raid." Illinois State Historical Society, *Transactions*, No. 12 (1907), 99–130; Gardner, Hamilton. "Captain Philip St. George Cooke and the March of the First Dragoons to the Rocky Mountains in 1845." *Colorado Magazine*, XXX (1953), 246–269; Godfrey, Calvin P. "General Edward S. Godfrey." *Ohio Archaeological and Historical Quarterly*, XLIII (1934), 61–98; Goplen, Arnold O. "The Historical Significance of Fort Lincoln State Park." *North Dakota History*, XIII (1946), 151–221; Graham, William A. "The Custer Myth." *American Heritage*, V (1954) 30–35; Hale, Henry. "The Soldier, the Advance Guard of Civilization." Mississippi Valley Historical Association, *Proceedings*, VII (1913–14), 93–98; Hoekman, Steven. "The History of Fort Sully." *South Dakota Historical Collections and Report*, XXVI (1952), 222–277; Johnson, Roy P. "Jacob Horner of the 7th Cavalry." *North Dakota History*, XVI (1949), 75–100; Karnes, Thomas L. "Gilpin's Volunteers on the Santa Fe Trail." *Kansas Historical Quarterly*, XXX (1964), 1–14; King, James T. "Needed: A Re-evaluation of General Crook." *Nebraska History*, XLV (1964), 223–235; Loyola, Sister Mary. "The American Occupation of New Mexico. 1821–1852." *NMHR*, XIV (1939), 34–75, 143–199, 230–286; Lynne, Donald M. "Wilson's Cavalry at Nashville." *Civil War History*, I (1955), 141–159; Mattison, Ray H. "Fort Rice—North Dakota's First Missouri River Military Post." *North Dakota History*, XX (1953), 87–108; *Id.* "The Army Post on the Northern Plains, 1865–1885." *Nebraska History*, XXXV (1954), 17–43; *Id.* "The Military Frontier on the Upper Missouri." *Ibid.*, XXXVII (1956), 159–182; Monaghan, Jay. "Custer's 'Last Stand'—Trevilian Station, 1864." *Civil War History*, VIII (1962), 245–258; Nesbitt, Paul. "Battle of the Washita." *Chronicles of Oklahoma*, III (1925), 3–32; Ogle, Ralph H. "Federal Control of the Western Apaches, 1848–1886." *NMHR*, XIV, XV (1939–40), 309–365, 12–71, 188–248, 269–331; Ramsdell, Charles W. "General Robert E. Lee's Horse Supply." *American Historical Review*, XXV (1930), 758–777; Roberts, Thomas D. "Resaca de la Palma, a Traditional Episode in the History of the Second Cavalry." *American Military History Foundation Journal*, I (1937), 101–107; Robinson, John C. "The Utah Expedition." *Magazine of American History*, XI (1884), 335–341; Stonesifer, Roy P., Jr. "The Union Cavalry Comes of Age." *Civil War History*, XI (1965), 274–283; Temple, Frank M. "Federal Military Defense of the Trans-Pecos Region, 1850–1880." *West Texas Historical Association, Yearbook*, XXX (1954), 40–60; Wallace, Edward S. "General Ranald Slidell Mackenzie: Indian Fighting Cavalryman." *Southwestern Historical Quarterly*, LVI (1953), 378–396; Wellman, Paul I. "Some Famous Kansas Frontier Scouts." *Kansas Historical Quarterly*, I (1932), 345–359; Welty, Raymond L. "Supplying the Frontier Military Posts." *Ibid.*, VII (1938), 154–169; Id. "The Policing of the Frontier by the Army, 1860–1870." *Ibid.*, VII (1938), 246–257; Id. "The Army Fort of the Frontier (1860–1870)." *North Dakota Historical Quarterly* II (1928), 155–167; Id. "The Frontier Army on the Missouri River, 1860–1870." *Ibid.*, II (1928), 85–99; Wemett, W. M. "Custer's Expedition to the Black Hills in 1874." *Ibid.*, VI (1932), 292–301; Wolff, Leon. "Black Jack's Mexican Goose Chase." *American Heritage*, XIII (1962), 22–27, 100–106; Young, Otis E. "Dragoons on the Santa Fe Trail in the Autumn of 1843." *Chronicles of Oklahoma*, XXXII (1954), 42–51; Id. "Military Protection of the Santa Fe Trail and Trade." *Missouri Historical Review*, XLIX (1954), 19–32; Id. "The United States Mounted Ranger Battalion, 1832–1833." *Mississippi Valley Historical Review*, XLI (1954), 453–470.

MISCELLANEOUS BOOKS: Andrews, J. Cutler. *The North Reports the Civil War* (1955); Beers, Henry P. *The Western Military Frontier, 1815–1846* (1935); Bender, Averam B. *The March of Empire. Frontier Defense in the Southwest, 1848–1860* (1952); Beyer, Walter F. & O. F. Keydel. *Deeds of Valor.* 2v. (1906); Blay, John S. *The Civil War. A Pictorial Profile* (1958); Boniface, John J. *The Cavalry Horse and His Pack* (1903); Brill, Charles J. *Conquest of the Southern Plains* (1938); Brimlow, George F. *Cavalryman Out of the West. Life of General William Carey Brown* (1944); Brogan, Evelyn. *Famous Horses of American History* (1923); Brown, Mark H. *The Plainsmen of the Yellowstone* (1961); Carter, William H. *Horses, Saddles and Bridles* (1918); Id. *The Life of Lieutenant General Chaffee* (1917); Catlin, George. *The Manners, Customs, and Condition of the North American Indians.* 2 v. (1841); Catton, Bruce. *A Stillness at Appomattox* (1954); Id. *Glory Road* (1952); Clarke, Dwight L. *Stephen Watts Kearny* (1961); Cleaves, Freeman. *Rock of Chickamauga. The Life of General George H. Thomas* (1948); Clendenen, Clarence C. *The United States and Pancho Villa* (1961); DeVoto, Bernard. *The Year of Decision, 1846* (1943); Downey, Fairfax. *Indian-Fighting Army* (1944); Dupuy, R. Ernest. *Men of West Point. The First 150 Years of the United States Military Academy* (1951); Dunn, J. P. *Massacres of the Mountains* (1886); Dyer, Brainerd. *Zachary Taylor* (1946); Dyer, John P.

The Gallant Hood (1950); Estergreen, M. Morgan. Kit Carson (1962); Farshler, Earl R. The American Horse Saddle (1938); Freeman, Douglas Southall. R. E. Lee. 4 v. (1935); Furniss, Norman. The Mormon Conflict (1960); Foreman, Grant. Fort Gibson (1936); Id. Pioneer Days in the Early Southwest (1926); Ganoe, William A. The History of the United States Army (1942); Graham, W. A. The Story of the Little Big Horn (1926); Hafen, LeRoy R. & Francis M. Young. Fort Laramie (1938); Id. & W. J. Ghent. Broken Hand. The Life Story of Thomas Fitzpatrick, Chief of the Mountain Men (1931); Hagedorn, Hermann. Leonard Wood (1931); Henry, Robert S. The Story of the Mexican War (1950); Hergesheimer, Joseph. Sheridan (1931); Hollon, W. Eugene. Beyond the Cross Timbers. The Travels of Randolph B. Marcy (1955); Hunt, Aurora. Major General James Henry Carleton (1958); Johnson, Virginia W. The Unregimented General. A Biography of Nelson A. Miles (1962); Johnston, William P. The Life of Albert Sidney Johnston (1878); Karsner, David. John Brown (1934); King, James T. General Eugene A. Carr (1963); Knight, Oliver. Following the Indian Wars (1960); Lockwood, Frank C. The Apache Indians (1938); Lummis, Charles F. The Land of Poco Tiempo (1893); McClellan, H. B. The Life and Campaigns of Major-General J. E. B. Stuart (1885); Marti, Werner H. Messenger of Destiny. The California Adventures, 1846–1847, of Archibald H. Gillespie, U. S. Marine Corps (1960); Martin, Sidney W. Florida During the Territorial Days (1944); Mason, Emily V. Popular Life of Gen. Robert Edward Lee (1872); Milton, George F. Conflict. The American Civil War (1941); Monaghan, Jay. Custer (1959); Nye, W. S. Carbine and Lance. The Story of Old Fort Sill (1938); Parks, Joseph H. General Edmund Kirby Smith, C. S. A. (1954); Pelzer, Louis. Henry Dodge (1911); Id. Marches of the Dragoons in the Mississippi Valley (1917); Pride, Woodbury F. The History of Fort Riley (1926); Pringle, Henry F. Theodore Roosevelt (1931); Rea, Ralph R. Sterling Price (1959); Reavis, Logan. The Life and Military Services of Gen. William Selby Harney (1878); Rickey, Don, Jr. Forty Miles a Day on Beans and Hay. The Enlisted Soldier Fighting the Indian Wars (1963); Richardson, Rupert N. The Comanche Barrier (1933); Id. & Carl C. Rister. The Greater Southwest (1934); Riis, Jacob A. Theodore Roosevelt (1904); Rister, Carl C. Robert E. Lee in Texas (1946); Id. Border Command. General Phil Sheridan in the West (1944); Rodenbough, Theo. F. Sabre and Bayonet (1886); Rosebush, Waldo E. Frontier Steel. The Men and Their Weapons (1958); Russell, Don. One Hundred and Three Fights and Scrimmages. The Story of General Reuben F. Bernard (1936); Ruth, Kent. Great Day in the West. Forts, Posts, and

Rendezvous Beyond the Mississippi (1956); Shannon, Fred A. The Organization and Administration of the United States Army, 1861–1865. 2v. (1928); Spaulding, Oliver L. The United States Army in War and Peace (1937); Stackpole, Edward J. Sheridan in the Shenandoah (1961); Stewart, Edgar I. Custer's Luck (1955); Stong, Phil. Horses and Americans (1939); Tebel, John & Keith Jennison. The American Indian Wars (1960); Toombs, Samuel. New Jersey Troops in the Gettysburg Campaign (1888); Vestal, Stanley. Kit Carson (1928); Id. War Path and Council Fire (1948); Villard, Oswald G. John Brown (1943); Whitman, S. E. The Troopers (1962); Wellman, Paul I. Death on Horseback (1934); Woodward, Arthur. Lances at San Pascual (1948); Young, Otis E. The West of Philip St. George Cooke (1955).

Index

Index

Index

Index

About the Author

JAMES M. MERRILL is a native Californian. He was born in Los Angeles, educated at Pomona College and Claremont Graduate School, and received his doctorate at UCLA.

During the Second World War he served in the Merchant Marine and in the United States Navy.

In 1952 he joined the faculty of Whittier College as Associate Professor of History. He is now Visiting Professor of History at the University of Delaware.

He is the author of THE REBEL SHORE: the story of Union Sea Power in the Civil War; QUARTERDECK & FO'C'S'LE; UNCOMMON VALOR; and TARGET TOKYO, the Halsey-Doolittle Raid.

Dr. Merrill is married and has two children.

PRINTED IN U.S.A.

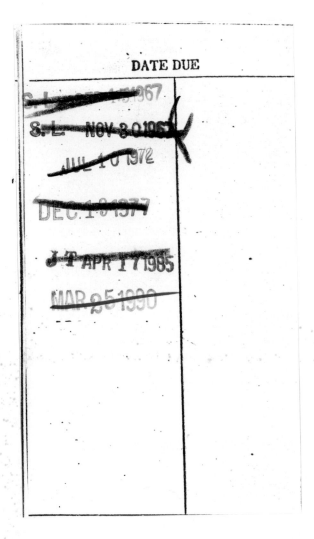